Zoomorphic Form *(Ink and water colour on paper)*

The English Writings of Rabindranath Tagore

The English Writings of Rabindranath Tagore

Volume Eight

Miscellaneous Writings

Introduction by

Mohit K. Ray

ATLANTIC

PUBLISHERS & DISTRIBUTORS (P) LTD

Published by

ATLANTIC

PUBLISHERS & DISTRIBUTORS (P) LTD

B-2, Vishal Enclave, Opp. Rajouri Garden,
New Delhi-110027
Phones : 25413460, 25429987, 25466842

Sales Office
7/22, Ansari Road, Darya Ganj,
New Delhi-110002
Phones : 23273880, 23275880, 23280451
Fax : 91-11-23285873
web : www.atlanticbooks.com
e-mail : info@atlanticbooks.com

ISBN 81-269-0761-4 (Vol. VIII)
ISBN 81-269-0666-9 (Set)

Printed in India
at Syndicate Binders, NOIDA (U.P.)

CONTENTS

CONVERSATIONS AND INTERVIEWS

PREFACE

One distinctive feature of the Volumes V-VIII—a feature that marks them out from the previous volumes—is that these volumes include many writings, speeches and utterances of persons other than Tagore. The exigency of the situation and the special character of these volumes make it obligatory to use others' writings, particularly when publishing conversations, interviews, etc.

The volumes offer a wide spectrum of Tagore's English prose pieces—lectures, essays, letters, speeches, tributes, and conversations and interviews. In range and depth these writings show how myriad-minded Tagore was, and how true is Aldous Huxley's assessment that 'he was at once a great idealist and a practical man of actions'. He was a poet with a soaring imagination reaching unimaginable heights, a thinker of the highest order who could also be equally concerned with the miserable condition of the village farmers and engaged in co-operative movement and rural reconstruction. A lover of children, he would write poems for children, write textbooks for them, and would also make a fine analysis of the crisis of civilization. A man of remarkable courage of conviction, he would not hesitate to renounce his knighthood and yet would have his own views about nationalism and would be critical about it. It may not immediately concern us here but the fact remains that the same man started painting when he was around seventy and left us a legacy of some two thousand doodles and paintings which have been praised highly by connoisseurs. A few specimens used in these volumes will justify the accolades. A singer himself, he has left us a collection of, again, some two thousand songs. These facts do not immediately concern us here but they are relevant in giving us an idea of the mighty stature of Tagore about whom we can always say what Arnold said about

Shakespeare: "Others abide our questions; Thou art free./ We ask and ask, thou smilest and art still, outtopping knowledge." And, unlike Shakespeare who remained confined only to drama and poetry, Tagore traversed all the fields of literary universe and whatever he touched turned into gold. He was not only a 'world poet', 'a great sentinel' or 'a universal man' but also an artist of the highest order.

We begin this set of volumes with the speech that Tagore delivered at Stockholm in 1921. Since Tagore could not attend the Nobel Award Ceremony at Stockholm in 1913, this speech may be regarded as 'the Nobel Prize Acceptance Speech'. The speech very succinctly describes 'the growth of a poet's mind'. We learn about his early exposure to Nature, how he 'used to live in utmost seclusion in the solitude of an obscure Bengal village by the river Ganges in a boat house', his growing love for the children, his translation of the *Gitanjali* 'without having any desire to have them published, being diffident of my mastery of that language', his enthusiastic reception in the West, his faith in the cultural heritage of India, for all its splendours and wisdom and wealth, his identification of the spirit of India as 'the ideal of unity' which he considers as 'the highest aim of our spiritual exertion to be able to penetrate all things with one soul, to comprehend all things as they are, and not to keep out anything in the whole universe—to comprehend all things with sympathy and love'. The speech, in brief, gives us an idea, though in an embryonic form, of the quality and substance of Tagore's vision of man and India. All his writings can be seen as elaborate manifestations of this vision in diverse forms.

ESSAYS

Thoughts from Rabindranath Tagore was first published by Macmillan, New York, in 1921 under the title *Thought Relic*, with 103 pages. The next edition edited by C.F. Andrews came out in 1929 under the title *Thoughts from Tagore* divided into three parts and containing 192 passages. The passages are meditative in nature.

The first edition of *The Religion of Man*, originally delivered as Hibbert Lectures at Manchester College, Oxford, in May

1930, was published by Allen and Unwin in 1930. Tagore made many major corrections in the edition and Macmillan, New York, brought out the second edition, incorporating all these changes, in 1931. The text reproduced here is the second edition. It should, however, be borne in mind, that these lectures are different from Kamala lectures delivered in Calcutta, published as *Mānuṣer Dharma* (Religion of Man) in Bengali, though there is a marked affinity in tone and temper.

Man was originally delivered as a course of three lectures, at Andhra University, in 1933.

Letters to a Friend, a revised and enlarged edition of *Letters from Abroad* (1922), was published by George Allen and Unwin, London, in 1928. The Preface and the first two essays are written by Charles Freer Andrews (1871–1940). These are also reproduced for a proper understanding of the letters. It is for the same reason that Andrews has presented the letters in several chapters with introductory notes. The letter dated 21 April was actually written not to Andrews but to Rothenstein with a copy to Andrews who by mistake included it in the volume.

Mahatmaji and the Depressed Humanity was published by the Visva-Bharati Bookshop, Calcutta, in 1932. The book contains lectures, essays, telegrams, etc., occasioned by Gandhi's decision to 'fast unto death' in protest 'against the communal award by Prime Minister Ramsay MacDonald'.

East and West, containing the letters exchanged between Gilbert Murray (1866–1957) and Tagore, was first published in Paris in 1935. Murray, because of his Greek scholarship and love of liberal values, was a great admirer of the poetry of Tagore.

LECTURES AND ADDRESSES

Race Conflict, originally an address delivered at the Congress of the National Federation of Religious Liberals held at Rochester, New York, in 1912, was published in *The Modern Review* in 1913.

The Spirit of Japan, originally a lecture delivered in Japan in 1915, was first published in *The Modern Review* in June 1917.

The Meeting of the East and the West, a critique of the contemporary political situation in India and originally published in the *Manchester Guardian,* was reprinted in *The Modern Review* in June 1918.

At the Cross Roads, also an essay on the political situation in India, was published in *The Modern Review* in July 1918.

The Message of the Forest, originally a lecture delivered in Bangalore on the occasion of the Festival of Fine Arts in January 1919, was published in its revised and enlarged version in May 1919.

Construction Versus Creation, originally an address delivered at the Gujarat Literary Conference, Ahmedabad, on 2 April 1920, was included in *Letters and Addresses,* edited by Anthony X. Soares and published in 1920.

A Cry for Peace was first published in *The Modern Review* in May 1919.

The Call of Truth, a criticism of Gandhi's non-cooperation movement, was published in *The Modern Review* in October 1921.

The Union of Cultures was published in *The Modern Review* in November 1921. The idea contained in the essay later crystallized in the form of Visva-Bharati, an international university.

A Vision of India's History was first published in *Visva-Bharati Quarterly* in 1923.

The Way to Unity was published in *Visva-Bharati Quarterly* in July 1923.

International Relations, originally a lecture delivered in Japan, was first published in *Visva-Bharati Quarterly* in 1924.

The Indo-Iranians was first published in *Visva-Bharati Quarterly*, Vol. 1, No. 3, October 1922.

Notes and Comments was first published in *Visva-Bharati Quarterly* in January 1924.

The Fourfold Way of India was first published in *The Modern Review* in August 1924.

The Schoolmaster was published in *The Modern Review* in October 1924.

City and Village, originally a lecture delivered in Turin, Italy, was published in *Visva-Bharati Quarterly* in October 1924.

The Voice of Humanity, originally a lecture delivered at Milan, during his first visit to Italy under Mussolini, was published in *Lectures and Addresses* in 1928.

The Indian Ideal of Marriage, based on the Bengali essay *Bhāratīya Bibāher Ādarśa* was published in *Visva-Bharati Quarterly* in July 1925.

The Cult of the Charka was published in *The Modern Review* in September 1995.

Judgment was published in *Visva-Bharati Quarterly* in October 1925.

The Philosophy of Our People, originally delivered as the Presidential Address at the First Indian Philosophical Congress in 1925, was published in *Visva-Bharati Quarterly* in January 1926.

The Rule of the Giant, originally a lecture delivered at Dhaka University, was published in *Visva-Bharati Quarterly* in July 1926.

The Meaning of Art, originally a lecture delivered at Dhaka University, was published in *Visva-Bharati Quarterly* in April 1926.

Notes and Comments, originally published in *Atlantic Monthly*, was reprinted in *Visva-Bharati Quarterly* in April 1927.

The Principle of Literature was first published in *Visva-Bharati Quarterly* in July 1927.

The Function of a Library was published in *Visva-Bharati Bulletin* in January 1929.

On Oriental Culture and Japan's Mission, originally a lecture delivered in Tokyo on 15 May 1929, was published by Indo-Japanese Association, Tokyo.

Ideals of Education, originally an address delivered in Tokyo in 1929, was published in *Visva-Bharati Quarterly* in April-July 1929.

The Philosophy of Leisure, originally an address delivered in Canada, was published in *Visva-Bharati Quarterly* in April-July 1929.

India and Europe was published in *Visva-Bharati Quarterly* in April-July 1929.

Wealth and Welfare was published in *The Modern Review* in February 1930.

The Educational Mission of the Visva-Bharati, originally a lecture broadcast by Radio New York, was published in *The Modern Review* in June 1931.

Meeting of the East and the West, originally an address delivered at a reception in New York in 1930, was published in *Visva-Bharati Quarterly,* Vol. 8, Part-3, 1930-31.

My Pictures was first published in *The Modern Review* in December 1930.

The First and the Last Prophets of Persia, a summary of a speech delivered at New History Society, New York in 1930, was published in *Visva-Bharati Quarterly*, Vol. 8, Part-4, 1931-32.

My School was first published in *The Modern Review* in January 1931.

International Goodwill is a summary of the speech at the All Peoples' Association, London, on 8th January 1931.

Lectures in Iran and Iraq are lectures that Tagore delivered during his visits to Iran and Iraq in 1932.

Asia's Response to the Call of the New Age, originally an address delivered in Teheran, was published in *The Modern Review*, October 1932.

Can Science be Humanised? was published in *Visva-Bharati News*, August 1934.

Rammohun Roy, originally the Presidential Address at Rammohun Roy Death Centenary, was published in *The Modern Review* in March 1933.

To the Youth of Hyderabad, originally a lecture delivered in Hyderabad in 1933, was published in 1963 (with a brief note by Padmaja Naidu).

Women's Place in the World is originally an address delivered at the All-India Women's Conference, Calcutta, in 1933-34 (24 Dec-2 Jan).

Reply to the Madras Corporation Address was first published in *Visva-Bharati News* in November 1934.

The Religion of an Artist was first published in *Visva-Bharati Quarterly* in April 1926 under the title "Meaning of Art", and later a revised version was published in *Contemporary Indian Philosophy* in 1936. It was also published in book form by Visva-Bharati in 1953.

To the Citizens of Delhi was first published in *Visva-Bharati News*, May-June 1936.

The Communal Award, originally the Presidential Address at a Conference held in Calcutta in 1936 to discuss the Communal Award, was first published by Dr Radhakumud Mukherjee.

Address at the Parliament of Religions, originally the Presidential Address at the Sri Ramakrishna Centenary Parliament of Religions, Calcutta, in March 1937, was published in *Visva-Bharati Quarterly* in May 1937.

China and India, originally an address delivered on the occasion of opening the 'Cheena Bhavan' at Santiniketan on 14 April 1937, was published by Prabhat Kumar Mukherjee.

To Subhas Chandra Bose is a translation by Tagore himself of his original Bengali address entitled *Deśañayak* written in May 1939.

Convocation Address at Gurukula Kangri, convocation address to the graduates of Gurukula Kangri, is available in typescript at Rabindra Bhavan, Santiniketan.

Crisis in Civilisation, Tagore's last public address, delivered on 14 April 1941, was published in *Visva-Bharati News*, Vol. 9, No. 2 and in *The Modern Review* in May 1941.

MISCELLANEOUS WRITINGS

A. Open Letters, Speeches, Tributes, etc.

The letter *The Problem of India* was first published in *The Modern Review* August 1910.

The letter *Spiritual Civilisation* was first published in *Visva-Bharati News* in October-November 1933.

National Language of India, Part 1 & 2 were published on 21 January 1918 and 26 March 1937, respectively.

The Object and Subject of a Story was first published in *The Modern Review* in September 1918.

The letter *Vernaculars for the M.A. Degree* was published in *The Modern Review* in November 1918.

The letter *Hindu Intercaste Marriage Validating Bill*, originally sent to the Editor of *Bharat Sevak*, was reprinted in *The Modern Review* in February 1919.

This Youth which Lies Hidden in My Heart was published in *The Modern Review* in February 1919.

On Some Educational Questions, first published in *The Mysore Economic Journal* under the title "Sir Rabindranath Tagore's Views on Some Educational Questions", was reprinted in *The Modern Review* in April 1919.

Poet's Contribution to Your Noble Work is Tagore's response to Gandhi's letter requesting him for a message on the occasion of launching 'Satyagraha' against the 'Rowlatt Act'.

The letter *When Badges of Honour Make Our Shame Glaring* evinces Tagore's reaction to the Jallianwallabagh Massacre.

A Great Crime ... in the Name of Law is Tagore's message to the first memorial meeting of the Jallianwallabagh Massacre, held in Bombay on 13 April 1923.

On British Mentality in Relation to India was published in *The Modern Review* in April 1921.

The Efficacy of Ahimsa was published in *The Bengalee* on 3 February 1922.

Message to the Young was published in *Visva-Bharati News* in July 1934.

Introducing Elmherst appeared on the occasion of Elmherst's arrival at Santiniketan in 1921.

Farewell to Dr. M. Winternitz was reprinted in *Visva-Bharati Quarterly,* October 1923.

To My Ceylon Audience was published in *Visva-Bharati Quarterly* in January 1924.

The *Letter to Lord Lytton* was written on 22 August 1924 in reaction to Lord Lytton's comment on Indian women.

The letter *Birth Control Movement* written on 30 September 1925 to Margaret Sanger, Editor, *Birth Control Review,* was published in *Amrita Bazar Patrika* on 5 January 1926.

Knighthood was published in *The Modern Review* in February 1926.

Deshbandhu Chittaranjan Das is Tagore's message of condolence on the death of Chittaranjan Das on 16 June 1925.

Romain Rolland was written in 1925 and included in *Rolland and Tagore* (1945), edited by Alex Aronson.

Farewell Address to Carlo Formichi was originally delivered in 1925. Later it was published in *Visva-Bharati Quarterly* in 1926.

Philosophy of Fascism was published in *Manchester Guardian* on 5 August 1926.

Fascism Denounced, a rejoinder to Formichi's letter (*Manchester Guardian,* 25 August 1926), was published in *Manchester Guardian* on 15 September 1926.

Protest against the Policy of Repression was published on 3 February 1927.

Henry Barbusse's Appeal: Tagore's Response was published in *Visva-Bharati Bulletin* in July 1927.

Freedom, a letter to J.T. Sunderland (who was writing a book on Indian struggle for independence) was written in February 1927.

Mother India, the first letter registering Tagore's protest against Catherine Mayo's *Mother India*, was first published in *Manchester Guardian* in October 1927; the second letter was addressed to the editor, *Nation,* New York, on 9 December 1927.

Colour Prejudice, a letter—Tagore's protest against colour prejudice—was published in *The Modern Review* in April 1928.

To the World League for Peace was written on 3 September 1928.

At the Immigration Office, originally published in *The Japan Adviser,* Tokyo, was reprinted in *Visva-Bharati Quarterly* in November 1929.

East is East was published in *Visva-Bharati Quarterly* in April-July 1929.

Protest Against the Arrest of Mahatma Gandhi was published in *Manchester Guardian* on 16 May 1930.

India: An Appeal to Idealism was published in *Spectator* on 7 June 1930.

Race and Colour Prejudice was published in *The Friend* on 13 June 1930.

Faith in British Justice was published in *Spectator,* London, on 30 August 1930.

Message to the Quaker Society of Friends was published in *Visva-Bharati Quarterly,* Vol. 8, Part-4.

I am Proud of My People was published in *Natal Witness* on 20 September 1930.

Statement Contradicted was published in *The New York Times* on 10 October 1930.

The Women's International League, originally published in *Pax International,* was reprinted in *The Modern Review* in November 1930.

The Colour Bar was published in *Spectator* on 17 April 1931.

Takagaki: Professor Nokuzo Takagaki was a Japanese expert in *Jujitsu*, and came to Santiniketan in 1929, and stayed for about two years.

India and Britain was published in *The Times* on 16 May 1931, and later in *The Modern Review* in July 1931.

On Proselytism was published in *Indian Social Reformer*, Bombay on 11 July 1931.

Sarnath is the text of the message sent by Tagore on the inauguration of the reconstructed *Vihar* at Sarnath.

Imprisonment of Gandhi is the cable sent by Tagore in protest against government repression.

Message to Iraq Air Force was sent to the Priest of the Iraq Air-Force on 13 April 1932.

The World's Children was published in *The World's Children* in September 1932.

Appeal to America was published in *Dharma*, New York in July-December 1932.

Welcome Address to Professor Davoud is the text of the formal welcome speech of Tagore on 9 January 1933.

On the Centenary of Wilberforce is the text of the message sent to the Centenary Celebration Meeting at Hull in honour of William Wilberforce.

Deshapriya J.M. Sengupta was published in *Visva-Bharati News* in August 1933.

Homage to Islam is the message on Sirat un Nabi that was published in *Forward* on 27 November 1933. The other message was published in *The Peshwa*, Delhi, in February 1936.

Bihar Earthquake and the Mahatma is Tagore's reaction to Mahatma's observations on the calamity on 15 January 1934.

The letter *Protest Against the Nazis* was published in *Israel's Messenger* on 3 August 1934.

My Ideals with regard to the Sreebhavana was published in *Visva-Bharati News* in August 1934.

Communal Award: To Madan Mohan Malviya is statements recording Tagore's position in regard to the Communal Award made by Ramsay McDonald.

Farewell to Abdul Ghafar Khan: Abdul Ghafar Khan came to visit Santiniketan to meet his son who was then a student at Kalabhavan.

My Young Friends was published in *Visva-Bharati News* in December 1934.

A Letter to an English Friend was published in *Visva-Bharati News* in December 1935.

Ishopanishat was published in *Visva-Bharati News* in April 1935.

Ramchandra Sharma Undertakes Fast: Tagore's Appeal was occasioned by Ramchandra Sharma's fast to stop animal sacrifice in the Kalighat temple in September 1935.

A Message of Condolence to Maharajkumari Vidyavati Devi of Kasmunda on the occasion of her personal bereavement.

To Indian National Congress was published in *Visva-Bharati News* in January 1936.

The Rice We Eat was published in *Visva-Bharati News* in January 1936.

Message to World Peace Congress was sent to Brussels on 5 September 1936.

New Education Fellowship was published in *Visva-Bharati News* in February 1936.

The English in India was published in *Manchester Guardian* on 2 October 1936.

Spanish Civil War was published in a pamphlet entitled *Spain* (Calcutta) in March 1937.

Appeal to the United Party of Sind was published in *The Hindu* on 25 April 1937.

In Defence of the Workers on Strike was published in *The Hindu* on 30 April 1937.

On India was published in *Visva-Bharati News* in July 1937.

Appeal for Andaman Prisoners was occasioned by the demand of the release of the Andaman prisoners in August 1937.

In Response to Rasbehari Bose's Appeal was Tagore's response to Rashbehari Bose's cable on the issue of Indo-Japanese friendship.

Vande Mataram was written in response to Jawaharlal Nehru's request to dispel confusions regarding the song.

Appeal to Journalists was published in *The Amrita Bazar Patrika* on 25 December 1937.

Jagadish Chandra Bose was published in *Visva-Bharati News* in December 1937.

The British Constitution in India was published in *Manchester Guardian* on 10 March 1938 and reprinted in *Visva-Bharati News* in April 1938.

To the People of China: Section 1 was published in *Visva-Bharati News* in July 1938 and Section 2 was published in *The Amrita Bazar Patrika* on 26 December 1939.

'Fascism' of the State of Travancore was published in *The Amrita Bazar Patrika* on 6 October 1938.

Letters to Czechoslovakia records Tagore's sympathy for the suffering Czechoslovakians.

Tagore and Noguchi was published in *Visva-Bharati Quarterly* in November 1938 under the title "Poet to Poet".

W.B. Yeats was published in *Hindusthan Standard* on 1 January 1939.

Bihar Cooperative Federation: 21st Conference was published in *Hindusthan Standard* on 22 August 1939.

A Tribute to Mahatma Gandhi was published in the Commemoration Volume, edited by Dr S. Radhakrishnan, on the occasion of the 70th birthday of Mahatma Gandhi in 1939.

European Order and World Order was published in *The Modern Review* in February 1940.

Freedom of Mind was first published in different newspapers on 4 February 1940, and reprinted in *Visva-Bharati News* in February 1940.

Telegram to Roosevelt is Tagore's telegram to Roosevelt on the occasion of the fall of Paris in June 1940.

Bengal's Great Inheritance records Tagore's reaction to the Secondary Education Bill (December 1940).

Man's Lost Heritage was published in *Visva-Bharati News* in November 1940.

Welcome to Xu Beihong was published in *Visva-Bharati News* in February 1940.

Message to 'Forward' was published in *The Modern Review* in February 1941.

Reply to Miss Rathbone records Tagore's reaction to Miss Rathbone's 'Open Letter to Indian', published in June 1941.

B. On Books

Thirty Songs from the Punjab and Kashmir is Tagore's Foreword to the book that was published in February 1913.

To the Nation is an Introduction to the English translation of Paul Richard's book, published in New York in 1917.

The Web of Indian Life is an Introduction to Sister Nivedita's book *The Web of Indian Life*, written on 21 October 1917.

A Great Channel for Communication is a Foreword to the Bengali Book of English Verse, published by Longman's Greene & Co., Bombay, 1918.

The Robbery of the Soil is an Introduction to L.K. Elmherst's book *The Robbery of the Soil.* It was read as lecture on 28 July 1922.

Zoroastrian Hymns is an Introduction, originally published by Macmillan, New York, in 1924.

The Case for India was published in *The Modern Review,* March 1931.

Voiceless India is Foreword to the book published in 1930 from America.

Christ was published in *Visva-Bharati News,* March 1933.

Rebel India is Tagore's review of the book, published in *The Modern Review* in January 1933.

Preface to 'Deliverance' is Preface to Sarat Chandra Chatterjee's *Niskriti* translated by Dilip K. Roy, and published in 1944.

When Peacocks Called is Foreword to Hilde Seligman's *When Peacocks Call* (1940).

CONVERSATIONS AND INTERVIEWS

Marguerite Wilkinson and Tagore was published in *The Touchstone,* New York, in February 1921.

Benedetto Croce and Tagore was published in *Visva-Bharati Quarterly,* October 1936.

Romain Rolland and Tagore was published in *Rolland and Tagore* (Visva-Bharati, 1945).

Salvadori and Tagore was published in *Visva-Bharati Quarterly,* October 1926.

Angelica Balban and Tagore was printed in *My Life as a Rebel,* published in New York (1965).

Interview with F.L. Minigerode was published in *The Weekly Press*, New Zealand, 2 December 1926.

H.G. Wells and Tagore was published in *A Tagore Reader* [Ed. Amiya Chakrabarty], Boston, 1961.

Einstein and Tagore was published in *The New York Times* on 10 August 1930.

Conversations in Russia was published in *The Modern Review* in November-December 1930.

Interview with the 'Jewish Standard': On the Palestinian Problem was published on 28 November 1930 (reprinted in *Rabindra-Bhavana,* autumn, 1990).

Interviews in Persia was originally published in *Parasya-Yatri* in 1933.

Tagore on Films was published in *The Observer,* London, on 8 August 1925.

MOHIT K. RAY

MISCELLANEOUS WRITINGS

A. Open Letters, Speeches, Tributes, etc.

1. THE PROBLEM OF INDIA

Myron H. Phelps, Esq.
New York

My Dear Sir,

I am exceedingly gratified to receive your very kind letter and to know of your desire for our welfare.

In regard to the assistance you expect from me, I am afraid that as I have never been used to express myself in the English language I shall not be able to give an adequate or effective idea of what I feel to be the truth about our country. However I shall attempt as best I may to give you an outline of my views, more as a response to your message of goodwill than with the hope of rendering any help in your friendly endeavours. One need not dive deep, it seems to me, to discover the problem of India; it is so plainly evident on the surface. Our country is divided by numberless differences—physical, social, linguistic, religious, and this obvious fact must be taken into account in any course which is destined to lead us into our own place among the nations who are building up the history of man. The trite maxim 'History repeats itself' is like most other sayings but half the truth. The conditions which have prevailed in India from a remote antiquity have guided its history along a particular channel, which does not and cannot coincide with the lines of evolution taken by other countries under different sets of influences. It would be a sad misreading of the lessons on the past to apply our energies to tread too closely in the footsteps of any other nation, however successful in its own career. I feel strongly that our country has been entrusted with a message which is not a mere echo of the living voices that resound from Western shores, and to be true to her trust she must realize the Divine purpose that has been manifest throughout her history; she must become conscious of the situation she has been instrumental in creating, of its meaning and possibilities.

It has ever been India's lot to accept alien races as factors in her civilization. You know very well how the case that proceeds from colour takes elsewhere a most virulent form. I need not cite modern instances of the animosity which divides white men from negroes in your own country, and excludes Asiatics from European colonies. When, however, the white-skinned Aryans on encountering the dark aboriginal races of India found themselves face to face with the same problem, the solution of which was either extermination, as has happened in America and Australia, or a modification in the social system of the superior race calculated to accommodate the inferior without the possibility of either friction or fusion, they chose the latter. Now the principle underlying this choice obviously involves mechanical arrangement of juxtaposition, not cohesion and amalgamation. By making very careful provision for the differences, it keeps them ever alive. Unfortunately, the principle once accepted constitution of the race even after the stress of the original necessity ceases to exist.

Thus secure in her rigid system of seclusion, in the very process of inclusion, India in different periods of her history received with open arms the medley of races that pour in on her without any attempt at shutting out undesirable elements. I need not dwell at length the evils of the resulting caste system. It cannot be denied; and this is a fact which foreign onlookers too often overlook, that it has served a very useful purpose in its day and has been even up to a late age, of immense protective benefit to India.

It has largely contributed to the freedom from narrowness and intolerance which distinguishes the Hindu religion and has enabled races with widely different culture and even antagonistic social and religious usages and ideals peaceably side by side—a phenomenon which cannot fail to astonish Europeans who, with comparatively less jarring elements have struggled for ages to establish peace and harmony among themselves. But this very absence of struggle, developing into a ready acquiescence in any position assigned by the social system, has crushed individual manhood and has accustomed us for centuries not only to submit to every form of domination, but sometimes actually to venerate the power that holds us down. The assignment of the business of government almost entirely to the military class reacted upon the whole social organism by permanently, excluding the rest of the people from all political co-operation, so that now it is hardly surprising to find the almost entire absence of any feeling of common interest, any sense of national responsibility, in the general consciousness of a people of whom as a whole it has seldom been any part of their pride, their honour, their *dharma,* to take thought or stand up for their country. This completeness of stratification, this utter submergence of the lower by the higher, this immutable and all-pervading system, has no doubt imposed a mechanical uniformity upon the people but has at the same time kept their different sections inflexibly and unalterably separate, with the consequent loss of all power of adaptation and re-adjustment to new conditions and forces.

The regeneration of the Indian people, to my mind, directly and perhaps solely depends upon the removal of this condition whenever I realize the hypnotic hold which this gigantic system of cold-blooded repression has taken on the minds of our people whose social body it has so completely entwined in its endless coils that the free expression of manhood even under the direct necessity has become almost an impossibility, the only remedy that suggests itself to me and which even at this risk of uttering a truism, I cannot but repeat, is—to educate them out of their trance.

I know I shall be told that foreign dominion is also one of the things not conducive to the free growth of manhood. But it must be remembered that with us foreign dominion is not an excrescence the forcible extirpation of which will restore a condition of normal health and vigour. It has manifested itself as a political symptom of our social disease, and at present it has become necessary to us for effecting the disposal of all internal obstructive agencies. For we have now come under the domination not of a dead system, but of a living power, which, while holding us under subjection, cannot fail to impart to us some of its own life. This vivifying warmth from outside is gradually making us conscious of our own vitality and the newly awakened life is making its way slowly, but surely, even through the barriers of caste.

The mechanical incompatibility and consequent friction between the American colonies and the parent country was completely done away with by means of a forcible severance. The external force which in the eighteenth-century-France stood to divide class from class had only to be overcome by *vis major* to bring emancipation to a homogeneous people. But here in India are working deep-seated social forces, complex internal reactions, for in no other country under the sun has such a juxtaposition of races, ideas and religions occurred and the great problem which from time immemorial India has undertaken to solve is what in the absence of a better name may be called the race problem. At the sacrifice of her own political welfare she has through long ages borne this great burden of heterogeneity, patiently working all the time to evolve out of these warring contradictions a great synthesis.

Her first effect was spent in the arrangement of vast materials, and in this she has attained a perhaps somewhat dearly bough success. Now has come the time when she must begin to build, and dead arrangements must gradually give way to living construction, organic growth. If at this stage vital help has come from the West even in the guise of an alien rule, India must submit—may welcome it, for above all she must achieve her life's work.

She must take it as a significant fact in her history that when on the point of being overcome with a torpor that well nigh caused her to forget the purpose of what she had accomplished, a rude shock of life should have thus burst in upon her reminding her of her mission and giving her strength to carry it on. It is now manifestly her destiny that East and West should find their meeting place in her ever hospitable bosom. The unification of the East which has been her splendid if unconsciously realized in order that the process may be continued with equal success and England's contribution thereto utilized to full advantage.

For us, there can be no question of blind revolution, but of steady and purposeful education. If to break up the feudal system and the tyrannical conventionalism of the Latin Church which had outraged the healthier instincts of humanity. Europe had needed the thought-impetus of the Renaissance and the fierce struggle of the Reformation, do we not in a greater degree need an overwhelming influx of higher social ideals before a place can be found for true political thinking? Must we not have the greater vision of humanity which will impel us to shake off the fetters that shackle our individual life before we begin to dream of national freedom?

It must be kept in mind, however, that there never has been a time when India completely lost sight of the need of such reformation. In fact she had no other history but the history of this social education. In the earliest dawn of her civilization there appeared amidst the fiercest conflict of races factions and creeds, the genius of Ramachandra and Krishna introducing a new epoch of unification and tolerance and allaying the endless struggle of antagonism. India has ever since accepted them as the Divine will incarnate, because in their life and teachings her innermost truth has taken an immortal shape. Since then all the illustrious names of our country have been of those who came to bridge over the differences of colours and scriptures and to recognize all that is highest and best as the common heritage of Humanity. Such have been our Emperors Asoka and Akbar, our philosophers, Sankara and Ramanuja, our spiritual masters Kabir, Nanak, Chaitanya, and others not less glorious because knit closer to us in time and perspective. They belong to various sects and castes, some of them of the very 'lowest', but still they occupy the ever sacred seat of the *guru,* which is the greatest honour that India confers on her children. This shows that even in the darkest of her days the consciousness of her true power and purpose has never forsaken her.

The present unrest in India of which various accounts must have reached you, is to me one of the most helpful signs of the time. Different causes are assigned and remedies proposed by those whose spheres of activity necessarily lead them to a narrow and one-sided view of the situation—from my seclusion it seems to me clear, that it is not this or that measure, this or that instance of injustice or oppression, which is at the bottom. We have been on the whole comfortable with a comfort unknown for a long time, we have peace and protection and many of the opportunities for prosperity which thus imply, why then anguish at heart? Because the contact of East and West has done its work and quickened the dormant life of our soul.

We have begun to be dimly conscious of the value of the time we have allowed to slip by, of the weight of the clogging effete matter which we have allowed to accumulate, and are angry with ourselves. We have also begun to vaguely realize the failure of England to rise to the great occasion, and to miss more and more the invaluable cooperation which it was so clearly England's mission to offer.

And so we are troubled with a trouble which we know not yet how to name. How England can best be made to perceive that the mere establishment of the *Pax Britannica* cannot either justify or make possible her continued dominion, I have no idea; but of this I am sure that the sooner we come to our senses, and take up the broken thread of our appointed task, the earlier will come the final consummation.

1909

2. SPIRITUAL CIVILIZATION

In every age the spiritual ideal has found its highest expression in a few specially gifted individuals. Such are to be found in India even today, often in the most unlikely places—among the apparently sophisticated, as well as among the unlettered and outwardly uncultured—startling us with the wonderful depth of their spiritual perception and insight. I do not feel that India has lost her spiritual heritage, for it is clear to me that her highest thought and activity is still spiritual. In the old days, however, the simpler environment—the comparative freedom from so many diverse and conflicting interests—permitted of the easy permeation of this ideal, emanate though it did from a few isolated altitudes, through and through the lower strata—with the result that Truth was recognized and realized not only intellectually but also in the details of everyday life.

A distinguishing characteristic of this spiritual civilization, as I have explained in my former letter, was its inclusiveness, its all-comprehensiveness. Aliens were assimilated into the synthesis; their widely differing modes of thought and life and worship being given their due places in the scheme by a marvellous interpretative process. But while the evolution of the spirit thus proceeded upon highly complex lines, the growth of the material body went on in a simple unorganized fashion, so that the time arrived when the messages of the spirit could no longer find their way unimpeded throughout, resulting in differences of spiritual intensity, and consequent compromises and aberrations in the character of its manifestations. That is why high thinking and degenerate living are seen side by side; ideals are converted into superstitions; and the finest of inspirations reduced to grossness in action, wherever the vitalizing spiritual stream is deprived of its freedom of onward movement.

The problem of India therefore does not seem to be that of re-establishing its lost ideals, but rather of reforming its overgrown body so as to harmonise with and give free and fitting expression to its ever-living soul. In other words our problem is not spiritual but social—that of reviving, by organizing and adapting to its more complex environment, our fast disintegrating social system. It is our disorganized society which prevents our ideas and activities from being broad, the narrower self from being merged into or sacrificed for the sake of the greater—and our national experiences are being dissipated and wasted for want of a storing and co-ordinating centre. The workings of the spirit are seen as flashes but cannot be utilised as a steady flame.

In the west the situation seems to be just the opposite. There we see a highly organized body, as it were, of which the soul is dormant, or at least, not fully conscious. While our soul is in search of an adequate body for want of which it cannot give its inspirations effective shape, and succeeds only in displaying to the outside world various incongruities clothed in phantastic forms, we find the west deploring its lack of spirituality. But surely spirituality cannot be lacking where the larger self is finding such noble expression in comfort-scorning striving, in death-defying heroism. On what can this living for ideas be based if not on spirituality? As for the want of consciousness, does not that tend more and more to be remedied by the very activities to which so efficient an organism finds itself increasingly impelled?

It is only where life is petty and scattered, and society partitioned into mutually exclusive sects that the vision of the Great is lost—it is only there that the mental horizon becomes narrow, aspirations fail to soar high, and the spirit remains steeped in a perpetual despondency. Here and there some greater soul may succeed, like a cloud-topping peak, in rising into the serene atmosphere above; but the multitudes wallowing in the slough below are as devoid of material consolations as of clarity of spiritual perception, and an unmeaning repetition of ritual is the only lifelike response of which they seem capable.

If the spiritual genius of India is not to prove futile for the purposes of humanity then it needs must seek to acquire the art of body-building. May it not be possible, in that quest, to avail ourselves of the assistance of the West without treading that slippery path of imitation which leads only to self-destruction?

16 December 1911

3. NATIONAL LANGUAGE OF INDIA

I

Dear Mr Gandhi

I can only answer in the affirmative the question you have sent to me from Motihari. Of course Hindi is the only possible national language for inter-provincial intercourse in India. But about its introduction at the Congress I think we cannot enforce it for a long time to come. In the first place it is truly a foreign language for the Madras people, and in the second, most of our politicians will find it extremely difficult to express themselves adequately in this language for no fault of their own. The difficulty will be not only for want of practice but also because political thoughts have naturally taken form in our minds in

English. So Hindi will have to remain optional in our national proceedings until a new generation of politicians, fully alive to its importance, pave the way towards its general use by constant practice as a voluntary acceptance of a national obligation.

1918

II

Though of one Motherland, we have many mother tongues, which gives rise to the anomaly that though at heart we are united by more or less common feelings and common reactions, we are often reduced to the humiliation of borrowing the use of a foreign speech for making ourselves understood by each other as in the present instance. I who am acknowledged by you as the poet of your land have to be interpreted to you in a language not of this land. It is imperative, therefore, to organize an all-India movement to foster and spread the growth of a language which is potentially capable of being adopted as a common medium of communication between the different provinces. I say '*communication*' and not '*expression*' advisedly. For literary expression can truly be achieved only in a language to which we are born. Whatever the national convenience of a language that can facilitate inter-cultural communication in our country, it remains a mere convenience and cannot replace the value of one's native tongue as a vehicle of intimate self-expression.

However, I hope that the language which is to claim our allegiance as the *lingua-franca* will prove and maintain its complete freedom from any communal bias.

It must truly represent the double current of Sanskrit and Persian literatures that have been working side by side for the last many centuries and must boldly enfranchise all the words that have been naturalized by long use. I have in my institution at Santiniketan provision for the teaching Hindi as well as Urdu. I used to think that Hindi and Urdu were really one language written in two different scripts, with only a slight variation in emphasis on Sanskrit or Arabic words, according to the cultural association of the people who use them. But now I am told that these two are fast growing into two different languages, mutually distrustful. I hope those who have undertaken the lead in replacing English by a national medium of communication will realize their responsibility in this respect. I wish them all success.

27 March 1937

4. THE OBJECT AND SUBJECT OF A STORY

My writings do not please all my readers, but whenever they take the trouble to make me realize that fact, they usually employ a form of language in which I am no master. For this reason I never answer them.

But the letter, which has just reached me, contains to my surprise complaints, but no insults. It comes from a lady, who is a stranger to me, and it is evident that she has felt pain, though she has avoided giving it. Her letter which puts forward some questions for me to answer is unaddressed. From that I could infer that these questions come from her, as a representative of the public, and she wants the answer to be sent to the address of the same public.

First of all, she has asked me, with some dismay, what was my object in writing this story?

The answer to this is, that the true object of writing a story is story writing. In a word, I write a story because it is my wish. But this cannot be interpreted as an object, because when you say 'wish', you ignore all other aims. All the same, when people are expecting some object, it sounds like insolence, if you tell them that you have no object to speak of.

Yet, very often, an object is revealed to an onlooker which escapes the principal actor. The antelope does not know why its skin is marked; but those who write notes on the subject tell us, that the marks are there to make it less conspicuous to its pursuers. This guess may or may not be true, but it is quite evident that the object is not in the mind of the antelope.

But you may contend that the object which was in the mind of the Creator is manifested through the antelope; and that in like manner, the age in which he is born expresses its object through the author. It cannot be gainsaid, that the age acts, consciously or unconsciously, upon the author's mind, nevertheless, I assert that this action is that of an artist, not of a teacher. The age is weaving in our minds its web of many-coloured threads simply for the purpose of creation. If you must utilise it, then the object becomes yours. This modern age of our country's history has secretly touched with its brush the present author's mind, and the impressions of that touch have come out in this novel. These impressions are artistic impressions.

Let us take the example of a great writing, such as Shakespeare's *Othello*. If the poet were asked, what was his object in writing the play, it would drive him out of his wits of give a reply. If, after a great deal of cogitation, he came out with an answer, I am sure it would be a wrong one. If I happen to be a member of the 'Brahmin Association,' I should be certain that the poet's object was to offer sound advice to the world about respect for colour distinctions. If I am opposed to the emancipation of women, I should say that the poet wanted to prove the mistake of allowing women to mix freely with men. If I have a strong prejudice against the poet's moral ideals and intelligence, then I shall have no doubt that he was trying to prove, that devotion to one's husband leads to terrible consequences, or else that this play was a cruel irony against the simplicity of noble minds and a vindication of the villainy of Iago. But the real thing is this,—he has written a play. No doubt, the poet's likes and dislikes lie inherent in his work, and also the genius of his age and country,—not in the shape of moral lessons, but of artistic creation. That is to say, these belong to the very life and beauty of the play. When I see a Bengali before me, I see him one with his race and ancestry. I see no line of cleavage between his individuality and his race. So, also, in a poet's works, the individuality and the environment are vitally blended.

This is why I was saying that, when I am writing a story, my contemporary experience is woven into its fabric and also my personal likes and dislikes. But their coloured threads, tinged with life's own colour, are simply the materials which the artist has in his hands to use. If you read any object into the work, it is not mine but your own.

Rich men use the tails of yaks for making whisks; but the poor yak knows that the tail belongs to its own vital organizations and to cut it off and make it into an 'object' is absolutely alien to its nature.

My next point is that, when there is a conflict between my own ideals and those of my readers, the reader has the advantage of being able to inflict punishment. When a child has a fall, it kicks at the floor on which it fell; and it is a well-known fact that the generality of readers follow the same rule. But that the punishment is always just and inevitable, I do not admit.

Grown-up people may not be afraid of ghosts. They may even think it harmful to foster the fear of ghosts. Yet, when a grown up person reads a ghost story, he need not remember all this. For, in a story, the question of opinion does not matter; it is the enjoyment which is important.

When a man of real culture, who is a Christian judges some image of a Hindu god made by a Hindu artist, it will be a real help to him to forget, for the time, that he is a missionary. But, if unfortunately he cannot do so, then he must not blame the Hindu artist; for the latter naturally paints his picture according to his own faith and tradition; nevertheless, because it is a picture, there is something in it which is above his faith and tradition and that is the living spirit. If that spirit is unacceptable to one who is not a Hindu, then it is either due to the insensibility of the critic, in which case he is to blame, or it is due to the deficiency in the inspiration itself, in which case the blame must rest with the artist.

Englishmen have a special kind of kerosene lamp. Hindus had lamps of their own before these English lamps were introduced. The difference here lies in the lamps; but light is light, both to the Hindu and to the Englishman. There is every likelihood of a difference of opinion between my countrymen and myself as to what is good for my country. But if my story is a story, then, in spite of my opinions, it will float.

When, however, the opinions are of such a nature, that they cannot but deeply concern my readers, it would be foolish to expect from them that perfect detachment of mind which is necessary for true appreciation, and in that case, the lamp which bears the light becomes more important than the light itself.

Let us agree to this.

Then what is the advice which the author must follow? Should he change his opinion altogether with regard to the good and bad of his country? If his readers are incapable of doing so, simply for the sake of the story, what obligation has the author to play such more somersaults, simply for the sake of his readers? But if it is maintained that the cause of one's country is greater than the perfection of a story, then this holds good for the reader as well as for the writer.

It is the paramount duty of the author to fix his attention only on the perfecting of his story, not on the applause of his reading public. But if this duty, for some reason or other, becomes impossible, then let him think what is good for his country, and not merely that his country should think him good.

The second question which the writer puts is whether the story of this novel is imaginary or whether it has its basis in actual fact; and if the latter, then does that fact belong to some orthodox Hindu family,—or to some sect enamoured of its western culture?

My answer is,—the story portion, like that contained in most of my writings, is imaginary. But that is not a complete answer to my correspondent. There is an implication hidden in the question that such events as I have described are impossible in orthodox Hinduism.

An exact coincidence of an imaginary story with some real fact is nowhere possible, either in an orthodox family, or in a family that has drifted away from orthodoxy. You can merely gossip about things that have actually happened in some family; you cannot write a story about them.

The possibilities that lie deep in human nature are the basis of the plots of all the best stories and dramas in literature. There is external truth in human nature itself, but not in mere events.

Events happen in a different manner in different places. They are never the same on two occasions. But man's nature, which is at the root of these events, is the same in all ages; therefore the author keeps his eye fixed on human nature and avoids all exact copying of actual events.

The question reduces itself to this, whether human nature in orthodox Hindu families always follows the direction of the orthodox Hindu code. Does it never, on any provocation whatever, break away from its tether and run wild?

It is a matter of common observation, from the Vedic period up to the present, that the fight is endless between the outbreak of nature on the one hand and man's heroic remedies on the other. If there exists a Hindu society, where such a fight is altogether impossible, its address is concealed from us. Then further, one must know that where there is no possibility of evil, there can be no place for good. If it is absolutely impossible for a member of an orthodox Hindu family to go wrong, then the members of that family are neither good nor bad, but puppets worked by the texts of ancient scriptures.

We have seen the ugliest calumnies against women written in old Sanskrit verses, such as are rare in those authors who are proud of their western culture. This proves that our modern Bengali writers have a genuine regard for women. At the same time, one must fully admit that these ancient calumnies may be wrong, when applied to the whole of womankind. But if they were untrue even with regard to individual women, how did they come to be written at all?

So our discussion narrows itself down to this point, whether the impulse for evil, which is a fact of human nature, can be a proper subject for literature. The answer to this question has been given by literature itself, through all ages and all countries, and therefore it will not matter if I remain silent about it.

Unfortunately, in Bengali, the criticism of literature has resolved itself into a judgment of the proprieties which are necessary for orthodoxy. Our critics go to the extreme tenuity of debate as to the excellence of Bankim's heroines in their strict conformity with the canons of Hinduism. Whether the indignation which Bhramar showed against her husband took away from the transcendental preciosity of her Hindu womanhood; whether the inability of Surjamukhi to accept, as her friend, her co-wife, Kunda, has cheapened the value of her Hindu character; how far Sakuntala is the perfect Hindu woman and Dushyanta the perfect Hindu king,—these are the questions seriously discussed in the name of literary criticism. Such criticism can only be found in our country, among all the countries of the world.

There are a crowd of heroines in Shakespeare's dramas, but their excellence is not judged according to their peculiar English qualities; and even the most fanatical Christian theologians desist from awarding them marks, in order of merit, according to their degree of Christianity. But possibly I am spoiling my own cause by admitting this, because our modern Bengali takes a special pride in thinking that India has nothing in common with the rest of the world.

But India is not a creation of the Bengalis, and it had already existed before we began our literary criticism. The classification of heroines which we find in the rhetoric of ancient India, was not in accordance with the models put forward in the Laws of Manu. I am not for such classification at all, because literature is not science; if in literature heroes and heroines are introduced according to certain classified types, then such literature becomes a toy shop, not an ideal world of living creatures. If one must indulge in this absurd mania for classification, even in literature, then at least it should follow the line of human nature as much as possible, instead of being arranged on the wooden shelves of what is Hindu, and what is not.

My last request to my correspondent is this, that she should take me seriously when I say that I love my country. If I did not, then it would have been quite easy for me to become popular with my countrymen.

1918

5. HINDU INTERCASTE MARRIAGE

Sir,

In answer to your letter dated the 8th December, I hasten to answer that Hon. Mr Patel's Bill has my heartiest support.

It is humiliating to find that some of our countrymen are opposing this Bill under the notion that it will injure Hindu Society if it is passed. They do not seem to consider that those who are already willing to accept the social martyrdom should not have any further coercion, passive or active, from any governing power, to oblige them to observe against their will such conventions as are not based upon the foundation of moral laws. To say that Hindu Society cannot exist unless it has victims who are forcibly compelled to live the life of falsehood and cowardice, is tantamount to saying that it should not exist at all. Moreover, such an implication is a libel against the spirit of Hinduism, which all through its history has been accommodating differences of creeds and customs, allowing mixture of castes and making new social adjustments from the time of the Mahabharata until now when an alien Government has nearly succeeded in petrifying our social body with its rigid laws, depriving it of life's flexibleness and thus hastening its fatal stage of senility. No doubt, society everywhere looks upon with suspicion and treats with hostility those men who choose to think and act for themselves, who have an invincible love for intellectual and moral freedom. But the community, which goes beyond all limits of endurance, which takes every step to make it impossible for such men to live within its pale, the men who have the courage and honesty of their conviction and are, therefore, best fitted to fight for truth and righteousness is doomed to breed in terminable generations of slaves. Where the society is terribly effective in its weapons of persecution it is shameful to appeal to a foreign Government to stiffen by its sanction a social tyranny, to rob people of their right to the freedom of conscience and in the next moment to ask from the same Government a wider political emancipation. Those who feel no compunction in invoking the organized power of the

State to compel or help by its connivance a weak minority to submit to the worst form of social slavery, can certainly not be held as fit to claim a large share of such power.

19 December 1918

6. VERNACULARS FOR THE M.A. DEGREE

It is needless to say that it has given me great delight to learn of Sir Ashutosh's proposal for introducing Indian vernaculars in the university for the M.A. But at the same time I must frankly admit the misgivings I feel owing to my natural distrust of the spirit of teaching that dominates our university education. Vernacular literature, at least in Bengal, has flourished in spite of its being ignored by the higher branches of our educational organization. It carried no prospect of reward for its votaries from the Government, nor, in its first stages, any acknowledgment even from our own people. This neglect has been a blessing in disguise, for thus our language and literature have had the opportunity of natural growth, unhampered by worldly temptation, or imposition of outside authority. Our literary language is still in a fluid stage, it is continually trying to adapt itself to new accessions of thought and emotion and to the constant progress in our national life. Necessarily the changes in our life and ideas are more rapid than they are in the countries whose influences are contributing to build the modern epoch of our renaissance. And, therefore, our language, the principal instrument for shaping and storing our ideals, should be allowed to remain much more plastic than it need be in the future when standards have already been formed which can afford a surer basis for our progress.

But I have found that the direct influence which the Calcutta University wields over our language is not strengthening and vitalizing, but pedantic and narrow. It tries to perpetuate the anachronism of preserving the Pundit-made Bengali swathed in grammar-wrappings borrowed from a dead language. It is every day becoming a more formidable obstacle in the way of our boys' acquiring that mastery of their mother tongue which is of life and literature. The artificial language of a learned mediocrity, inert and formal, ponderous and didactic, devoid of the least breath of creative vitality, is forced upon our boys at the most receptive period of their life. I know this, because I have to connive, myself, at a kind of intellectual infanticide when my own students try to drown the natural spontaneity of their expression under some stagnant formalism. It is the old man of the sea keeping his fatal hold upon the youth of our country. And this makes me apprehensive lest the stamping of death's seal upon our living language should be performed on a magnified scale by our university as its final act of tyranny at the last hour of its direct authority.

In the modern European universities the medium of instruction being the vernacular, the students in receiving, recording and communicating their lessons perpetually come into intimate touch with it, making its acquaintance where it is not slavishly domineered over by one particular sect of academicians. The personalities of various authors, the individualities of their styles, the revelation of the living power of their language are constantly and closely brought to their minds—and therefore all that they need for their final degrees is a knowledge of the history and morphology of their mother tongues. But our students have not the same opportunity, excepting in their private studies and according to their private tastes. And therefore their minds are more liable to come under the influence of some inflexible standard of language manufactured by pedagogues and not given birth to by the genius of artists. I assert once again that those who, from their position of authority, have the power and the wish to help our language in the unfolding of its possibilities, must know that in its present stage freedom of movement is of more vital necessity than fixedness of forms.

Being an outsider I feel reluctant to make any suggestions, knowing that they may prove unpractical. But as that will not cause an additional injury to my reputation, I make bold to offer you at least one suggestion. The candidates for the M.A. degree in the vernaculars should not be compelled to attend classes, because in the first place, that would be an insuperable obstacle to a great number of students, including ladies who have entered the married state; secondly, the facility of studying Bengali under the most favourable conditions cannot be limited to one particular institution, and the research work which should comprehend different dialects and folk literature can best be carried out outside the class; and lastly, if such freedom be given to the students, the danger of imposing upon their minds the dead uniformity of some artificial standard will be obviated. For the same reason, the university should not make any attempt, by prescribing definite textbooks, to impose or even authoritatively suggest any particular line of thought to the students, leaving each to take up the study of any prescribed subject,—grammar, philology, or whatever it may be, along the line best suited to his individual temperament, judging of the result according to the quantity of conscientious work done and the quality of the thought-processes employed.

1918

7. 'THIS YOUTH WHICH LIES HIDDEN IN MY HEART'

It has given me great delight to be invited to this meeting for various reasons. In the first place, I have not been used to the four walls of meeting places, but I feel at home under the shades of great trees. It is needless for me to say to you that I am a great lover of nature. [Hear, hear.] And then again, the meeting here, under these large trees, of so many students is of really great gratification to me. For, let me make a confession to you—that I love all young men of all countries—young students especially. Please do not think that this is a piece of condescension from the hoary altitude of my age. [Laughter.] I have a genuine love for all young beings, as I told you. For, I feel in the inner core of my being the eternal presence of youth. Believe it that I feel in my heart of hearts that I have this gift of youth given to me. And this, though I have witnesses who bear false evidence [laughter] against this;—I mean my grey beard and hair, which —like professional witnesses in the law courts, whose profession it is to give false evidence [laughter]—contradict my inner youthfulness. [Hear, hear.] And I wish I could lay it open before your view,—this youth which lies hidden in my heart. I suppose it is difficult for you to believe that time is not absolutely fixed. I mean that a year does not consist of 365 days in all cases. The figure '20' is '20,' absolutely '20' and it can never be a day more than 20; or 57 cannot be less than 57 to you. Well, I suppose you have studied mathematics too much [laughter] and neglected poetry [laughter]. This gross superstition has been made firm in your mind. But time is elastic. There are men who are old, old not in the tenth century after Christ or tenth century before Christ, but in the 20th I mean; and some who are 57 like myself, but in reality not older than '27',—let us say. And so I find that I get on very well with all young men everywhere. And I am fortunate enough to see that in all places, they themselves had found out this weakness in me. They know that I love young people; I get on very well with them, better than with people who are of my own age [Laughter], because I find that most of the old men of my age have *opinions*. That is a great nuisance—I can tell you. [Laughter] I have not got any *opinions* till now; and, sometimes, people come to me and they think that I am old enough to give them advices and to tell my 'opinions' about things; and I have to look very grave and wise. But unfortunately I have to disappoint them. I say I have no 'opinions'. Opinions have not been formed in me, I do not know how to give advice. And so they have very scant respect for me; but, as I say, I am quite at home among students of all communities; and it is because they are so receptive and their minds not only receive the light, but also reflect it. And it is a great privilege to come in close contact with all young minds. It is a privilege which very few old people possess. They keep aloof from the young, and the young also keep aloof from the old. And that is unfortunate. But you know I have been living not only among the trees, but among the young boys, my own students. I have been fortunate enough to find my place in the heart of Nature, in the heart of the Youth of my country [Hear, hear]. And that is what makes it so fitting that the students of this place should invite me to this delightful spot, under the shade of these great trees. I have to thank you for this with all my heart, and I wish I could fittingly express my gratitude and my love to you in proper language. But you know this platform makes one feel so unnatural. This posture is not at all favourable for thinking or for giving expression to one's thoughts; and then the language is a great barrier. From my infancy I have been used to sitting quiet in secluded spots and thinking out my thoughts and giving expression to them. And I feel quite like a fish out of water when you put me up on the height of a wooden platform, [Laughter] and you ask me to address you in a language to which I was not born. And so, to save you from the infliction of a formal speech, I have to make it as brief as possible. [No, No.] This is my one little way of paying you back your kindness. Please don't think that I am wanting in the sense of gratitude and love, because I am wanting in my power to express my emotion in *English*; [Laughter] and with these few words I beg to take my seat, and thank you for all the good things you have spoken of me at this meeting, a great part of which has remained unintelligible to me though I could enter into the spirit of it; and it has come to me like the sunshine through the shade of the trees and yet beautiful through them; and your kindness has beamed upon me through your own language, through the barrier of a language which I do not understand, yet mellowing all that you have said, the kind words, the praises, and making it beautiful to my ears. And this is all that I can say to you; and I make you my *Namaskar*. —[*Report by* Mr S.G. Narasimhayya in *Karnataka*]

1919

8. ON SOME EDUCATIONAL QUESTIONS

I. UNIVERSITIES

(1) *Professors*: While for the routine work of the University classes, men may be appointed, as Assistant Professors, in consideration of their academical titles and diplomas, it would be a most serious blunder to select Professors for higher work on the same principle. For the latter have to be the leaders and

directors of thought. And none but such as have given unquestionable proof of originality and genius should be placed in such positions. It is because of this defect in our Universities that most of them have not been the success that they should otherwise have been.

(a) The right method of appointing Professors is to invite the leading writers and thinkers available, on any subject, irrespective of race, colour, creed or caste to deliver courses of lectures and to select the best from among such lecturers.

(b) Next, such Professors, when appointed, should be bound by a condition that within *three* years they should produce some original work and that in every three years succeeding, they should continue to give evidence of thought on original lines.

(c) The system of 'Exchanging' Professors of different Universities for short periods, as in America, should also be adopted.

High salaries must necessarily be paid. But that will be cheaper than the present system, which is more costly, in that it does not bring a corresponding return for the large sums spent.

(2) *Selection of Men for Specialization*: Now-a-days men are being deputed for special study not only within the University but also to places outside. But the results such men have thus far achieved, though in some cases really brilliant, yet in most cases have not been equal to the expectation. And that is because the selection is not rightly made. Mere academic titles are not a safe guide. Nor is the selection made by authorities competent to judge of the merits of such candidates. It is only when young men have been in close touch with Professors with originality of thought, that their merits and aptitudes for *original* work can be known. And this can be judged best not by ordinary lecturers, usually known as Professors; but by those who have done original or research work.

(a) There should be travelling scholarships to enable the students to visit different provinces in India collecting materials for their special studies from observation and submitting them to proper authorities.

(b) Professors, engaged in research work, should select students to collaborate with them. The mechanical portions of their work, such as collecting data from different sources, collating different versions of texts, drawing up concordances, and other such tasks, should be left to these students to carry out with the guidance of their professors.

(3) *Subjects of Study*: Another chief reason for the paucity of original thought and production in the existing Universities, is the viciousness of dividing the pupils energies and attention in the Collegiate stage. A grounding in general knowledge ought to be provided for up to the Entrance. But in the University, pupils should be allowed to bring up, for a degree, only *one* subject, in which the standard might be raised. Such a graduate will have greater depth, consequently greater love of his subject, greater aptitude for research work and better scope for manifesting originality, if he have any.

The Universities will then turn out a superior type of graduates, which alone could make for real advancement of knowledge in the land.

(4) *The Medium of Instruction in the University*: As a general rule the mother tongue, *if it be one of the leading* vernaculars of India, should be made the medium of instruction. But the adoption of this principle should be *gradual*. The sciences cannot be immediately taught in the vernacular. It is, therefore, necessary to *bifurcate* the courses of study in the University. Pupils desirous of bringing up humanistic subjects like History, Economics, Sociology and Philosophy, should be made to get their education in the vernacular. Pupils seeking to gain degrees in Science subjects should be instructed through the medium of English. The necessary books for the humanistic subjects may be translated *at once*. In the course of ten or fifteen years, all the courses may be given in the vernacular and the 'bifurcation' abolished. English should be universally taught as a second, but *compulsory* language.

(5) *Fine arts*: Instruction in fine Arts is an urgent necessity. For, these arts develop a province of the mind, which remains untouched by modern Indian education. This defective

development of the mind of our times has seriously stunted the growth of national life.

The first step must be to organize, under the direction of experts, a 'Museum' on the most scientific lines. Articles indicative of the life and culture of all the peoples of India, must be secured and then similar articles of other races and cultures of the world, as far as possible. They must be classified according to the purposes they were or are intended to serve; so that the underlying ideas may be studied not only from economic, historical or ethnological standpoints, but also from the ethical and aesthetical.

(6) *Sanskrit Education*: There is a false notion that Buddhistic culture is either antagonistic or alien to Hindu culture. But they are, in fact, more closely related than Aryan and Dravidian cultures. The study of the Buddhistic and the Pali literature should be combined with a study of Sanskrit literature. The Pehlavi literature should also be associated with it, for the same reason. Else, a comprehensive idea of Sanskrit *culture* cannot be attained.

II. WOMEN'S EDUCATION

Women's education cannot be the same as men's for the reason that women have a special duty to discharge towards society and humanity. It is not that every woman should be made to learn the culinary art or that she should have no higher ambition than to be a cook or a house-manager. Woman has a right to learn the sciences and arts that man learns and to enter, *as far as practicable,* the walks of life that man usually seeks. But it must not be forgotten that to her alone belongs one of the greatest privileges of life. Of Nature's endowments to man the most valuable is his 'individuality'. Its preservation and development is one of humanity's foremost concerns. This work can be done best only by woman. She must, therefore, be first trained for discharging this great duty of rearing up the real man of the future. And her studies must be subordinated to this end. Else, the very object of creation will have failed. The courses that have such an aim can be best given in the *Vernacular.*

III. PRIMARY AND SECONDARY EDUCATION

So far as the Primary stage goes, there is something to be said in favour of the old. Hindu method of teaching pupils one subject after another. It does not mean that the child should learn nothing of history or geography for months or years when it is engaged in the study of Language of Arithmetic. When Language is taken up, it should be the one subject of special and direct instruction. But the teacher and the parents may give the child talks on various topics or subjects *incidentally* in the garden, on the road, at dinner or elsewhere. Task work must be confined only to one subject. The talks should prepare the child for receiving instruction in other subjects, later on. In the High School or Lower Secondary stage, however, a number of subjects may be taught simultaneously.

The Mother tongue should be the medium of instruction. The fewer the textbooks the better in the Primary and the Lower Secondary stage. In the High school stage vernacular textbooks for all subjects should be prepared, without any further delay.

IV. EDUCATION IN GENERAL

All educational development must proceed from within outwards. It is really a spiritual process, not merely an intellectual or a mechanical one. The spirit being greater than the body and even the individual mind, education is a process covering the widest area. Education is, in a real sense, the breaking of the shackles of individual narrowness. The aim must, therefore, be to develop not only the *individual* aspect of the mind but also the *universal* or the *spiritual,* which is the chief characteristic of the ancient Hindu system. It is therefore necessary to bring *together* in every educational organization, *all* the different cultures found in India and, as far as possible, all the cultures of the world, all the phases of religion and art, in which the universal mind has expressed itself in different ages and countries, i.e., to co-ordinate these various cultures without attempting the suppression of the natural differences. The highest aim of education should be to help the realization of unity, but not of uniformity. Uniformity is unnatural. And in fact, its attainment is impossible. A sound educational system should provide for the development of variety without losing the hold on the basic or spiritual unity.

Hence the idea underlying the Bolepur school is to bring together pupils of all creeds and cultures and to help them to realize their spiritual brotherhood and to develop, freely and fully at the same time, their individual and racial characteristics.

V. A REAL INDIAN UNIVERSITY

There must be a place, if not in every province, at least in one centre in this vast country, to which the best intellects of India and even of the world outside, could be induced to resort, where they could meet, stay temporarily or permanently and impart their knowledge to the public. It will help to kill racial, sectarian, caste and other prejudices and be a real fountain of universal light. It is only Hindu States, whose rulers have in their veins flowing the ancient Aryan spiritual culture, based on 'unity' and 'universality' can realize its importance and organize a real university of this type, which will be India's educational contribution to the world's progress.

1919

9. 'POET'S CONTRIBUTION TO YOUR NOBLE WORK'

Dear Mahatmaji

Power in all its forms is irrational,—it is like the horse that drags the carriage blindfolded. The moral element in it is only represented in the man who drives the horse. Passive resistance is a force which is not necessarily moral in itself; it can be used against truth as well as for it. The danger inherent in all force grows stronger when it is likely to gain success, for then it becomes temptation.

I know your teaching is to fight against evil by the help of the good. But such a fight is for heroes and not for men led by impulses of the moment. Evil on one side naturally begets evil on the other, injustice leading to violence and insult to vengefulness. Unfortunately such a force has already been started, and either through panic or through wrath our authorities have shown us their claws whose sure effect is to drive some of us into the secret path of resentment and others into utter demoralisation. In this crisis you, as a great leader of men, have stood among us to proclaim your faith in the ideal which you know to be that of India,—the ideal which is both against the cowardliness of hidden revenge and the cowed submissiveness of the terror-stricken. You have said, as Lord Buddha has done in his time and for all time to come,—*Akkodhena jine kodham asādhum sādhunā jine*—'Conquer anger by the power of non-anger and evil by the power of good.'

This power of good must prove its truth and strength by its fearlessness, by its refusal to accept any imposition which depends for its success upon its power to produce frightfulness and is not ashamed to use its machines of destruction to terrorise a population completely disarmed. We must know that moral conquest does not consist in success, that failure does not deprive it of its dignity and worth. Those who believe in spiritual life know that to stand against wrong which has overwhelming material power behind it is victory itself,—it is the victory of the active faith in the ideal in the teeth of evident defeat.

I have always felt, and said accordingly, that the great gift of freedom can never come to a people through charity. We must win it before we can own it. And India's opportunity for winning it will come to her when she can prove that she is morally superior to the people who rule her by their right of conquest. She must willingly accept her penance of suffering,—the suffering which is the crown of the great. Armed with her utter faith in goodness she must stand unabashed before the arrogance that scoffs at the power of spirit.

And you have come to your motherland in the time of her need to remind her of her mission, to lead her in the true path of conquest, to purge her present day politics of its feebleness which imagines that it has gained its purpose when it struts in the borrowed feathers of diplomatic dishonesty.

This is why I pray most fervently that nothing that tends to weaken our spiritual freedom may intrude into your marching line, that martyrdom for the cause of truth may never degenerate into fanaticism for mere verbal forms, descending into the self-deception that hides itself behind sacred names.

With these few words for an introduction allow me to offer the following as a poet's contribution to your noble work:

I

Let me hold my head high in this faith that thou art our shelter, that all fear is mean distrust of thee.

Fear of man? But what man is there in this world, what king, O King of Kings, who is thy rival, who had hold of me for all time and in all truth?

What power is there in this world to rob me of my freedom? For do not thy arms reach the captive through the dungeon-walls, bringing unfettered release to the soul?

And must I cling to this body in fear of death, as a miser to his barren treasure? Has not this spirit of mine the eternal call to thy feast of everlasting life?

Let me know that all pain and death are shadows of the moment; that the dark force which sweeps between me and thy truth is but the mist before the sunrise; that thou alone art mine for ever and greater than all pride of strength that dares to mock my manhood with its menace.

II

Give me the supreme courage of love, this is my prayer,—the courage to speak, to do, to suffer at thy will, to leave all things or be left alone.

Give me the supreme faith of love, this is my prayer,—the faith of the life in death, of the victory in defeat, of the power hidden in the frailness of beauty, of the dignity of pain that accepts hurt but disdains to return it.

1919

10. 'WHEN BADGES OF HONOUR MAKE OUR SHAME GLARING'

TO LORD CHELMSFORD

Your Excellency,

The Enormity of the measures taken by the government in the Punjab for quelling some local disturbances has, with a rude shock, revealed to our minds the helplessness of our position as British subjects in India. The disproportionate severity of the punishments inflicted upon the unfortunate people and the methods of carrying them out, we are convinced, are without parallel in the history of civilized governments, barring some conspicuous exceptions, recent and remote. Considering that such treatment has been meted out to a population, disarmed and resourceless, by a power which has the most terribly efficient organization for destruction of human lives, we must strongly assert that it can claim no political expediency, far less moral justification. The accounts of the insults and sufferings undergone by our brothers in the Punjab have trickled through the gagged silence, reaching every corner of India, and the universal agony of indignation roused in the hearts of our people has been ignored by our rulers—possibly congratulating themselves for imparting what they imagine as salutary lessons. The callousness has been praised by most of the Anglo-Indian papers, which have in some case gone to the brutal length of making fun of our sufferings, without receiving the least check from the same authority, relentlessly careful in smothering every cry of pain and expression of judgment from the organs representing the sufferers. Knowing that our appeals have been in vain and that the passion of vengeance is blinding the noble vision of statesmanship in our Government which could so easily afford to be magnanimous, as befitting its physical strength and normal tradition, the very least that I can do for my country is to take all consequences upon myself in giving voice to the protest of the millions of my countrymen, surprised into a dumb anguish of terror.

The time has come when badges of honour make our shame glaring in the incongruous content of humiliation, and I for my part wish to stand, shorn, of all special distinctions, by the side of those of my countrymen who, for their so-called insignificance, are liable to suffer degradation not fit for human beings. And these are the reasons which have compelled me to ask Your Excellency, with due deference and regret, to relieve me of my title of knighthood which I had the honour to accept from His Majesty the King at the hands of your predecessor, for whose nobleness of heart I still entertain great admiration.

Yours faithfully,
Rabindranath Tagore
30 May 1919

11. 'A GREAT CRIME ... IN THE NAME OF LAW'

A great crime has been done in the name of law in the Punjab. Such terrible eruptions of evil leave their legacy of the wreckage of ideals behind them. What happened in Jalianwallah Bagh was itself a monstrous progeny of a monstrous war, which for years had been defiling God's world with fire and poison, physical and moral. The immenseness of the sin through which humanity had waded across its bloodred length of agony has bred collousness in the minds of those who have power in their hands with no check of sympathy within, or fear of resistance without. The cowardliness of the powerful who owned no shame in using their machines of frightfulness upon the unarmed and unwarned villagers, and inflicting unspeakable humiliations upon their fellow beings behind the screen of an indecent mockery of justice, and yet not feeling for a moment that it was the meanest form of insult to their own manhood, has become only possible

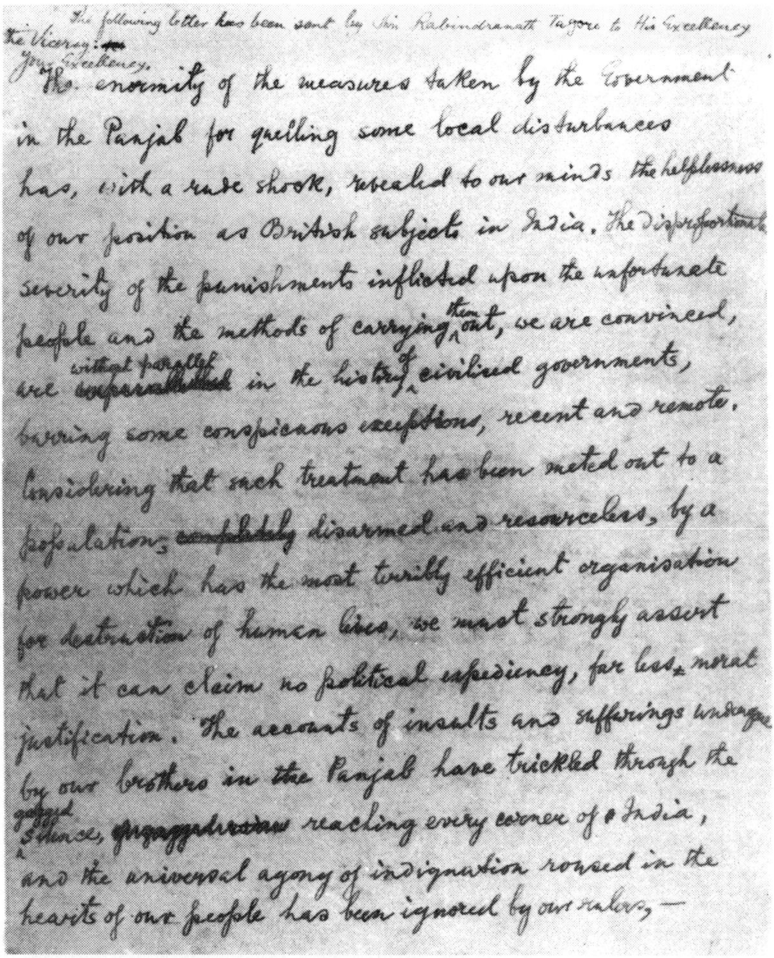

The following letter has been sent by Sir Rabindranath Tagore to His Excellency the Viceroy:

Your Excellency,

The enormity of the measures taken by the Government in the Panjab for quelling some local disturbances has, with a rude shock, revealed to our minds the helplessness of our position as British subjects in India. The disproportionate severity of the punishments inflicted upon the unfortunate people and the methods of carrying them out, we are convinced, are without parallel in the history of civilised governments, barring some conspicuous exceptions, recent and remote. Considering that such treatment has been meted out to a population, disarmed and resourceless, by a power which has the most terribly efficient organisation for destruction of human lives, we must strongly assert that it can claim no political expediency, far less moral justification. The accounts of insults and sufferings undergone by our brothers in the Panjab have trickled through the gagged silence, reaching every corner of India, and the universal agony of indignation roused in the hearts of our people has been ignored by our rulers,—

Facsimile of the draft of Tagore's letter to Lord Chelmsford renouncing knighthood

(*Courtesy*: Rabindra Bhavan, Visva-Bharati)

possibly congratulating themselves for imparting what they imagine as salutary lessons. This callousness has been praised by most of the Anglo-Indian papers which have in some cases gone to the brutal length of making fun of our sufferings, without receiving the least check from the same authority, ~~which is~~ relentlessly careful in smothering every cry of pain and expression of judgment from the organs representing the sufferers. Knowing that our appeals have been in vain and that the passion of vengeance is blinding the nobler vision of statesmanship in our Government, which could so easily afford to be magnanimous as befitting its ^physical^ strength and ~~it has~~ moral tradition, the very least that I can do for my country is to take all consequences upon myself in giving voice to the protest of the millions of my countrymen, surprised into a dumb anguish of terror. The time has come when badges of honour make our shame glaring in their incongruous context of humiliation, and I for my part wish to stand, shorn of all special distinctions, by the side of those of my countrymen who, for their socalled insignificance, are liable to

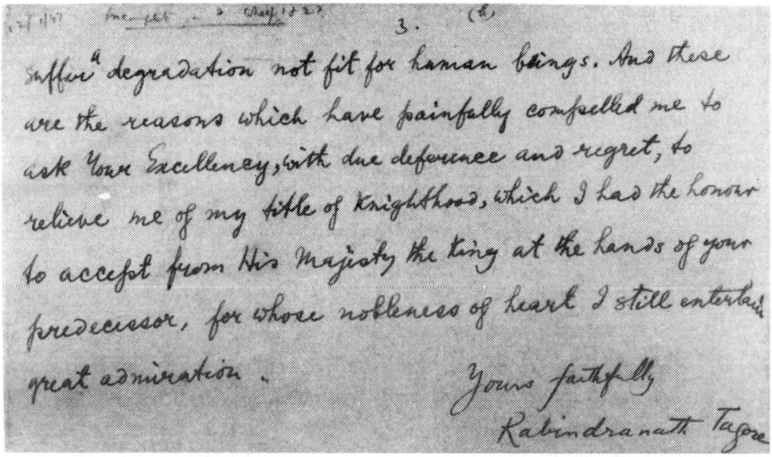

3.

suffer degradation not fit for human beings. And these are the reasons which have painfully compelled me to ask Your Excellency, with due deference and regret, to relieve me of my title of Knighthood, which I had the honour to accept from His Majesty the King at the hands of your predecessor, for whose nobleness of heart I still entertain great admiration.

Yours faithfully

Rabindranath Tagore

through the opportunity which the late war has given to man for constantly outraging his own higher nature, trampling truth and honour under foot. This disruption of the basis of civilization will continue to produce a series of moral earthquakes, and men will have to be ready for still further sufferings. That the balance will take a long time to be restored is clearly seen by the suicidal ferocity of vengefulness ominously tinging red the atmosphere of the peace deliberations.

But we have no place in these orgies of triumphant powers rending the world into bits according to their own purposes. What most concerns us is to know that the moral degradation not only pursues the people, inflicting indignities upon the helpless, but also their victims. The dastardliness of cruel injustice confident of its impunity is ugly and mean, but the fear and impotent anger which they are apt to breed upon the minds of the weak are no less abject. Brothers, when physical force, in its arrogant faith in itself, tries to crush the spirit of man, then comes the time for him to assert that his soul is indomitable. We shall refuse to be afraid and to own moral defeat by cherishing in our hearts foul dreams of retaliation. The time has come for the victims to be the victors in the field of righteousness.

When brother spills the blood of his brother and exults in his sin, giving it a high sounding name; when he tries to keep the blood stains fresh on the soil as a memorial of his anger, then God in shame conceals it under His green grass and the sweet purity of this flowers. We who have witnessed the wholesale slaughter of the innocent in our neighbourhood, let us accept God's own office and cover the blood stains of iniquity with our prayer:

Rudra yat te dakshinam mukham tena mam pahinityam.

With the graciousness, O, Terrible, for ever save us.

For the true grace comes from the Terrible, who can save our souls from the fear of suffering and death in the midst of terror and from vindictiveness in defiance of injury. Let us take our lesson from His hand even when the smart of the pain and insult is still fresh—the lesson that all meanness, cruelty and untruth are for the obscurity of oblivion, and only the Noble and True are for eternity. Let those who try to burden the minds of the future with stones, carrying the black memory of wrongs and their anger, but let us bequeath to the generations to come memorials of that only which we can revere—let us be grateful to our forefathers, who have left us the image of our Buddha, who conquered self, preached forgiveness, and spread his love far and wide in time and space.

13 April 1920

12. ON BRITISH MENTALITY IN RELATION TO INDIA

Recently I chanced to find a copy of Professor Lowes Dickenson's report of his travels in the East. It made me realize clearly the mentality of the British people in their relation to India. When the author indicates in it, the utter difference of their temperament from ours, it fills me with despair at the unnaturalness of our relationship, which is so humiliating on our side and so demoralising on theirs.

In the pamphlet, he quotes, with approval, a remark made to him by an Englishman, an officer, in India, whom he describes as 'intelligent and enlightened'. It is about the maintaining by Englishmen of an impassable social gulf between themselves and the people of India, and it says:

> *An Englishman cannot be expected to lose his own soul for the sake of other people's politics.*

Here the author parenthetically explains the word 'soul' by saying that it denotes the habits and traditions of one's race.

All this means that Englishmen feel a sense of irreconcilable contradiction between their nature and ours; and therefore we are like twins, who, by some monstrous freak of destiny, have been tied together back to back. He concludes the summary of his Report by saying:

'But my own opinion is that India has more to gain and less to lose than any other Eastern country by contact with the West.'

He contemptuously ignores the fact that where no communication of sympathy is possible, gifts can be hurled, but not given; that while counting the number of gains by the receiver, we also have to consider the fracture of his skull; and while thanking the doctor for the rest cure, we must hasten to negotiate with the undertaker for the funeral.

It is the very irony of fate for us to be blamed by these people about the iniquity of our caste distinctions. And yet, never, in the blindness of our pride of birth, have we suggested that by coming into contact with any race of men we can lose our souls, although we may lose our caste which is a merely conventional classification. The analogy would be perfect, if the division of the railway compartments, with its inequality of privileges, was defended by the railway directors as being necessary for the salvation of the passengers' souls.

Only think in this connections of the ideal which the life of Akbar represented. This Emperor's soul was not afraid, for its own safety, of the touch of a neighbouring humanity but of the want of touch. Aurangzeb, on the other hand, who was certainly 'intelligent and enlightened' and meticulously careful about keeping intact what he considered to be his soul, represented a force, insolent and destructive. Such an enormous difference in the ideals of these two most powerful monarchs of Moghal India sprang from fundamentally different interpretations of the word 'soul'.

Lowes Dickenson has mentioned about the possibility of India being benefited by her contact with the West. Very likely he meant the contact to be like that of the root of a tree with the water in the soil. I admit the light of Europe's culture has reached us. But Europe, with its corona of culture, is a radiant idea. Its light permeates the present age, it is not shut up in a single bull's eye lantern, which is some particular people from Europe who have come to us in India, yet we are repeatedly asked to be grateful to this bull's eye lantern and prostrate ourselves before it with loyalty and reverence. But this is not possible; for it is a mere lantern, it has no soul. Not only that, but it circumscribes the light to a narrow circle of barest necessity. The full radiation of European Culture has pervaded

Japan only because it has not come to her through an unnatural glare of a miserly lense, exaggerating the division between the small shining patch and the vast obscure.

It is our pride which seeks difference, and gloats upon it. But sympathy is a higher faculty, being our spiritual organ of sight: it has the natural vision of the *Advaitam*. The world is an ever moving multitude with an eternal unity of movements, which must not be retarded in any of its parts by a break of cadence. The world of man is suffering because all movements in its individual parts are not in harmony with one another and therefore with the whole: because the relationship of races has not been established in a balance of truth and goodness. This balance cannot be maintained by an external regulation, as in a puppet show. It is a dance which must have music in its heart to regulate it. This great music of love is lacking in the meeting of men which has taken place in the present age; and all its movements in their discongruity are creating complexities of suffering.

I wish I could write to you simple letters giving our detailed news. But the world-wide agony of pain fills my mind with thoughts that obstruct natural communications of personal life.

April 1921

13. 'THE EFFICACY OF AHIMSA'

LETTER TO NANALAL DALPATRAM

I believe in the efficacy of *ahimsa* as the means of overcoming the congregated might of physical force on which the political powers in all countries mainly rest. But like every other moral principle *ahimsa* has to spring from the depth of mind and it must not be forced upon man from some outside appeal of urgent need. The great personalities of the world have preached love, forgiveness and non-violence, primarily for the sake of spiritual perfection and not for the attainment of some immediate success in politics or similar department of life. They were aware of the difficulty of their teaching being realized within a fixed period of time in a sudden and wholesale manner by men whose previous course of life had chiefly perused the path of self. No doubt through a strong compulsion of desire for some external result, men are capable of repressing their habitual inclinations for a limited time, but when it concerns an immense multitude of men of different traditions and stages of culture, and when the object for which such repression is exercised needs a prolonged period of struggle, complex in character, I cannot think it possible of attainment. The conditions of South Africa (referring to the Passive Resistance of S. Africa and those in India) are not nearly the same, and fully knowing the limitations of my powers I restrict myself to what I consider as my own vocation, never venturing to deal with blind forces which I do not know how to control.'

3 February 1922

14. MESSAGE TO THE YOUNG

I have come to the time of my dismissal from life's workshop, barred from further earning. My old age keeps me pensioner to my departed days: I am only allowed to live upon my past achievement. The thoughts that I have thought, the dreams that I have dreamed, gradually matured and came to the season of fruitage, till some of them shrivelled and died and some were ripe for reaping and were garnered.

Though I confess that I began my youth in a comparatively remoter past from that of yours, do not imagine that I dwell in a time of dilapidated desolateness, and that I am no longer modern. Old age has not its reliable witness in any back number of the calendar, but in the stagnation of spirit that disclaims its own future.

It is cynicism, even though of the most modern make which is truly senile, for it has lost its vision of the beyond, the deeper meaning of existence. The cleverness which is up-to-date seems to exult when it proclaims that the doctrine of spirit has grown obsolete and that our present day education should rely only upon external forces and material foundations.

But I say over and over again that the impertinence of material dominion is extremely old; the revelation of spirit in Man is ever modern though born of an immemorial past. Occasionally it has its time of silence, it disappears from our view, so that its price has to be paid for winning it back.

And a poet's mission is to give breath to the voice which is yet inaudible in the air, to inspire faith in the dream which is unfulfilled; to bring the earliest tidings of the unborn flower to a doubting world.

I have often been asked for messages and it ever troubles me. It is like asking the tree to talk and the bird to lecture. As a poet it is for me only to maintain my instinct of happiness even when there is gloom on sky and land; the pulsation of light throbs in my own pulse when it vibrates in the unseen depth of the dark.

I am here to offer you that unreasoning joy of mine and a hope for life's renewal which thrills in the roots of our being when the spring unloosens the coils of the winter before we come to know it.

I hope that some profound dreamer will spring from your midst to sing a psalm of life everlasting and love that embraces all, and overcoming all differences, bridge the chasm of passions which has been widening for centuries. Age after age, in Asia great souls have heartened the world with showers of grace and immense assurance; Asia is again waiting for such world-spirits to come and carry on the work, not of fighting, not of profit-making but of interlinking bonds of human relationship.

Intently I hope that the time is at hand when we shall once again be proud to belong to a continent which produces the light that radiates through the storm-clouds of trouble and illuminates life's pilgrim path.

There was a time when Asia saved the world from barbarism. Then came the night, I do not know how. And when we were aroused from our stupor by the knocking at our gate, we were not prepared to receive Europe; for it came, not to give of its best, or to seek for our best; but heartlessly to exploit us for the sake of material gain. And Europe overcame Asia not through our admiration of her message of freedom and her service to humanity, but through her overpowering greed and the racial pride that humiliates. We did Europe injustice because we did not meet her on equal terms. The result was the relationship of the superior and the inferior; and since then we have been imagining that we are destitute. We are suffering from want of self-confidence. We are not aware of our own treasures.

Let us free ourselves from the meshes of self-abasement, the most deadly of all impositions from the West, let us prove that we are not beggars.

This is your responsibility. Recover from your own homes things that are of undying worth. Then you will be saved and will be able to save all humanity.

Some of us, in the East, think that we should ever imitate the West. I do not believe in it. For imitation belongs to the dead mould. Life never imitates, it assimilates.

What the West has produced is for the West, being native to it. But we of the East cannot borrow the Western mind nor the Western temperament. We want to master the idiom which belongs to our own genius, the river bed which naturally carries our own thought-streams to the ocean of world culture.

You know that fairy tale—the eternal story of youth which is current in almost all parts of the world. It is about the beautiful princess taken captive by some cruel giant and the young prince who goes out to free her from the dungeon. Do you not remember when you heard it in your boyhood, how your blood was stirred, how you felt yourselves setting out in the guise of that prince to rescue her back to freedom. Today the human soul is lying captive in the dungeon of a Giant Machine, and I ask you, my young princes, to light up the fire of enthusiasm in your hearts and rush to rescue the human soul from the tyranny of the relentless greed which keeps it chained.

My young friends, I gaze across the distance of age at your young faces, beaming with intelligence and eager interests. I am approaching the shore of the sunset-land. You stand over there with the rising sun. My heart reaches out to your hearts and blesses them.

I envy you. When I was a boy, in the dusk of the waning night, we did not fully know to what a great age we had been born. The meaning of that age has become clear today. I believe there are individuals all over the world this moment who have heard its call.

What a delight it may be for you, and what a responsibility this belonging to a period which is one of the greatest in the whole history of Man, when all races have come close to each other. We realize the immense significance of this age only dimly, in the light of a glowing fire of pain, and do not yet know what form it is going to take.

It is your mission to prove that love for the earth, and for things of the earth, is possible, without materialism, love without the vulgarity of avarice.

I am tired and old. This is perhaps my last meeting with you. With all my heart I take this occasion to entreat you not to allow yourselves to be awed by the insolence of vulgar strength, of stupendous size, nor lured by the spirit of storage by the multiplication of millions, without meaning and without end.

October 1922

15. INTRODUCING ELMHERST

As chairman, it is my primary duty to introduce to you Professor Elmherst, the lecturer of today's meeting. As my junior in years he has my affection. But deep in my heart I hold him in high regard. A time was when India saw a conflict between one race and another, one religion and another. During those medieval times of India's history saints like Ramananda broke through those barriers. They brought races and religions together and tried to bring about unity amongst Hindus and Muslims—so as to be able to deliver them out of the bounds of their narrowness. In Europe today we see the same spirit of conflict among nations. The countries there are torn by repeated wars. As a result, some of their men have started coming out into the wider world of humanity leaving behind the boundaries of nationhood and of caste and creed. By and by, we are bound to see a gradual expansion of such humanitarian work in the varied activities of men like Elmherst. And, as we come to know him through his work we shall learn to give him the respect due to him of our own accord.

After obtaining his Tripos in History from Cambridge Mr Elmherst had been to the United States to study Agriculture. I consider it necessary that I give you this background of his education. We do not wish nor expect that he should tell us something about the science of agriculture merely as an academic discipline. Nor is it the aim of today's lecture to deal with such eminently practical subjects as enriching the fertility of the soil or rotation of crops and so on. As a historian he must have studied the history of the human race in the wider perspective of man's relationship with the soil. We would like to hope that out of his study and reflection of this subject he will unfold to us his own ideas about the place that agriculture should occupy in the context of human life and civilization.

It has been my earnest desire for long that we in this country should deal with the problems of agriculture in a big way. I had sent some of our young men abroad to study agriculture so that on their return home they might tackle this problem and thus serve their motherland. During those days I had said in my article entitled *Swadeshi Samaj* that we have to reconstruct our national life with the village as the centre. To bring completeness of life to the village has been a dream of mine of long standing. That must be the reason why I shared this dream of mine with Mr Elmherst when I met him for the first time in the States. I had told him then that if he could come out to India he would have no dearth of work to do and that he might be of help in bringing to the Indian village the kind of fulfilment that I had envisaged. He readily agreed to my proposal, and, young though he be, did not hesitate in the least to take up this work with a full sense of responsibility and dedication. The way he is going ahead with this work amongst the peasantry of a country strange to him—is a marvel to watch.

One of the highlights of our Indian tradition is the legend of King Janaka who is reputed to have combined his quest for the highest truth (*Brahma*) with his knowledge of agriculture. For this wonderful synthesis that he achieved in the days of yore between the heavenly and the earthly, he is still considered to be the ideal monarch. It is in such context of the highest human ideal that we must regard the art of agriculture. If we fail to do so, this noble pursuit loses all its dignity. We cannot deny the hard truth that by looking upon agriculture as a daily repetition of drudgery our peasants humiliate themselves and wear the shibboleth of slavery of their own accord. By so doing they offer themselves for sale to the wealthy who live on the fruits of their toil. In Europe, they speak about the dignity of labour. But a peasant who is only a vassal or slave can claim no dignity. When a man exhausts all his wits plying the loom or driving a plough, he has no surplus left from cultivating his higher or nobler traits of humanity. He puts his hand to the job—but only as a machine or automation—and that is not conducive to his development as a complete human being. There can be no dignity in slaving for a wage. Manual work mechanically performed stultifies the mind and blunts the intellect. That is why a peasant drudging in a field excites only pity or contempt. Intellectuals have always looked down upon them because they find the churls have no vision, that their eyes cannot travel beyond the four corners of their fields. The intellectuals have felt that mere act of existence cannot make life worth-living.

But when a kingly sage like Janaka puts his hand to the plough, there can be no question of stultification or enslavement of the mind. When the time comes for our thinkers and intellectuals to take agricultural activities under their responsibility, the schism that at present exists between the hand and the brain for a large section of our population, will vanish. It is my earnest desire that having that aim in mind we do not grudge rendering help and cooperation to the lecturer in reaching that goal. Pray do not look upon him as a stranger from a distance simply because he is a foreigner. As he has dedicated himself to the service of mankind, he is one of us, and there can be no humiliation in accepting what he has to give. If one could see the work that he has initiated in our villages by joining hands with the local peasants, one cannot but entertain the highest regard for his enterprise. I therefore commend him and his lecture today to your best attention.

1922

16. FAREWELL TO DR M. WINTERNITZ

Acharya M. Winternitz,

Before you came to us we had been aware of your reputation as one of the foremost scholars whose knowledge comprehended an amazingly vast field of Indian literature. We felt grateful to you for having accepted our invitation and were proud to be able to receive you as our honoured guest. On the day when we must bid you farewell, let us assure you that our love for your personality has become equal to our reverence for your scholarship, and that though in outward appearance the time of your stay with us has been short, spiritually it has acquired a permanence in our heart.

Through the reticence of your modesty has sweetly shone the love of truth, and the love of man which is so completely free from race prejudice, from the narrow spirit of national egotism. Your intellectual outlook has found its moral background in the unity of man; and this has strengthened our love for the Visva-Bharati ideal. In fact, your personal contact with the inmates of this *Asrama* has been a living contribution to the building up of our Institution which for its materials must never depend upon bricks and mortar, rules and regulations, but upon its faith in human history as the history of the ceaseless endeavour to reach the highest expression of the spiritual meaning of existence.

It is needless to tell you that we started our Visva-Bharati with the expectation of attracting round it, from all parts of the world, individuals who, in the present turmoil of contradiction, still cherish hope in the ultimate triumph of the *Shantam* and *Shivam,* who in the light of the *Advaitam* will recognize themselves as brothers when they meet, though belonging to different climates and races. We have found you, dear friend, as one such, and our brothers' greetings we offer to you at this time of our parting.

1922

17. TO MY CEYLON AUDIENCE

It struck my heart with dismay, when I visited Ceylon, to find that the people there have lost the consciousness of their unity with their Indian kinsmen. Not having in their mind a continental background for their culture and aspiration, they have permitted their intellectual and spiritual individuality to miss its shelter, and easily to drift into the vagabondage of imitation.

They seem to have forgotten that political division is merely a division of property through which we can change our residence, but not our brotherhood.

When the mouth of the branch of a great river is choked up, the branch becomes reduced to a stagnant pool; the pulsation of the ocean heart no longer reaches it, nor the living message that flows from the hoary height of the inaccessible. A community, cut off from its parent stem by disastrous oblivion, is sure to forget the great meaning of its own personality, and thus to fall a prey to the force of other personalities and be bent and clipped and hammered by them to their purposes. A tree grows in its own shape and finds its fulfilment, but when cut off from its root it is, as timber, at the mercy of the dealers who turn it into toys of their fancy.

Life is original; it is adventurous; it seeks itself in endless experiments, the outcome of its spontaneous creative impulse. The people, who passively lend themselves to imitation, prove that life has lost its best claim on their hearts. It is the temptation of *Māra,* the evil spirit of Untruth, which whispers to us that we can be better than we are by seeming to be something else.

Thus we yield ourselves to being slowly robbed of the best gift given to us by God,—the dignity of our individual existence with its infinite possibilities of creation. We must never allow this to happen on either side of the water that divides this island of Ceylon from India.

Our subconscious self has the accumulation of ages of creative memory, wherein has grown in secret the racial genius which creates. The whole current of a people's history generates its own special energy of guidance in this region lying beneath the surface-consciousness of our mind. This is why, when we try to imitate some other people's history, we remain so pathetically unaware of the absurdities that are produced.

There can be no doubt that Ceylon's subconscious mind, its racial mind, has unbroken connection with that of India; the language which she speaks has all the subtle modulations, her physical organism all the characteristic gestures, that belong to it. When her conscious self tries to ignore this, and attaches itself to some alien mentality, then its progress, like that of a three-legged race in which legs belonging to different individuals are tied together, takes on a gait which is neither efficient, nor graceful.

All our efforts which are unmixed imitations are lame, for in them our conscious will ignores the co-operation of its great partner, our fundamental personality, which nevertheless goes on working in the subsoil of our consciousness. History, properly studied, saves us from these unrhythmic strivings which go contrary to the direction of our inmost nature; and Ceylon if she would do herself justice, must acknowledge that her intellectual and spiritual history runs in one stream with the cultural history of India.

The great religion of the Buddha had once spread its living spirit of Unity over the greater part of Asia. It drew race together and turned their hope and faith away from the turmoil of self-seeking.

True, the modern facilities of science have also established human communication across geographical barriers; but in this, man has only utilised physical forces to overcome physical obstructions. Buddhism was the first spiritual force, known to us in history, which drew close together such a large number of races separated by most difficult barriers of distance, by differences of language and custom, by various degrees and divergent types of civilization. It had its motive power, neither in international commerce, nor in empire-building, nor in scientific curiosity, nor in a migratory impulse to occupy fresh territory. It was a purely disinterested effort to help mankind forward to its final goal.

The religion, which flowed from the comprehensive mind of Buddha, has its negative aspect,—the control of passion and renunciation of self,—for purifying spiritual ideas and religious phraseology from all narrowness, anthropomorphic, or egotistic; it is the path of discipline through elimination. But this cannot be the whole of it; and that this has not been all, is amply proved by the direction and form which Buddhism has naturally taken in the greater part of the Buddhistic world.

A seed has, as a portion of its body, the sheath which is hard, which is for its protection; but it also has its kernel which grows, which takes it out of its obscurity and spreads its branches wide. The special aspect of Buddhism, that has grown and spread its branching life far away from its mother soil, that has subdued the savage in the races which were primitive, and inspired in them art and literature, must have been its religious nucleus, carrying in itself the vital principle of Buddha's teaching. This life force, which is the positive element in Buddhism, has neither been lost in India herself; it is still working in the heart of even her lattermost religions in various shapes.

I have lately been reading a book about Buddhism, written by one who professes this religion. Our Buddhist author has tried to prove, that though Buddhism had its origin in geographical India, neither did its seed come from the Indian culture, nor did its root draw sap from the Indian mind. In other words, he would make out that it was an accident, which had no previous history, no natural genesis in a continued line of ancestors. In his zeal, the author is acrimoniously violent in the assertion that Buddhism as a religion is absolutely contrary to whatever preceded it in the religious history of India.

The child in the very process of birth manifests an apparent antagonism to the mother. All the same, the birth can never be a repudiation of the parent. There can be no question that Buddhism was one of the great products of the mother-heart of India.

We are free to admit that after centuries of its domination there was, outwardly a violent reaction against it. But when the history of that period is thoroughly investigated, I have no doubt that it will be found that what was forcibly thrown out was no part of the original idea of Buddhism, but a medley of miscellaneous aberrations, interpolated mostly from the dense tangle of non-Aryan superstitions.

That which I value most in my religion or my aspiration, I seek to find corroborated, in its fundamental unity, in other great religions, or in the hopes expressed in the history of other peoples. Each great movement of thought and endeavour in any part of the world may have something unique in its expression, but the truth underlying any of them never has the meretricious cheapness of utter novelty about it. The great Ganges must not hesitate to declare its essential similarity to the Nile of Egypt, or to the Yangtse-Kiang of China. Only a water spout displays a sudden arrogance of singularity and vanishes in the void, leaving mother Nature ashamed of so monstrous a production!

Whenever we find, in the immensity of the human mind the prototype of something which we hold most precious in ourselves, we should rejoice. The pride of special possession can cling only to those results of pot culture, which have merely market value. But great truths, like great monarchs of the forest, disdain to exhibit any extravagant speciality, which may offer temptation to those who are jealous of their proprietary right in rareness. The great is never alone; it has its aristocracy of the sublime, its common kinship of the immortal.

This is why, because I consider Buddhism to be one of the greatest religious achievements of man, I find a delight in discovering some of its essential similarities, not only to the spiritual thought of ancient India, but to that of other great religions as well. Is it right that we should have pride merely in some special production of man, but not in Man himself? Only those, who have no respect for humanity as a whole, can believe that Truth, in its supreme aspect, has been reached only once by one chosen people, leaving no alternative to others but to borrow from it, or else to live in utter spiritual destitution.

I cannot accept from anybody the statement, that Buddhism was a freak of human nature, and that as a religion, utterly unlike any other religion in the world, it is not only unrelated, but contradictory to its spiritual surroundings; that it is the science and art of self-extinction referring to a world where there is no true principle of unity anywhere, within man, or outside him.

Once again I assert that no religion whatsoever can for a moment stand on the basis of negation. It must have some great truth in its heart which is positive and eternal, and for whose sake Man can offer all that he has, and be glad. And, in this, Buddhism must have its inherent relation and resemblance to that spiritual endeavour in ancient India which led men to leave aside their material possessions and seek the fulfilment of their life.

And what is this truth which the Buddha preached, which is eternal? It is *Dharma,* difficult to be rendered in English. Perhaps it may be translated as the 'highest ideal of perfection'. Certainly it is not a logical abstraction, nothing which is merely subjective. It is a reality which has to be reached, and according to the degree of our relationship with it, we attain the fulfilment of life. So this *Dharma* and the *Brahma* of our Upanishads are essentially the same, in regard to that which is supreme Reality.

The Buddhist *Dharma* does not consist in mere reason, blind and dark. It comprises within itself the highest spiritual enlightenment; it is eternally true for all beings; its laws are not restricted to any boundary of outward circumstances. Therefore it has the principle of reality, wisdom, and infinity. Likewise it has been said in the Upanishad: *Satyam, Jnanam, Anantam, Brahma,—Brahma is truth, wisdom, and eternity.* Then again, *Dharma* has not merely its reality, like the universal force of gravitation; it has its moral value, it leads us to peace, goodness and love. Similarly the *Brahma* of the Upanishad, who is *Satyam,* is also *Santam, Sivam, Advaitam,* which means that in *Brahma* is peace, goodness and union.

Dharma in Buddhism, or *Dharma Kāyā*, as it has been termed in some of the Buddhist scriptures, is an eternal reality of Peace, Goodness and Love, for which man can offer up the homage of his highest loyalty, his life itself. This *Dharma* can inspire man with almost superhuman power of renunciation, and through the abnegation of self, lead him to the supreme object of his existence, a state that cannot be compared to anything we know in this world; and yet of which we can at least have a dim idea, when we know that it is only to be reached, not through the path of annihilation, but through immeasurable love. Thus, to dwell in the constant consciousness of unbounded love is named by Lord Buddha: *Brahma-Vihara, —moving in Brahma.*

However, let me not dwell too long on my own idea about the essential points of resemblance between the truths of Buddhism and the truths inculcated in the Upanishads. Those who want to indulge their sectarian pride by believing that they only are the fortunate people in the world, in possession of religion absolutely solitary in its singularity, I shall leave to their exultation. But I cannot allow the historical link of Buddhism with India's mind to be ignored, and I must assert that the truest relationship among human beings is that of ideals; a relationship more real indeed than even the kinship of blood.

What is this Visva-Bharati, this international institution—I was asked to explain. It may not be out of place to reproduce in our journal the explanation which I gave of the Visva-Bharati ideal to my Ceylon audience.

The word 'international' may sound too indefinite,—its meaning appearing large only because of its vagueness, like water acquiring volume by turning into vapour. I do not believe in an internationalism which is amorphous, whose features are broadened into flatness. The internationalism of Visva-Bharati must be the internationalism of India, with its own distinct character.

The true universal finds its manifestation in the individuality which is true. Beauty is universal, and a rose reveals it because, as a rose, it is individually beautiful. By making a decoction of a rose, jasmine and lotus, you do not get to a realization of some larger beauty which is interfloral. The true universalism is not the breaking down of the walls of one's own house, but the offering of hospitality to one's guests and neighbours.

Like the position of the earth in the course of its diurnal and annual motions, man's life, at any moment, must be the reconciliation of its two movements, one round the centre of its own personality, and another whose centre is in a luminous ideal comprehending the whole human world. The international endeavour of a people must carry the moment of the people's own personality round the great spirit of man. The inspiration must be its own, which is to help it in its aspiration towards fulfilment. Otherwise, mere cosmopolitanism but drifts on the waves, buffeted by wind from all quarters, in an imbecility of movement which has no progress.

One of the objects of Visva-Bharati is concerned with the personality of the people she represents,—to rescue this personality from the dimness of ignorance. As a people we must be fully conscious of what we are. It is a truism to say that the consciousness of the unity of a people implies a knowledge of its parts as well as of its whole. But, we not only have no such knowledge of India, we do not even have an eager desire to cultivate it.

By asserting our national unity with vehemence in our patriotic propaganda, we assure ourselves that we possess it, and thus continue to live in a make-believe world of political day-dreams. The greater part of Bengal's knowledge of the Punjab consists in its relative position upon the maps of India, —a mere outline of information of a dead kind. How many Bengalis are there, who have studied the message of Nanak that has come to us through the Sikhs? And are there students in the Punjab, who have tried to understand the Vaishnavism of Chaitanya, and what place it occupies in the religious culture of India? India is the one place in the world, where the science of Ethnology can be studied with the full advantage; and yet it has never, aroused any enthusiasm in our students.

The fact is, we have a very feeble human interest in our own country. We love to talk about politics and economics; we are ready to soar into the thin air of academic abstractions, or to roam in the dusk of pedantic wildernesses; but we never care to cross our social boundaries and come to the door of our neighbouring communities, personally to inquire how they think and feel and express themselves, and how they fashion their lives.

The love of man has its own hunger for knowing. Even if we lack this concerning our fellow-beings in India, except in our political protestations, at least love of knowledge for its own sake could have brought us close to each other. But there also we have failed and have suffered. For weakness of knowledge is the foundation of weakness of power. Until India becomes fully distinct in our mind, we can never gain her in truth; and where truth is imperfect, love can never have its full sway. 'Know thyself,' for the giving of self is waiting for that knowledge. One of the endeavours of Visva-Bharati is to help us to *know* ourselves; and then along with it, her other mission will be fulfilled which is to inspire us to *give* ourselves.

What has given such enormous intellectual power to Europe is her concentration of mind. She has evolved a means by which all the countries of that continent can think together. Such a great concert of ideas, by its own pressure of movement, naturally wears away all her individual aberrations of thought and extravagances of unreason. It keeps her flights of fancy close to the limits of reticence. All her different thought-rays have been focussed in one common culture, which finds its complete expression in all the great European universities.

The mind of India, on the other hand, is divided and scattered; there is no one common pathway along which we can reach it. Up to the present, in all our patriotic endeavours, our effort has been to establish our unity on the basis of our common interest in the political or economic situation. It is like gathering coals for our railway journey, while the locomotive is nowhere to be found!

So I must guard myself against the least chance of my audience carrying away the belief that Visva-Bharati bases its ideal upon any ulterior expectation, political or otherwise. Its one object is to help each student to realize his personality, as an individual representing his people, in such a broad spirit, in such an unobstructed sunshine of spiritual expansion of consciousness, that he may know how it is the most important fact of his life for him to have been born to the great world of man.

1922

18. LETTER TO LORD LYTTON

Your Excellency,

I am being urged by my countrymen to assist them in giving expression to their sense of indignation at the remark made by your Excellency in referring to the complaint regarding police outrages on Indian woman.

There can be no room for doubt that the great majority of my countrymen who have come across your Excellency's reported words have been profoundly hurt by what they have taken them to mean—a meaning so far as I am aware which has upto now have not been authoritatively stated to have been wrongly attributed to those words.

At the same time knowing what I do of your excellency personally and of the traditions of chivalry which are your inheritance, I find if extremely difficult to believe that it could have been your Excellency's intention to cast aspersions on the fair names of the women of our country or even to hurt the feelings of my countrymen.

So I feel that I owe it to your Excellency, no less than to myself, frankly to write and ask what your Excellency's real meaning was, before saying anything further about the matter.

Trusting your Excellency will excuse any liberty which I may have unknowingly taken.

1924

19. BIRTH CONTROL MOVEMENT

Dear Margaret Sanger,

I am of opinion that the Birth Control movement is a great movement not only because it will save women from enforced and undesirable maternity, but because it will help the cause of peace of lessening the number of surplus population of a country, scrambling for food and space outside its own rightful limits. In a hunger-striken country like India it is a cruel crime thoughtlessly to bring more children to existence than could properly be taken care of, causing endless sufferings to them and imposing a degrading condition upon the whole family. It is evident that the utter helplessness of a growing poverty very rarely acts as a check controlling the burden of over-population. It proves that in this case nature's urging gets the better of the severe warning that comes from the providence of civilized social life. Therefore, I believe, that to wait till the moral sense of man becomes a great deal more powerful than it is now and till then to allow countless generations of children to suffer privations and untimely death for no fault of their own is a great social injustice which should not be tolerated. I feel grateful for the cause you have made your own and for which you have suffered.

'I am eagerly waiting for the literature that has been sent to me according to your letter, and I have asked our Secretary to send you our Visva-Bharati Journal in exchange for your Birth Control Review.'

1926

20. 'KNIGHTHOOD'

Being aware that a discussion has been raised in regard to my Knighthood, I feel it right to put clearly my own view of it before the public. It is obvious that it was solely to give utmost emphasis to the expression of my indignation at the Jallianwalla Bagh massacre and other deeds of inhumanity that followed it that I asked Lord Chelmford to take it back from me. If I had not fully realized the value of this title, it would have been impertinent on my part to offer it as a sacrifice when such was needed in order to give strength to my voice. I have not the overweening conceit discourteously to display an insincere attitude of contempt for a title of honour which was conferred on me in recognition of my literary work. I greatly abhor to make any public gesture which may have the least suggestion of a theatrical character. But in this particular case I was driven to it when I hopelessly failed to persuade our political leaders to launch an adequate protest against what was happening at that time in the Punjab.

A title of personal distinction for some merit that has a universal value is never a reward of favour. To show honour where it is truly due is the responsibility of the party who does it and any token of it should not be thrown away, unless for an exceptional occasion or purpose which is painfully imperative. I am not callously insensitive to the approbation which I have been fortunate enough to gain from outside my own country, and for the same reason, I also feel proud that men like Jagadish Chandra Bose and Prafulla Chandra Ray have won a title valuable like any other real recognition which our country may rightfully claim. The only complaint that can be made is that this title is fast losing its distinction through its heterogenous associations and that the above-named illustrious countrymen of ours are made to put up with too many strange bed-fellows in the career of glory. While concluding I confess to an idiosyncrasy, which has already been pointed out to the Editor of this journal, that I do not like any addition to my name,—Babu or Sriyut, Sir Doctor, or Mr., and least of all, Esquire. A psycho-analyst may trace this to a sense of pride in the depth of my being and he may not be wrong.

February 1926

21. DESHBANDHU CHITTARANJAN DAS

Man truly reveals himself through his gift, and the best gift that Chittaranjan has left for his countrymen is not any particular political or social programme, but the creative force of a great aspiration that has taken a deathless form in the sacrifice which his life represented.

1925

22. ROMAIN ROLLAND

While in America, I had occasion to talk about the rapid and enormous growth of organizations which attain their irresistible efficiency by eliminating the personal man and concentrating the mechanical one in a huge lump of system. I spoke of the spread of callousness and the deadening of the moral sense of responsibility in consequence of the machine representing man in most of his activities. Cruelty and injustice of an appalling kind have today been made easily possible, because they can be done through an organized elemental force which ruthlessly takes a direct path towards the fulfilment of its purpose, trampling down all other considerations. We have seen how the church can be blood-thirsty, while the religion it represents is humane; how it is possible to cheat on a wholesale scale in the name of business, while the respectability of the shares of profit remains untouched; how gross falsehoods are deliberately used for poisoning their victims by governments whose members have gentlemanly manners and traditions. When in loyalty to such gigantic institutions men commit terrible wrongs, they feel something like a religious exultation which smothers their conscience. It is the modern form of fetish worship with its numerous rituals of human sacrifice, in the shadow of which all other religions have faded into unreality.

One of my hearers who was in sympathy with my thoughts asked me how it could be possible to fight these organizations without setting up others in their place. My answer was that my reliance is on those individuals who have made human ideals living in their personality. They may look small and weak by the side of the power they resist, as does a plant by the side of a huge, frowning boulder. But the plant has the magic power of life. It gradually creates its own soil with its own constant emanations, and its defeat and death are a prelude to a victorious resurrection. I believe that when anti-human forces spread their dominion, individuals with firm faith in humanity are born, who become acutely conscious of the menace to man and fearlessly fulfil their destiny through insult and isolation. We came to know such a man in England in the person of E.D. Morel who is dead now, but who can never die. When we see them, we know that the living spark of human spirit is not yet extinct and that there is hope. Human civilizations have their genesis in individuals, and they also have their protectors in them. One of the few proofs that the present day is not utterly barren of them is the life and work of Romain Rolland. And that the present day needs him most is proved by the scourging he has received from it, which is a true recognition of his greatness by his fellow-beings.

1925

23. FAREWELL ADDRESS TO CARLO FORMICHI

Dear Friend,

The happy time of our meeting in Santiniketan, in the atmosphere of rich leisure and peaceful cooperation, has at last come to its end, and your departure from our midst draws near. The very few weeks that you have been able to give us contain in them a full harvest of friendship that in the normal course of things would require the sunshine of a lifetime to mature. I know that our scholars here, with whom you worked, and who have come to appreciate heartily the value of the help you rendered and of the kindness you showed to them, will always remember you with grateful admiration. Your scholarship has most impressed us for its living and luminous quality of imagination; we have realized that your study of Indian culture does not merely reveal a scientific mind, but a personality full of sympathetic insight. Having the noble modesty of the truth-seeker, your unbiased mind could come into intimate touch with the ideal India, with all that is immortal in her of beauty and truth. Your discriminate appreciation has helped our students in directing their loyalty to the best that India has achieved in her intellectual and spiritual adventures—loyalty which is needed for the building up of a fruitful future on the promise of a fertile past.

In your own nature you have brought to us a gift which is not merely an outcome of a studious, scholarly training, but something native to the kindly soil of your mother country. It is that generosity of heart which has the magic power of bidding open the door of the inner sanctum of an alien race. I shall always remember the happiness of those days which we shared together when profuse welcome was lavished upon us by the springtime in the eastern districts of our province, when all along our path we were repeatedly roused by the loud greetings of colour from the extravagant *kinshukas,* from the *ashoka* groves, blossoming with wistful reminiscences of a far-away lyric age in India. It made me feel proud of your companionship when I realized how easily your own accommodating kindliness found its way into the hospitality of our people, across the natural boundaries of unaccustomed habits and manners.

Your arrival in our *ashrama* was accompanied by the gift of an Italian library from your country, surprising in its magnificence. It has already aroused in our students a desire to honour it by owning it truly, thereby directly reaching that great source of inspiration which, in a period of new birth in European history, brought out such a variegated luxuriance of intellect and art on the western continent. This library has been a generous invitation to our people by your country to the feast of soul in that guest-house of hers which is open to all time and to all humanity.

You were a worthy bearer of this message from your own land; but being a true lover of India, you must also act as messenger on our behalf in carrying our assurance to Italy that this friendly beckoning of hers has given a permanent direction to our mind in its communication with herself. And all this is in accord with the ideal of Visva-bharati which, as you know, is to realize the freedom of pathway along the vast realm of man, widening our consciousness of the unity of spirit in the different human races. Your genial presence among us, the valuable service you have rendered to our *ashrama,* the precious token of sympathy you brought to us from your country and the masterly exposition you gave us of the gradual course of the spiritual illumination running through the period of Vedic India, has greatly strengthened our cause, creating a strong link with Italy in our bond of human solidarity.

In this connection I must mention the name of your former pupil Dr. Tucci, who is still with us and for the loan of whose services I cannot enough thank your government. He has studied with an amazing comprehensiveness, along with most of the other phenomena of ancient Indian culture, the greatest period of India's history; he has pursued the triumphant career of Buddhism in distant countries, following almost obliterated indications across the sand-buried antiquities, among the records of a startled history that has lost the memory of its own language. He can best remind the modern children of India of what has been the most glorious self-revelation in the annals of their ancestors. That was her ideal of universal sympathy—made uniquely real in the relationship which India at one time established with the neighbouring and distant countries through her self-conquering messengers, unarmed and unafraid, without greed and devoid of material means,—the ideal which urged one of her mightiest emperors in the hey day of his power to transfer the progress of his conquest and the expansion of his empire from the political to the moral plane.

It is our desire to proclaim this richest birth-right of ours as Indians, our faith in this *dharma* which enjoins every man to realize, through the cultivation of *maitri,* the truth of his own self in the Truth which dwells in the All. You who come as a voice from across the seas giving harmony to the voice of the Eternal in the aspiration of India, you who allow us to realize in yourself the spiritual kinship of love and disinterested service,—you have helped us in this dark age of international suspicion and jealousy to light our lamp, which is dedicated to the divine spirit of *maitri,* acknowledged by Visva-bharati as the true ideal of India. And, therefore, our farewell today contains within it the deeper silent welcome of all days to our world of endeavour which will always carry in its heart the memorial of the best that your own life has offered to its creation.

Before we part, allow me to say that my relation with you is not merely through the cause I cherish in our institution. It is warmly personal and is intimately associated with my love for Italy and with the exuberant welcome which I received from her. If, owing to my increasing weakness and ill-health, I am prevented from claiming her hospitality ever again, her touch will always remain with me in the many relics of our meeting and the permanent representation you leave behind in the *ashrama* of the treasure of her thoughts and dreams, and of the large-heartedness of her people.

1925

24. PHILOSOPHY OF FASCISM

REFUSAL OF SUPPORT

My mind is passing through a conflict. I have my love and gratitude for the people of Italy. I deeply appreciate their feeling of admiration for me, which is so genuine and generous. On the other hand, the Italy revealed in Fascism alienates itself from the ideal picture of that great country which I should love to cherish in my heart.

You know I had my first introduction to Italy when I was invited to Milan last year. It takes a long time to study the mind of a people, but not long to feel their heart when that heart opens itself. I was in the city only for a very few days, and in that time I realized that the people loved me. Rightly or wrongly, one can claim praise as one's desert, but love is a surprise every time it comes. I was strongly moved by that surprise when I found loving friends and not merely kind hosts in the people of Italy. It grieved me deeply, and I felt almost ashamed when I suddenly fell ill and had to sail back home before I could fulfil my engagements in all the other towns.

Then followed the magnificent gift from Mussolini, an almost complete library of Italian literature, for my institution.

It was a great surprise to me. In this greeting I felt the touch of a personality which could express itself in this direct manner in an appropriate action of unstinted magnificence. This helped me to make up my mind to visit Italy once again, in spite of the misgivings created by the reports reaching us in India about the character of the Fascist movement. I had neither the qualifications nor any inclination to dabble in the internal political issues of the European countries. For this reason I wanted to keep my mind neutral when I came to Italy. But we live in a whirlwind of talk today, and an individual like myself is compelled to contribute to that universal noise, dragged by the chain of *Karma,* as we say in our country. I allowed myself to fall a victim to this relentness *Karma,* with its ever lengthening coil of consequence, when I succumbed to the importunity of the interviewers in Italy.

THE INTERVIEWS IN ITALY

The interview is a dangerous trap in which our unwary opinions are not only captured but mutilated. Words that come out of a moment's mood are meant to be forgotten; but when they are snapshotted, most often our thoughts are presented in a grotesque posture which is chance's irony. The camera in this case being also a living mind, the picture becomes a composite one in which two dissimilar features of mentality have made a *mesalliance* that is likely to be unhappy and undignified. My interviews in Italy were the products of three personalities—the reporter's, the interpreter's, and my own. Over and above that, there evidently was a hum in the atmosphere of another insistent and universal whisper which, without our knowing it, mingled in all our talks. Being ignorant of Italian I had no means of checking the result of this concoction. The only precaution which I could take was to repeat emphatically to all my listeners that I had as yet no opportunity to study the history and character of Fascism.

Since then I have had the opportunity of learning the contents of some of these interviews from the newspaper cuttings that my friends have gathered and translated for me.

And I was not surprised to find in them what was, perhaps, inevitable. Through misunderstanding, wrong emphasis, natural defects in the medium of communication, and the pre-occupation of the national mind, some of these writings have been made to convey that I have given my deliberate opinion on Fascism, expressing my unqualified admiration.

This time it was not directly the people of Italy whose hospitality I enjoyed, but that of Mussolini himself as the head of the Government. This was, no doubt, an act of kindness, but somewhat unfortunate for me. For always and everywhere official vehicles, though comfortable, move only along a chalked path of programme too restricted to lead to any places of significance, or persons of daring individuality, providing the visitors with specially selected morsels of experience.

The only opinions I could gather in such an atmosphere of distraction were enthusiastically unanimous in praise of Mussolini for having rescued Italy in a most critical moment of her history, from the brink of ruin.

ABSURD TO IMAGINE THAT I COULD SUPPORT IT

In Rome I came to know a professor, a genuinely spiritual character, a seeker of peace who was strongly convinced not only of the necessity but of the philosophy of Fascism. About the necessity I am not competent to discuss, but about the philosophy I am doubtful. For it costs very little to fashion a suitable philosophy in order to mitigate the rudeness of facts that secretly hurt one's conscience. One statement which particularly surprised me, coming from the mouths of fervent patriots, was that the Italian people owing to their unreasoning impulsive nature, had proved their incapacity to govern themselves, and that, therefore, in the inevitable logic of things, they lent themselves to government from outside by strong hands.

However, these are facts that immediately and exclusively concern Italy herself, though their validity has sometimes been challenged by European critics. But whatever maybe the case as to that, the methods and the principles of Fascism concern all humanity, and it is absurd to imagine that I could ever support a movement which ruthlessly suppresses freedom of expression, enforces observances that are against individual conscience, and walks through a bloodstained path of violence and stealthy crime. I have said over and over again that the aggressive spirit of Nationalism and Imperialism, religiously cultivated by most of the nations of the West, is a menace to the whole world. The demoralisation which it produces in European politics is sure to have disastrous effects, especially upon the peoples of the East who are helpless to resist the Western methods of exploitation. It would be most foolish, if it were not almost criminal, for me to express my admiration for a political ideal which openly declares its loyalty to brute force as the motive power of civilization. That barbarism is not altogether incompatible with material prosperity may be taken for granted, out the cost is terribly great; indeed it is fatal. The worship of unscrupulous force as the vehicle of nationalism keeps ignited the fire of international jealousy, and makes for universal incendiarism, for a fearful orgy of devastation. The mischief of the infection of this moral aberration is great because today the races of humanity have come close together, and any process of destruction act going does its work on an enormously vast scale. Knowing all this, could it be believed that I should have played my fiddle while an unholy fire was being fed with human sacrifice?

FASCISM AN AMERICAN INFECTION?

I was greatly amused when reading a Fascist organ to find a writer vehemently decrying the pantheistic philosophy of the passive and the meditative East, and contrasting it with the vigorous self-assertion and fury of efficiency which he acknowledges to have been borrowed by his people from their modern schoolmasters in America. This has suggested to my mind the possibility of the idea of Fascism being actually an infection from across the Atlantic.

The unconscious irony in the article I refer to lies in the fact of the writer's using with unction the name of Christianity in this context—a religion which had its origin in the East. He evidently does not realize that if Christ had been born again in this world he would have been forcibly turned back from New York had he come there from abroad—if for no other reason, then certainly for the want of the necessary amount of dollars to be shown to the gatekeeper. Or if he had been born in that country, the Ku Klux Klan would have beaten him to death or lynched him. For did he not give utterance to that political blasphemy, "Blessed are the meek", thus insulting the Nordic right to rule the world, and to that economic heresy, "Blessed are the poor?" Would he not have been put in prison for twenty or more years for saying that it was as easy for the prosperous to reach the Kingdom of Heaven as for the camel to pass through the eye of a needle?

CHRISTIANITY AND EUROPEAN POLITICAL THOUGHT

The Fascist professor deals a penthrust against what he calls our pantheism; but that is a word that has no synonym in our language, nor has the doctrine any place in our philosophy. He does not seem to have realized that the idea of Christian theology, that God remains essentially what he is while manifesting himself in the Son's being, belongs to the same principle as our principle of immanence. According to this doctrine the divinity of God accepts humanity for its purpose of self-revelation and thus bridges the infinite gulf between the two. This idea has glorified all human beings, and has had the effect in the Christian West of emancipating individuals from the thraldom of absolute power. It has trained that attitude of mind which is the origin of the best internal politics of the Western peoples. It has helped to distribute the power of government all over the country, and thus has given it a permanent foundation which cannot be tampered with or destroyed by the will of one individual or the whim of a group. This consciousness of the dignity of the individual has encouraged in the West the freedom of conscience and thought. We in the East come to Europe for this inspiration. We are also dreaming of the time when the individuals belonging to the people of India will have courage to think for themselves and express their thoughts, feel their strength, know their rights, and take charge of their own government.

AGGRANDISEMENT OF THE SLAVE STATE: A LESSON FROM INDIA

The Fascist writer I have quoted is evidently fascinated by the prospect of the economic self-aggrandisement of the nation at the cost of the moral self-respect of the people. But it is the killing of the goose for the sake of golden eggs. In the olden civilizations the slavery of the people did build up for the time being powers of stupendous splendour. But this spirit of slavishness constantly weakened the foundations till the towers came down into the dust, offering as their contribution to humanity ruins haunted by venerable ghosts.

In bygone days in India the State was only a part of the people. The mass of the population had its own self-government in the village community. Dynasties changed, but the people always possessed the power to manage all that was vital to them. This saved them from sinking into barbarism, this has given our country a continuity through centuries of political vicissitudes.

Our Western rulers have destroyed this fundamental structure of our civilization, the civilization based upon the obligations of intimate human relationship. And therefore nothing today has been left for the people through which they can express their collective mind, their creative will, or realize the dignity of their soul, except the political instrument, the foreign model of which is always present before their envious gaze. We come to Europe for our lesson in the mastery of this instrument, as Japan has done and has been successful in her purpose. But must our friend the Fascist philosopher come to us to copy our political impotence, the result of the surrender of freedom for centuries to the authority of some exclusive reservoir of concentrated power, while rejecting our great ideal of spiritual freedom, which has its basis in the philosophy that infinite truth is everywhere, that it is for everyone to reach it by removing the obstruction of the self that obscures light!

IMPRESSION OF MUSSOLINI

I am sure you will be interested to know what was the impression that I have carried away from my interview with Mussolini. We met only twice, and our meetings were extremely brief, owing very likely to our difficulty of communication through the slow and interrupted medium of an interpreter.

In a hall of which the great size is accentuated by an unusual bareness of furniture, Mussolini has his seat in a distant corner. I believe this gives him the time and space to observe visitors who approach him, and makes him ready to deal with them. I was not sure of his identity while he was walking towards me to receive me, for he was not tall in proportion to his fame that towers high. But when he came near me I was startled by the massive strength of his head. The lower part of the face, the lips, the smile, revealed a singular contradiction to the upper part, and I have often wondered since then if there was not a secret hesitation in his nature, a timid doubt which was human. Such an admixture of vacillation in a masterful personality makes his power of determination all the more vigilant and strong because of the internecine fight in its own character. But this is a mere surmise.

For an artist it is a great chance to be able to meet a man of personality who walks solitary among those who are mere fragments of a crowd which is always on the move, pressed from behind. He is fully visible in his integrity above the lower horizon obstructed by the dense human undergrowth. Such men are the masters of history, and one cannot but feel anxious least they miss their eternity by using all their force in taking the present by the throat, leaving it dead for all time. Men have not altogether been rare who furiously created their world by trampling human materials into the shape of their megalomaniac dreams, to burden history at last with the bleached bones of their short-lived glory; while there were others, the serene souls, who with the light of truth and magic of love have made deserts fruitful along endless stretches of grateful years.

SUSPENDED APPRAISEMENT

But to be honest, I must confess that I cannot fully trust my own impression, caught from a momentary glimpse of Mussolini in which mingled the emphasis of the surroundings in which I was placed. There have been times when history has played tricks with man and through a combination of accidents has magnified the features of essentially small persons into a parody of greatness. Such a distortion of truth often finds its chance not because these men have an extraordinary weakness of those whom they lead. This produces a mirage that falsifies the real and startles our imagination into a feeling of awe and exaggerated expectation.

To be tortured by tyranny is tolerable; but to be deluded into the worship of a wrong ideal is humiliating for the whole age which has blundered into submission to it. If Italy has made even a temporary gain through ruthless politics she may be excused for such an obsession; but for us, if we believe an idealism, there can be no such excuse. And therefore it would be wise for us to wait before we bring our homage to a person who has suddenly been forced upon our attention by a catastrophe, till through the process of time all the veils are removed that are woven round him by the vivid sensations of the moment.

My letter has run to a great length. But I hope you will bear with it, knowing that it has helped me in making my thoughts clear about my experience in Italy and also in explaining the situation in which I have been placed. This letter which I write to you I shall make use of in removing the misstanding that has unfortunately been created in the minds of those who are in harmony with my ideals about the problems of the present age.

Vienna, 20 July 1926

25. FASCISM DENOUNCED

Sir, Professor Formichi is one of my best friends in Europe, and I do not wish to enter into a controversy with him about a subject that has already given him pain. It is enough that there has been a misunderstanding for which I myself must acknowledge my own share of the blame.

The literature that had reached me before I started for Italy was full of condemnation against Fascism and its leaders. And this was why it amazed me when the magnificent gift of an Italian library came to our Institution directly from Mussolini, proving in a most appropriate manner his appreciation of our own cause. This generous expression of sympathy was followed by his lending to Santiniketan the service of Dr. Tucci, for whose scholarship I have an unbounded admiration. When, owing to this fact, my mind was hesitating between the two contrary inclinations, every evidence in favour of the present Government of Italy brought great relief to me. Such evidences appeared to me at that time as numerous, and what gave a special weight to them was the favourable testimony of some English residents in Italy, whom I chanced to meet. All this helped to make me feel at ease when I enjoyed the hospitality of the Italian Government, also to cherish the expectation that a channel of communication would be opened through Italy that would bring India closer into touch with Europe. There was every chance of such an expectation being fulfilled because of the fact that in the present-day Italy a human personality could make its mind work directly, and not through the wilderness of pulleys and wheels of a complex machinery of administration.

It may be because of the great attraction that we have in the East not so much for an efficient organization as for some living genius in all departments of society that I was naturally drawn to the vision of a creative mind, working in the person of Mussolini, moulding the destiny of Italy, infusing life into her from his own abundant life when she showed any sign of feebleness. That such was the case had often been declared to me by all types of men, commencing with the captain of the steamer that brought me to Europe and ending with a professor who believed in a spiritual significance of civilization. For some time I felt almost elated with the idea that an object-lesson was being offered by Italy to show that an ample room could be made for human personality in the heart of a political machine, modulating its rhythm in sympathy with the movement of a great living mind.

But this does not at all mean that I had any sympathy for the methods of Fascism, the nature of which I gradually came to learn at a later date. Even during my stay in Italy I was shocked and surprised when an Englishman in Rome, in his talk to me, tried to defend the Italian Government for forcing the teaching of Roman Catholicism through its educational institutions, saying that the State as an organism has the natural right, for the sake of its welfare, to choose its own particular religion and never to allow individuals in exercise their own choice. We personally know from the modern instances in India what a blind power of darkness religious sectarianism does represent, often giving rise to a fury of blasphemous inhumanity. European history also reveals the terrible danger of an epicureanism of destructive passion when religion makes its alliance with physical force and material power. The talk with the Englishman suddenly made me aware for the first time in my tour, of the stifled voice and tortured conscience in Italy of the dominance of ruthless coercion that stood darkly hidden behind the screen on which was thrown the shadow picture of prosperity and peace. It struck me all the more strongly because I knew that there was a time when Mussolini had openly expressed his hatred of all religions in an extravagant language of abhorrence. For the first time it made me suspect that possibly there was something unnatural in the high-pitched protestation of happiness by the people whom I met, that it rang loudly upon the dread hush of a universal fear.

I need not go into detail about the communications that were poured upon me by the victims of Fascism when I came out of Italy. I felt bound to assure my friends that the rumour which spread the impression that I supported Fascism as an ideal was unjust to me, that I still decried the despotic intimidation of spirit that humiliates the inner man in order to decorate him with a costly semblance of an outer glory.

At the same time I must confess that the more one studies the conditions of the different European Governments the more one is convinced that political freedom of the people, however desirable as an idea cannot be attained merely through the help of an organization. Like the spiritual freedom in an individual, it can only be won by a nation through self-discipline, through a self-respecting trustworthiness that naturally produces mutual trust, through voluntary submission to law and order. Where mastery of self is feeble the tyranny from outside compulsion is inevitable. It has become evident to us all that the best instrument of the freedom for the people has been created and mastered by the British nation only because it is one with its own character.

September 1926

26. PROTEST AGAINST THE POLICY OF REPRESSION

According to the teaching of our modern law-givers we refuse to believe that our countrymen who are being punished without trial are guilty of any crime. Taking shortcuts in law is like setting the whole house on fire in order to roast one's pig,—it is the primitive form of despotism. That we are amazed at such instances happening to us, is the best compliment that can be paid to the British administration in India. For we know that even in the West there are governments which in their attempt to enforce loyalty have no scruple in blindly applying the hasty method of punishment that has no restriction of law. The mind of the rulers whose misfortune is to govern a people that are physically helpless, is daily being sucked into the depths of demoralisation. For want of adequate resistance they are too often tempted to simplify the problem of administration by breaking through the barriers of their own law, thus not only doing injustice to their subjects, but much more so to themselves. As they have partially paralysed their own courts of justice, which represent their conscience, we have no other recourse but to appeal to the higher nature of the British people, and to remind them that civilization takes infinite trouble to prove itself, to keep the lamp of its best ideals from being extinguished,

—and that is why it is more afraid of the innocent being punished than of the chance of escape of the guilty.

We cannot claim the sympathy of kinship from our ruling race, while on the other hand, we only make our impotence ludicrous when we insinuate retaliation—our only claim is the claim of humanity which if refused comes secretly to hurt those who ignore it.

February 1927

27. HENRY BARBUSSE'S APPEAL: TAGORE'S RESPONSE

TO THE FREE SPIRITS

Since eight years that the war is over, the state of war is going on. In almost every country the essential liberties are threatened by violence. First one could believe that these were the last waves of a storm which would gradually subside, the consequence, fatal but transitory, of the pressure formerly exercised on martyrized peoples who reconquer their rights. But the mean interests of some groups or individuals have incorporated these blind forces; they have made of violence a system of government. Under the name of Fascism we see everywhere crushed or threatened all the conquests of freedom, that had been achieved by centuries of sacrifices and strenuous efforts: freedom of association, freedom of press, freedom of opinion, and even Conscience itself, all are persecuted. We can no longer remain silent in the presence of this bankruptcy of progress.

We think that the time has come to ask all the persons who exercise in our times any intellectual and moral influence in the world, to unite in a committee destined to struggle against the barbarous tide of Fascism.

In every country, under more or less open forms, but more and more audaciously and criminally, everywhere in forms more and more organized every day, a white terror is let loose on the populations, and the most sacred principles of individual and collective freedom.

Against this state of things which multiplies the acts of violence, the most inexcusable and indeniable crimes, and threatens to bring about hideous occurrences, the public opposition of men who are universally admired and respected will build an effective barrier. The mere fact of such an international committee being constituted would have a capital repercussion over opinion, would enlighten it, attract its attention, and incite the masses to manifest their will in the sense of their interests and destinies. This initiative would also constitute an act of salutary pressure over the governments who manifest for Fascism an inadmissible helpfulness and complicity.

That is not all. Every day from Italy, Spain, Poland, from the Balkans, from everwhere, the echoes of numberless crimes and coups, reach us. Measures of reprisals deprive of their sustenance crowds of brave and loyal citizens. A shocking misery resigns in certain circles because of the dictature of the Fascist reaction. One of the first tasks of the committee will be to hold out their hand to these victims, to these martyrs, and to study the problem of their relief.

Once the Committee is constituted, outside every political party, uniquely on the plane of justice, reason and democratic progress which are in peril, this Committee will decide through what means its high and righteous mission can be realized.

It is therefore an adhesion of principles that we request from each of those to whom we address this appeal.

Henry Barbusse

THE APPEAL REFERRED TO IN THE LETTER

Dear and Eminent Colleague, Dr. Rabindranath Tagore,
Santiniketan, Bolpur

Allow me to join a personal appeal to the one included herewith and to which I am requesting you to adhere. Your name is one of those which impose themselves in a league of great honest people who would stand up to oppose and fight the invading barbarity of Fascism.

I have worded this appeal spontaneously, without listening to any suggestion of a political order, or anything like it: I have only followed the feeling of solidarity and the voice of common sense. The evil is not without remedy. Something can be done, and what can be done before all with regard to the frightful proportions Fascism has taken, is to raise a moral protest, to mobilize the real public consciousness, and to give an explicit voice to the reprobation which is to be heard everywhere.

I must add that concerning the tenor of this appeal, I have exchanged views with Romain Rolland who is heartily with me, and who also thinks that a levy of free spirits, a protest of enlightened and respected persons is the only thing likely, if it is organized and continuous, to put a stop to an abominable state of things.

Finally I inform you that I intend to create very soon an international review: *Monde* (World), whose mission it will be to diffuse the great human principles among the present international chaos, to struggle against the reactionary spirit and propaganda. This publication can become an important tribune in the intellectual, artistic, moral, and social planes, if personalities like yourself want it. It will be a vehicle for the voice of the Committee and will embody its high protest.

I would be thankful to you for telling me whether you accept to be considered as an occasional contributor to *Monde*.

I would also be obliged to you for answering me, with regard to the appeal, in a letter which I could utilise in case of need by publishing it partly or in extracts.

With my feelings of high and devoted consideration.

Henry Barbusse

TAGORE'S REPLY

Dear Friend,

It is needless to say that your appeal has my sympathy, and I feel certain that it represents the voices of numerous other who are dismayed at the sudden outbursts of violence from the depth of civilization.

It is natural to expect in primitive peoples their faith in ceremonies of power-worship dripping with human blood; their awe-struck veneration for the relentless physical force that, at first, coerces and then fascinates its victims into the abject obedience of slavery. Such a mental attitude only indicates an immaturity of moral consciousness which, like the thoughtless cruelty of adolescence, can claim a future of growth for its rectification.

But when a similar phenomenon makes its appearance among cultured peoples it proves the second infancy of senility that has lost its control over animal passions. Its greed is not of impulsive youth, but of a hardened old age efficiently unscrupulous. Its infection is noxious because while it exhales from its core an unwholesome odour of decay and death, its outer skin swells and glows with an exultant flush of rottenness.

Therefore I rejoice at the fact that there are individuals who still believe in a higher destiny of man, proving in their suffering the deathless life of the human soul ever ready to fight its own aberrations.

You ask me for occasional contributions to your proposed international review *Monde,* which I shall remember when I have a little leisure, which is growing scarcer as I grow older.

Cordially Yours
Rabindranath Tagore
July 1927

28. FREEDOM

Dear Dr. Sunderland,

I had the pleasure of your personal acquaintance when I visited America and, along with many others of our countrymen, I know you, as a true friend of India. I am sure that there are very few who are as worthy as yourself to stand up for her rights and vindicate her honour.

Perhaps you are aware that I have not taken any active part in the political movement lately started in India with the object of gaining *Swaraj*. It is needless to say that I also dream of freedom for my motherland, but I know that neither the path towards it nor its instrument and expression can be copied from the history of other nations. So long as the bulk of our people remains steeped in ignorance, unable to know its own mind, it can never attain emancipation for the purpose of its self-revealment in politics according to its own temperament and need.

I have been in the West and one thing that has strongly impressed my mind is the fact that there are nations who are technically free, and yet, like a bird that has hurt its wings, have not gained true freedom, remaining incapable of building up and using a perfect medium of political self-expression. There is every sign of their lapsing into slavery, voluntarily surrendering their freedom of self-government into the hands of the few who have the power to subjugate their minds into a dumb and blind obedience.

Freedom, like all the other best things in life, cannot be given from outside, but has to be won through the awakened personality of the people truly claiming it with intelligence, feeling and active will. We know it from our own national experience that the mere geographical fact of a country can never attract from its people a true feeling of loyalty and love, that our country must be our own creation, that its health, wealth and wisdom must represent the combined self-discipline of an intelligent and continual public service.

I know that the government by foreigners who must, by every means, cling to their possession of our land because of its vital necessity for themselves, can never allow us our full opportunity for serving our country and moulding her destiny according to her own best interest. All the same, it has to be admitted, that the people who cannot intimately identify their own selves with their motherland through comprehensive knowledge, love and labour, the constant co-operation of their intellect and will, have not the real possession of their country, and therefore for them foreign subjection is the inevitable outcome of their lack of such moral grip upon their environment.

It is a truism to say that freedom cannot be built upon a foundation of unreality. Our want of ordinary human interest not only in our neighbouring provinces, but in communities not our own, is darkly dense among us; the communication of mutual sympathy and understanding between ourselves is barred at every step by caste and communal obstructions and religious fanaticism. The unreasoning acceptance of practices and prohibitions in minute details of life, the complete sacrifice of individual initiative forced upon our unthinking millions by a system of social tyranny more perfectly organized than in any other country of the world, the terribly efficient machinery for a wholesale manufacture of cowards and slaves constantly working in our domestic surroundings, these are the powerful enemies that are in alliance with the evil star of our political misfortune. Our immediate duty is to fight them, to conquer our country from the age-long domination of an intellectual and moral inertia, from the crude materialism ruling in the guise of piety causing immense dissipation of energy and unmeaning suffering and degradation.

In countries where the mind is alive and active, the different problems such as politics and economics have their meaning. But where the mind itself is smothered under a load of dead things, under the pressure of automatic habits inherited from a primitive past, all our powers must be directed towards rescuing it from the debris of a ruined antiquity. That means widespread education. Of course, we in the name of humanity, have the right to appeal to our rulers to help us in this object. And yet that appeal may be in vain, or ludicrously meagre in its response, owing to a parsimonious budget bursting with its burden of military and punitive expenditure. But there is nothing, except our own apathy, to prevent ourselves, from utilising all our resources and organizing a system of national education that will include in its functions an active and direct guidance of the life of the people, helping them to realize the dignity and freedom of their creative spirit. Only when they are conscious of the real meaning of self-rule within themselves, can they successfully strive to establish it over their outer circumstances.

February 1927

29. MOTHER INDIA

I

Sir

While travelling in this land of Bali, I have just chanced upon a copy of the New Statesman of the 16th of July, containing the review of a book on India written by a tourist from America. The reviewer, while supporting with an unctuous virulence all the calumnies heaped upon our people by the authoress, and while calling repeated attention to the alleged common Hindu vice of untruthfulness even amongst the greatest of us, has made public a *malicious piece of fabrication* not as one of the specimens picked up from a show-case of wholesale abuse displayed in this or some other book, but as a gratuitous information about the truth of which the writer tacitly insinuates his own personal testimony. It runs thus: 'The poet Sir Rabindranath Tagore expresses in print his conviction that marriage should be consummated before puberty in order to avert the vagaries of female sexual desire....'

'We have become painfully familiar with deliberate circulation of hideous lies in the West against enemy countries, but a similar propaganda against individuals, whose countrymen have obviously offended the writer by their political aspiration, has come to me as a surprise....'

II

Sir,

I came to know from the advertising columns of your paper that Miss Katherine Mayo's 'Mother India' has been lauded by Arnold Benett as 'a shocking book, in the honourable sense'.

Unfortunately, for obvious reasons, there is a widely prevalent wish among the race that rules India to believe any detraction that may bring discredit upon India, and consequently the kind of shocks that Miss Mayo has manufactured offers them a delicious luxury of indignation. The numerous lies mixed with facts that have been dexterously manipulated by her for the production of these shocks are daily being exposed in our journals; but these will never reach the circle of readers which it is easy for Miss Mayo to delude. Along with other eastern victims of lying propaganda, we in India also must defencelessly suffer mudbesmearing from unscrupulous literature: for your writers have their machinery of publicity which is cruelly efficient for raining slanders form a region usually unapproachable by us, shattering our fair name in an appallingly wholesale manner.

I happen to be one of those whom the writer has specially honoured with her attention and selected as a target for her midnight raid. Difficult though it is for me completely to defend myself from such a widespread range of mischief, I must try through your organ to reach the ears of at least some of my friends, who are on the other side of the Atlantic and have, I hope, the chivalry to suspend their judgment about the veracity of these shocking statements made by a casual tourist against a whole people, before lightly believing them to be honourable.

For my own defence, I shall use the following extract from a paper written by Mr. Natarajan, one of the most fearless critics of our social evils. He has incidentally dealt with the incriminating allegation against me deliberately concocted by the writer out of a few sentences from my contribution to Keyserling's 'Book of Marriage'—cleverly burgling away their true meaning and shaping them into an utterly false testimony for her own nefarious purpose. Mr. Natarajan writes as follows:

'Tagore sets forth his own ideal of marriage in five long pages at the end of his paper (Keyserling, p. 117 *et seq.*) "Let me," he begins, as an individual Indian, offer in conclusion my own personal contribution to the discussion of the marriage question generally.' He holds that the marriage system all over the world—and not only in India—from the earliest ages till now, is a barrier in the way of the true union of man and woman, which is possible only when 'Society shall be able to offer a large field for the creative work of women's special faculty, without detracting from the creative work in the home.'

'If Miss Katherine Mayo was not a purblind propagandist but an honest enquirer, and if she had the patience to read Tagore's essay, she might have asked any one in Calcutta what the age of marriage of girls is in Tagore's own family. That she was determined to discredit the poet is evident.'

Let me ask some of your readers to read my paper on Hindu marriage in Keyserling's book and challenge in fairness to me, Miss Mayo to prove that it was my own opinion as she asserts that child marriage is "a flower of the sublimated spirit a conquest over sexuality and materialism won by exalted intellect for the eugenic uplift of the race," implying "the conviction, simply, that Indian women must be securely bound and delivered before their womanhood is upon them if they are to be kept in hand."

Let me in conclusion draw the attention of your readers to another amazing piece of false statement in which she introduces me, with a sneer as a defender of the "Ayurvedic" system of medicine against Western medical science. Let her prove this libel if she can.

There are like myself other numerous witnesses who, if they find their access to the Western readers, will be able to place their complaints before them, informing them how their views have been misinterpreted their words mutilated and facts tortured into a deformity which is worse than untruth.

November 1927

30. COLOUR PREJUDICE

I have read the letter of Mr. Habib Motan dated November 19, 1927, addressed to the Agent-General, protesting against any Indian being invited to attend Fort Hare Natevi College, for University education. In this published letter, he states that 'it is humiliating to the Indian sentiment, and to the Indian National Honour and Civilization to think that our Agent-General is trying to bring us down to such a low level. Such colour prejudice, from an Indian, who has himself suffered from the racial prejudice of the European, is to me revoking in the extreme. It is neither in accord with Indian sentiment or with Indian National Honour and Civilization. Our only right to be in South Africa at all is that the native Africans, to whom the soil belongs, wish us to be there. To insult them publicly as Mr. Habib Motan has done, in their open letter,—both by the words I have quoted, and by others are equally contemptuous—is an act which needs immediate repudiation from all right-minded men.

April 1928

31. TO THE WORLD LEAGUE FOR PEACE

In our political ritualism, we still worship the tribal god of our own make and try to appease it with human blood. This fetishism is blindly primitive and angers truth that leads to death dealing conflicts. To many of us it seems that this blood-stained idolatory is a permanent part of human nature. But we know in our past history, there have been things born of dark unreason producing phantoms of fear in our mind and ferocity of suspicion. Within the boundaries of night they also had loomed large and appeared as everlasting. But a great many of them have already vanished, making the social life of a fruitful peace possible in civilized communities.

Let us, today, by the strength of our own faith prove that the homicidal orgies of a cannibalistic politics are doomed, in spite of contradictions that seem overwhelmingly formidable.

1928

32. AT THE IMMIGRATION OFFICE

I was asked by the US Immigration Authorities at Vancouver to go to their office in person with my papers. My secretary had asked the Immigration Officer to fix an hour for the examination and at the appointed hour, I went to the office. After I had waited for about half-an-hour, the officer came to the door, saw me and without taking any notice of me, went on talking to some one who had then come. After finishing that, he silently beckoned to me to come into the room and then curtly pointed to a chair with a nod of his head. I was then asked the usual questions about my ability to pay my passage, whether I had independent means of livelihood as long as I remained in the States, and I was warned of the penalty that I shall incur if I overstayed in the States the period of time allowed to me by the officer.

I had visited the States before but I never had such experience. I thought of cancelling my proposed visit to the States; but I had already reserved my accommodation in the train and said good-bye to my friends. I arrived at Los Angeles, and I felt something in the air—a cultivated air of suspicion and general incivility towards Asiatics. I was assured that the Immigration Regulations were made in the application particularly humiliating to all Asiatics. I felt that I should not stay in a country on sufferance. It was not a question of personal grievance or of ill-treatment from some particular officer. I felt the insult was directed towards all Asiatics, and I made up my mind to leave a country where there was no welcome for ourselves.

...I have great regard for your people. But I have also my responsibility towards those whom you classify as coloured people of whom I am one. I am a representative of Asiatic peoples and I could not remain in a country where Asiatics were not wanted.

...I am very glad that the officer did not treat me differently because I might have some reputation but treated me as an Oriental and as a coloured man. The ordinary civility between gentleman and gentleman was lacking in his treatment but this was entirely due to the fact that he had been dealing with Asiatics and the Immigration Regulations had given his attitude of mind.

11 May 1929

33. 'EAST IS EAST'

Dear Madam,

Each people has its physical environment given to it, and social surroundings created by itself. Its history is its continual adjustment to these, through modifications of its inner and outer world. If in the midst of this, some alien element is thrust upon a particular people—some human power which has its own distinct evolution, its separate need, its special object which is not only not coincident with that of the other, but very often hurtfully antagonistic,—a confusion results, and this people, in its perplexity, can never show itself to its best advantage.

Europe today is the dominant factor in the human world, but unfortunately she has come to the Far East, not with an ideal, but with an object that primarily concerns her own self-interest. This naturally makes the Eastern peoples suspicious and nervously eager in their turn to exploit the circumstances for their own profit; but, not having the power in their hands, and being therefore unequally matched, they cannot afford to be frank in their manner and method. They have become accustomed to being misunderstood, which helps them to develop, for the sake of self-respect and self-protection, the habit of hiding their thoughts. This is what makes it difficult for the Western individuals who have a natural gift of sympathy and the desire to deal with their fellow-beings in the East in a spirit of justice and love.

You will surely understand why, generally, a Chinese may feel constrained to shut his heart, and even reveal the worst side of his nature, to the European,—member of a race that, for the sake of profit, felt no compunction in drugging the whole great people of China, and humiliating them because they showed resistance. If the Europeans had come to China to offer to her the best that their own civilization had produced, China also, in her relationship to them, would have had the opportunity to do herself justice, and show to them her best side.

Allow me to assure you that your letter has given me genuine pleasure for which I thank you.

1929

34. PROTEST AGAINST THE ARREST OF MAHATMA GANDHI

Mahatmaji has been arrested without having been given a chance of coming to mutual understanding with the Government. It only shows that of the two partners in the building of the history of the people of India can be superciliously ignored according to our rulers. However, the fact has to be accepted as a fact, and we must prove to the world that we are important, more important than the other factor which is merely an accident. But if we lose head and give vent to a sudden fit of political insanity, blindly suicidal, a great opportunity will be missed. The despair itself should give us the profound calmness of strength, the grim determination which silently works its own fulfilment without wasting its resources in puerile emotionalism and self-thwarting destructiveness. This is the moment when it should be easy for us to forget all our accumulated prejudices against our kindreds, when we must do our best to combine our hands in brotherly love even with those who have roughly rejected our call of comradeship, when we must claim of us an intense urge of co-operation with all different parts of our nation. This is the kind of catastrophe which rarely comes to a people with a shock that brings to a focus our scattered forces and shortens the difficulties of our creative endeavour in the building of our freedom.

The primitive lawlessness of the law-makers should forcibly awaken us to our own ultimate salvation in above which owns no defeat in the face of a power which barricades itself with an indiscriminate suspicion that its blind panic cannot define. This is the time when we must never forget our responsibility to prove ourselves morally superior to those who are physically powerful in a measure that can defy its own humanity.

May 1930

35. INDIA: AN APPEAL TO IDEALISM

I find it difficult to do my duty today in a spirit of patience and calmness, and at the same time to do justice to the Indian cause, to myself and my friends in this country. For the atmosphere of mutual relationship between India and Great Britain has grown dark with suspicion and suffering.

It is my desire in this article to write concerning a reconciliation between two peoples who for over a century have had a close connection with each other, and yet are still separated by a moral distance more difficult to overcome than mountains and seas. In this sensitive age of new awakening, the human in us in India has felt the indignity and pain of being dealt with by an abstraction of a government from across a dark chasm of impersonal aloofness, devoid of the light of imagination and the living touch of sympathy. This large gap in humanity has offered a breeding-place to a diseased political condition in our history that is crying for a cure. It can only be affected by a generous co-operation from both sides, by a union of minds which know how to make proper allowance for weakness in human nature, and at the same time maintain firm faith in it where it is great.

Our task is every day growing harder: for the situation, is solely left in the hands of the politicians, who represent the organization and not the humanity of a people. And therefore any appeal today is to that idealism which has made English history glorious, and which must extend its glory in an alien country.

Once Asia in her spring time of exuberant life offered the world her spiritual ideals. Today Europe in the illumination of her intellect has brought her science and also her spirit of service. But unfortunately she has not come to Asia to reveal the generosity of her civilisation, but to seek an unlimited field for her pride and power, trying to make these things eternal. She has come with her need and not with her wealth; and therefore she has belied her own mission and used the truth itself for a utilitarian purpose of self-aggrandisement. In order to wake her up to her own responsibility Asia must refuse weakly to yield her contribution to the impious belief that dehumanised power can succeed for ever with the help of science.

The people of England appear doomed to remain ignorant of the true state of things that prevails today in India. For in critical times like those Governments which have their faith in the short cut of punitive force for the speedy solution of their problems become more afraid of the higher spirit of their own people than their enemies themselves. And therefore they create in the surrounding air the smoke screens of obscurity and calumny in order to hide their own method of action and discredit that of their opponents. This has been amply proved in the late war. The organized power has the organ of a magnified voice; but we who have no proper means of publicity nor the bond of kinship with the British people to make it easy for us to gain credence, must resignedly accept all misrepresentation as the bitterest part of our national penance, the unavoidable penance for our own long history of weakness. Yet I cannot allow this occasion to pass by without declaring that with few exceptions, inevitable in the present atmosphere of panic and defiance, India in this trial has maintained her dignity of soul. Even through distortion and suppression of truth, and circulation of untruth with belated contradiction in small letters, the fact glimmers out that our people, with a pious determination, has kept unshaken the difficult ideal which they have accepted from their great leader Mahatma Gandhi, who upholds the noblest spirit of India, the spirit of Buddha himself. To us who are away from our homes there has reached the voice of the sufferers across the barriers of silence and the sea, carrying above the smothered cry of pain, the exaltation of a fulfilled vow under extreme provocation. My prayer for my people is not for the cessation of their suffering, but for the keeping up of their trust in the power of the human spirit which shows itself in all its might of truth among those who are physically weak; for we have both the occasion and the responsibility to prove this not only on behalf of India, but of all humanity.

For the sake of justice I must declare that in such a conflict between an unarmed people and a government in possession of unlimited power of destruction, our sufferings would have been terribly greater under any imperialistic rulers other than the British; and the fact that our country even in her desperate effort of utter defiance should still feel resentful at the acts of injustice due to methods of coercion hastily improvised, is an evidence of her strong faith in the standards of justice and humanity possessed by the British nation. It also shows our lack of direct experience of any great political revolution. In fact, if the lesson of history must be acknowledged, our people should never murmur against violence on the part of their rulers when normal conditions of government have been upset. We must expect this and face it, and never complain and blame the government for the drastic measures which we have deliberately made inevitable, while fully, I hope, anticipating the consequence. To light the fire and then complain that it burns in absurdly childish. And, therefore, we should, in all fairness, take upon ourselves the ultimate responsibility of the flogging and shooting, of injuries and indignities, of indiscriminate methods of striking terror into the hearts of a helpless multitude and of the awful fact that the majority of victims must necessarily be innocent in a catastrophic outrage of this nature. None of us can cowardly claim immunity or mitigation of suffering, when, even if rashly, the subversive forces of history have brought down upon our country in the hope of building her history upon a new foundation.

The only thing which is most important for us to remember is that we should heroically uphold our own *Dharma* and refuse to accept defeat by offering violence in return.

June 1930

36. RACE AND COLOUR PREJUDICE

I regard the race and colour prejudice which barricades human beings against each other as the greatest evil of modern times, which should be overcome if humanity must be realized as one spirit.

The different paths along which progress may be made towards recovery from this evil are manifold. My own stress would be laid upon elevation of the public mind and the collection and dissemination of accurate scientific knowledge as against the pseudo-science and pseudo-religion which, in this disguise of truth are treacherously dealing mortal blows to truth herself.

There should be a united effort to combine the emotional forces of religion, in its broadcast sense, with the spread of education based on fully ascertained truth concerning the human race as a whole.

1930

37. FAITH IN BRITISH JUSTICE

Sir,

A fact of very grave significance at present crisis in the British rule in India has sorely puzzled my mind. I am impelled to write about it, for I find that its importance is not understood in England even by those who are in touch with Indian affairs.

At Dacca in Eastern Bengal, there have been communal riots in which men of vicious character have been brought in so as to increase the mischief, and unspeakable atrocities have occurred. Yet, according to reports which have reached me, the police have either stood idly by or allowed the evil to go on with indifference and contempt. While the news of a motor accident in Europe causing a few casualties is circulated in all your newspapers, these crying evils continuing from day to day in the capital city of East Bengal (whereby the whole neighbourhood was terrorized and all work paralysed) have hardly found any mention in English journals. The number of deaths, the loss of property, the daily sufferings and terrors caused by these events have been enormous; and yet they have been ignored with a strange ominous silence. If a single English man were injured, or the comforts of English residents were menaced such silence would hardly be kept. Is it any wonder, then, that we are led to regard ourselves as of no interest or importance in the eyes of the British people, who have taken upon themselves the gratuitous task of our trusteeship? Is it strange that we consider such silence as artificially imposed rather than naturally occurring?

We have not the least doubt that the most expensively and elaborately organised power which the British Government has in India is more than sufficient in checking at once any symptoms of violence in our communal relationship. We have been brought up for a long time past on this belief. What has now occurred at Dacca had happened in a somewhat similar manner a few years ago in Calcutta and had been loudly proclaimed in the English Press. What is remarkable in the present instance is that amid an almost complete silence in the British Press a state of anarchy continued in Dacca for a unconscionably long time. The opinion formed about this arresting silence by our own people is unlikely to be accepted by the people of England.

Here comes the real meaning of our helplessness. For the British people have their comfortable faith in the conduct of their own officials who rule over an alien people. They feel little direct responsibility. Therefore, when our evidence is pitted against that of their own official representatives, we have little chance of credence. Let us acknowledge that this is natural; yet at the same time we should be allowed for the same reason to have faith in our own people when under conditions like the present they suffer and complain. For we are very unequally matched; and while your opinion vitally affects us at every point our opinion may easily remain unnoticed or else be even suppressed by you. But silenced though our people may be and ineffectual in their struggle, we judge; and in the end it 'does' matter. I know from my own correspondence that this event at Dacca has alienated, more than anything else in Bengal the sympathies of those who were still clinging their faith in British justice. Other happenings had shaken public confidence, but this has struck at its very foundation.

1930

38. MESSAGE TO THE QUAKER SOCIETY OF FRIENDS

By segregating ethics to the Kingdom of Heaven and depriving the Kingdom of Earth from its use man has up to now never seriously acknowledged the need of higher ideals in politics or in practical affairs. That is why when disagreements occur between individuals, violence is not encouraged but punished; but when the combatants are nations, barbaric methods are not only not condemned but glorified. The greatest of men like Buddha or Christ have from the dawn of human history stood for the ideal of non-violence, they have dared to love their enemies and defied tyrannism by peace, but we have not claimed the responsibility they have offered us.

Fight is necessary in this world, combat we must and relentlessly against the evils that threaten us, for by tolerating untruth we admit their claim to exist. But war on the human plane must be what in India we call—*Dharma-Yuddha*—moral warfare, in it we must array our spiritual powers against the cowardly violence of evils. This is the great ideal which Mahatma Gandhi represents, challenging his people to fearlessly apply man's highest strength not only in our individual dealings but in the clash of nation and nation.

In the barbaric age man's hunger did not impose any limits on its range of food, which included even human flesh but with the evolution of society this has been banished from extreme possibility: in a like manner we await the time when nothing may supposedly justify the use of violence whatever consequences we are led to face. Because, success in a conflict may be terrible defeat from the human point of view, and material gain is not worth the price we pay at spiritual cost. Much rather should we lose all than barter out soul for an evil victory. We honour Mahatma Gandhi because he has brought this ideal into the sphere of politics and under his lead India is proving everyday how aggressive power pitifully fails when human nature in its wakeful majesty bears insult and pain without retaliating. India today inspired by her great leader opens the new chapter of human history which has just begun.

1930

39. 'I AM PROUD OF MY PEOPLE'

In the Indian endeavour to pursue the ideals of the Mahatma in the fight for freedom, success may or may not be achieved. But I am proud of my people that they fight for higher ideals. India must be an example to the whole world.

What kind of government India will have cannot be foreseen. Governments develop through centuries, and should India obtain self-government this must be in accord with the character of the Indian people and with the peculiar circumstances. For the form of government suitable for India can develop only out of the atmosphere of Indian life.

It is certain that India will have her own constitution, for India's problems are as unique as her own mental constitution. India is India.

20 September 1930

40. STATEMENT CONTRADICTED

To The Editor, New York Times,

I cannot allow to remain uncontradicted some misstatements of my view about the present Indian problem in the report of the interview with me which has appeared in your paper of this morning issue. Let it definitely be known that according to me it is the opportunity for self-government itself which gives training for self-government, and not foreign subjection, and that an appearance of peace superficially maintained from outside can never lead to real peace, which can only be attained through an inevitable period of suffering and struggle.

October 1930

41. THE WOMEN'S INTERNATIONAL LEAGUE

The Women's International League for Peace and Freedom has done valuable work in bringing to bear upon the civilization of the West the ideals of spiritual life which demand social service and belief in non-violence to establish the future civilization of humanity. Women are naturally gifted with the power of peace and the modern age needs their active co-operation in its effort to unite the different peoples of the world on the basis of mutual understanding. I am glad to know that the W.I.L. has accepted its full share of responsibility in this great work.

I am sure our women of India will be happy to join hands with their sisters in the West in their service to humanity, and that the visit of the representative of WI.L. to India, which I hear is being arranged for will help to bring India and Europe closer together in lasting bonds of comradeship.

November 1930

42. THE COLOUR BAR

Sir,

An Englishman finds his mental comfort disturbed when he has to deal with differences that are foreign to him, for he has inherited an intense consciousness of race individuality from an ancestry brought up in geographical segregation. A marked difference in colour which makes too conspicuous the difference in race produce in his conventional mind an aggressive sense of alienation. The same thing happens with regard to a different dress, as I have often noticed in my case even in a metropolis like London or in American towns, where, curiously enough, strangers are less tolerated in their strangeness than in England. In the continental countries of Europe I have never once aroused among those with whom I travelled, their sense of the comic by my costume, which I am sure, has not the slightest element of the ludicrous, specially when compared with their own. It is from the same cause that an Englishman feels not merely amused but positively irritated at the wrong pronunciation of his language by foreigners who cannot help being foreigners in the habits of their tongues.

It is a sign of national provincialism thus to associate natural differences in others with inherent inferiority and disagreeableness. Of all peoples in India, we in Bengal suffer from this imperfect adaptability of imagination which causes arrogance. It is owing to our provincialism, for we have been accustomed for centuries to live in a remote corner developing our race mannerism. The Bengali people are prone to keep themselves isolated when in unaccustomed surroundings, and they have an unenviable talent of making themselves unpopular with the people of other provinces of India.

Up to a certain point this tendency of aloofness has its advantage in emphasizing individuality which helps to conquer opportunities for itself, and Bengali people undoubtedly did utilize that advantage, capturing special privileges long before others were ready in the field. But when history has to be made great through perfect co-operation with neighbours, through a spirit of mutual concession and understanding, our ungenerous habit of jealous self-assertiveness offers obstacles, and we are likely to recede into the background.

The stubborn insularity of the Englishman has helped him in the beginning of his career of conquest. He naturally failed to identify himself even in a slight degree with the Indian people whom he ruled from a supercilious distance. This proud detachment has no doubt helped him in ruling a foreign race with a vigorous efficiency. But such an imperfect relationship in human affairs maintained by force cannot last long. At last the time inevitably comes when history has to be made great upon a positive basis of co-operation, and not merely upon the negative basis of law and order. It is not the race which can rule that has the historical fitness to survive, but the race which understands, which has the sympathetic imagination—in other words, the moral power of adaptability. After all, in the long run it will come true that the meek shall inherit the earth. Colour prejudice shows the lack of the power of social adaptation. Our own history began with it, and though India desperately tried some kind of mechanical race adjustment, she has failed in giving birth to a living political organism owing to this abnormal caste consciousness that obstructs the stream of human sympathy and spirit of mutual co-operation. This is the reason why, in spite of the fact that India has produced a series of great minds, she has not produced a great organic history; and it has yet to be seen if such a history is in the making in which two peoples of different colours can have a perfect bond of life from across the sea.—I am, Sir, & c.

April 1931

43. TAKAGAKI

To Dr. B.C. Roy, M.D. F.R.C.S., Mayor of Calcutta Corporation, Calcutta

Dear Dr Roy,

Please accept my sincere congratulations on your election as the Mayor of Calcutta Corporation.

I wrote sometime ago to Srijukta Subhas Chandra Bose about our Jiu-jitsu professor, Mr Takagaki but apparently he has not been able to reply to it as he is touring about in East Bengal. May I now put before you the case of Professor Takagaki whom as you may know, I brought from Japan specially for the purpose of giving a thorough training in the art of Jiu-Jitsu to the students of Bengal. Professor Takagaki comes of a highly distinguished family in Japan and is one of the most well-known experts in Jiu-Jitsu in that country. When I found that our countrymen did not properly realize the importance of the visit of Professor Takagaki to our country, I had to take up myself the entire financial responsibility of his travel and stay in this country. I engaged his services for two years and boys and girls of our institution have received instruction from him with remarkable results. Our students gave a demonstration of Jiu-Jitsu in Calcutta at which several members of the Corporation were present, and I was told that they all appreciated it very much.

It will be a great pity if Professor Takagaki has to be sent back to Japan without the student community in Calcutta ever getting the opportunity of mastering from him the art of self-defence and physical training which I need hardly point out is specially required by our boys and girls. Professor Takagaki, has to make definite arrangements from now for his future programme, and therefore I am writing to you requesting the Corporation to take advantage of his presence in our country and to engage him for giving instructions to the students in Calcutta. Professor Takagaki is willing to remain in Calcutta for the purpose if suitable arrangements are made for him.

I do hope that my appeal will find response in the Calcutta Corporation and that both yourself and Srijukta Subhas Chandra Bose will consider the proposal favourably and retain the services of Professor Takagaki for a cause which concerns the well-being of the students of Bengal.

With kind regards,
Yours sincerely
Rabindranath Tagore
1931

44. INDIA AND BRITAIN

From the depths of the present atmosphere of suffering, the cry has come for the inauguration of a new age of faith and reconciliation, for a fellowship of understanding between races and nations alienated by cruel politics and diplomacy. We in India are ready for a fundamental change in our affairs which will bring harmony and understanding into our relationships with those who have inevitably been brought near to us. We are waiting for a gesture of goodwill from both sides, spontaneous and generous in its faith in humanity, which will create a future of moral federation, of constructive works of public goods, of the inner harmony of peace between the peoples of India and England.

The visit of our friends from England has confirmed the immediate possibility of such intimate fellowship and truth in our mutual relationship, and I feel called upon to appeal to all who have the welfare of humanity at heart to come forward at this critical hour and courageously take upon themselves the task of fulfilling the moral responsibility which is before us of building upon the bare foundation of faith, of acceptance of truth in a spirit of generous, mutual forgiveness.

The memory of the past, however painful it may have been for us all, should never obscure the vision of the perfect, of the future which it is for us jointly to create. Indeed, our experience of the futility of suspicion and hostility must inspire us with a profounder belief in the truth of the simple fellowship of hearts, in the mighty power of creative understanding between individuals as well as Nations inspired by a common urge of love.

March 1931

45. ON PROSELYTISM

I have read your letter with pleasure. I have only one thing to say: it is this: Do not be always trying to preach your doctrine, but give yourself in love. Your Western mind is too much obsessed with the idea of conquest and possession; your inveterate habit of proselytism is another form of it. Christ never preached himself or any dogma or doctrine; he preached the love of God. The object of a Christian should be to be like Christ—never like a coolie recruiter trying to bring coolies to his master's tea garden. Preaching your doctrine is no sacrifice at all—it is indulging in a luxury far more dangerous than all the luxuries of material living. It breeds an illusion in your mind that you are doing your duty—that you are wiser and better than your fellow-beings. But the real preaching is in being perfect, which is through meakness and love of self-dedication. If you have strong in you your pride of race, pride of sect, and pride of personal superiority, then it is no use to try to do good to others. They will reject your gift, or even if they do accept it they will not be morally benefitted by it—instances of which can be seen in India every day. On the spiritual plane you cannot *do* good until you *are* good. You cannot preach the Christianity of the Christian sect until you be like Christ—and then you do not preach Christianity, but the love of God, which Christ did.

July 1931

46. SARNATH

The spiritual illumination in India, which ages ago shed its radiance over the continent of Asia, raised its memorial on the sacred spot near Benares where Lord Buddha had proclaimed to his, disciples his message of love's supreme fulfilment. Though this monument representing the final hope of liberation for all peoples was buried under dust and forgotten in India, the voice of her greatest son still waits in the heart of silent centuries for a new awakenment to hearken to his call.

Today when in spite of a physical closeness of all nations a universal moral alienation between races has become a fateful menace to all humanity, let us, in this threatening gloom of a militant savagery, before the widening jaws of an organized greed, still rejoice in the fact that the reopening of the ancient monastery of Sarnath is being celebrated by pilgrims from the West and the East.

Numerous are the triumphal towers built to perpetuate the memories of injuries and indignities inflicted by one murdering race upon another, but let us once for all, for the sake of humanity restore to its full significance this great memorial of a generous past to remind us of an ancient meeting of nations in India for the exchange of love, for the establishment of spiritual comradeship among races separated by distance and historical traditions, for the offering of the treasure of immortal wisdom left to the world by the Blessed One to whom we dedicate our united homage.

December 1931

47. IMPRISONMENT OF GANDHI

CABLE TO RAMSAY MACDONALD

The sensational policy of indiscriminate repression being followed by Indian Government starting with imprisonment of Mahatmaji is most unfortunate in causing permanent alienation of our people from yours making it extremely difficult for us to co-operate with your representations for peaceful political adjustment.

January 1932

48. MESSAGE TO IRAQ AIR FORCE

From the beginning of our days man has imagined the seat of divinity in the upper air from which comes light and blows the breath of life for all creatures on this earth. The peace of its dawn, the splendour of its sunset, the voice of eternity in its starry silence have inspired countless generations of men with an ineffable presence of the infinite urging their minds away from the sordid interests of daily life. Man has accepted this dust-laden earth for his dwelling place, for the enacting of the drama of his tangled life ever waiting for a call of perfection from the boundless depth of purity surrounding him in a translucent atmosphere. If in an evil moment man's cruel history should spread its black wings to invade that realm of divine dreams with its cannibalistic greed and fratricidal ferocity then God's curse will certainly descend upon us for that hideous desecration and the last curtain will be rung down upon the world of Man for whom god feels ashamed.

April 1932

49. THE WORLD'S CHILDREN

I am glad to identify myself with the objects of the Save the Children International Union, which seems to me to be the most vital and profoundly significant movement in modern Europe.

The rich success that has already been achieved by this Union, in spite of partial response from the public, inadequate means, and inclement political circumstances, only confirms its unchallengeable truth and urges us to join hands, fearlessly, with this movement for the protection of humanity.

War and hostility, incipient and unashamed, still poison the atmosphere of the modern age—the age, externally, of unbridled greed, competition, and tribal hatred. The one promising sign, however, is the emergence in every country today of idealists who unswervingly keep to their indwelling humanity and uphold the banner of fellowship and amity in the face of adversity and persecution.

The Save the Children International Union is to me a most precious manifestation of this idealism and it is a direct answer to the merciless spirit of organized militarism which wreaks havoc and ruin on the face of our fair earth.

I appeal to all men of faith and love to respond to the noble idealism of this Union by offering all possible help to establish it on a permanent basis.

September, 1932

50. APPEAL TO AMERICA

Owing to increasing facilities to communication the different countries and peoples of the world have now been brought closer together than before but this external proximity has yet to be transformed into spiritual unity by the united endeavour of individuals and nations. Till this has been achieved the very fact of our material linkedness will be grievously hurtful to the different peoples which is evidenced just now when disturbances in remote parts of the world helplessly drag into the common net of suffering people who are far removed from the scene of action.

The need of recognizing this urgent fact of our inescapable relatedness in the modern age can no longer be shelved by diplomatic machinations of frenzied politics. Nations like America, therefore, who because of their central geographical position are able to take a more detached view of events should now come forward and offer to lead the human world toward a future of mutual understanding and harmonious co-operation.

America with her internal unity of purpose, her resources of power, and her noble traditions of freedom is peculiarly fitted to exercise this sagacity of mind, and her moral influence is already one of the most powerful assets in the comity of nations. America is young, she has the fire of creative energy, and unfettered by any complicated heritage of ranking political memories of the past, she is free to develop a great edifice of human solidarity. With her gifts of applied science she can liberate the human spirit from the dominance of privation and disease, she can evolve purposive Government of the peoples of the world from her own experience of combining diverse races into one democracy in interdependence; she can fearlessly take her stand against exploitation of weaker peoples and uphold the sacred right of human honour above the din of clamorous greed.

My appeal to the America of today is founded on my profound belief in her moral integrity and her true mastery of the resources of power.

December 1932

51. WELCOME ADDRESS TO PROFESSOR DAVOUD

To Aga Poure-Davoud,

We welcome you who have come as a messenger of the great Persian civilization to our land; we welcome you on behalf of Santiniketan and of India.

In different chapters of our history India has communed with your culture; through art and literature and philosophy we have built up a comradeship of civilization. Those were the golden days of Asia's self-expression, when in spite of barriers of language and distance her neighbouring continents carried on a commerce of the spirit, rich in the wealth of realization, of wisdom garnered from many fields of effort and achievement.

Centuries of oblivion have intervened, the dust of time has covered up relics of India's kinship with Iran. But the memory of that ancient union still runs in our blood, and in this great age of Asia's awakening we are once more discovering our affinities, we are rescuing from the debris of vanished ages the undying memorials of our co-operation.

You have come to us with that message of Asia's awakening. Once more we are to light our lamps which ages ago Iran and India placed together on the altar of Asia's common culture. The hymns we then sung in languages closely allied will yet again reverberate under Asia's sky; we shall unite our hearts and our minds in quest of the inmost truths of our soul.

We of Asia are profoundly grateful to your great Monarch who with his indomitable personality and far-reaching creative vision has ushered in a new age in Persia and inspired the neighbouring countries with a spirit of self-reliance and hope. We take this occasion to offer him our deep appreciation of his gracious friendliness in having invited me to his kingdom and given me a taste of Persia's magnanimous hospitality, and in thus lending your services to our Visva-Bharati in Santiniketan. No more wonderful manner of expressing his cordial fellowship could be chosen than thus sending to us one of the noblest emissaries of Persia's culture.

Great is our joy today that we welcome you, our friend from Iran, to this *ashrama* of Santiniketan, where we have taken up the task of revealing the deepest mind of Asia. May our collaboration bind Persia and India close together in ties of intimate comradeship, uniting us once again in the responsibility jointly shared of restoring to the modern age the great gift which Asia has to offer to humanity.

January 1933

52. ON THE CENTENARY OF WILBERFORCE

A century has passed since Wilberforce showed a noble courage to condemn the thriving business of slave hunting. It is right that we should remember it with proper ceremony and bring our homage to the memory of the great man. But at the same time this should be the occasion for us to acknowledge with shame that the evil has not died with his own death, that in the dark corners of civilization slavery still lurks hiding its name and nourishing its spirit. It is there in our plantations, in factories, in business offices, in the punitive department of government where the primitive vindictiveness of man claims special privilege to indulge in fierce barbarism. A considerable section of men still seems to have an innate sympathy for the strong seeking victims in its chase of profit and power and what is worse there are terrible movements of benevolent idealism relentlessly smothering freedom in its path of ruthless recruitment. Humanity ever waits for the voice of judgment against uncontrolled cultivation of slavery which invades all parts of the civilized world offering enormous bribes to the conscience of man spreading a callousness of heart that is unashamed of its hooliganism.

July 1933

53. DESHAPRIYA J.M. SENGUPTA

Jatindra Mohan is one of those valiant fighters for the country's cause to whom no sacrifice was too great for the uplift of his motherland. He gave up his lucrative profession, with his whole family embraced a life of suffering and sacrifice by throwing himself in the very thick of the struggle. A man of noble manners and winning courtesy, he was a most beloved political leader of India. India can ill-afford to lose such a leader at this critical juncture in her national life.

There can be but little doubt that his untimely death was hastened by his long incarceration as a political prisoner. He was a man of peace and refinement but when his country called he rejoiced to offer his life at the alter of his country's freedom. The memory of such a life nobly lived and freely given is at once India's glory and shame.

August 1933

54. HOMAGE TO ISLAM

SIRATUN NABI

Islam is one of the few great religions of the world and the responsibility is immense upon its followers who must, in their lives, bear testimony to the greatness of their faith. Our one hope of mutual reconciliation between the communities inhabiting India, of bringing about a truly civilized attitude of mind towards each other in this unfortunate country depends not merely on the realization of an intelligent national self-interest, but on the eternal source of inspiration that comes from the immortal lines of these messengers of truth who have been the beloved of God and lovers of men. I take this advantage of this auspicious occasion today when I may join my Moslem brothers in offering my homage of adoration to the grand prophet of Islam and invoke his blessings for India which is in dire need of succour and solace.

26 November 1933

MESSAGE FOR THE PROPHET NUMBER OF THE PESHWA

I take this opportunity to offer my homage of veneration to the Holy Prophet Mohammad, one of the greatest personalities born in this world, who has brought a new and potent force of life into human history, a vigorous ideal of purity in religion, and I earnestly pray that those who follow his path will justify their noble faith in their life and the sublime teaching of their master by serving the cause of civilization in building the history of the modern India, helping to maintain peace and mutual goodwill in the field of our national life.

27 February 1936

55. BIHAR EARTHQUAKE AND THE MAHATMA

It has caused me painful surprise to find Mahatma Gandhi accusing those who blindly follow their own social custom of untouchability for having got down God's vengeance upon certain parts of Bihar, evidently specially selected for His desolating displeasure! It is all the more unfortunate, because this unscientific and materialistic view of things is too readily accepted by large sections of our countrymen.

I keenly feel indignity of it when I am compelled to utter the truism that physical catastrophes have their inevitable and exclusive origin in a certain combination of physical facts. Unless we believe in the inexorableness of universal laws, in the working of which God himself never interferes, imperilling thereby the integrity of His own creation we find it impossible to justify His ways on occasions like the one which has so sorely stricken us in an overwhelming manner and scale.

If we associate the ethical principles with cosmic phenomena we shall have to admit that human nature is morally superior to a Providence that preaches lessons on good behaviour in orgies of the worst behaviour possible. For we can never imagine any civilized ruler of man making indiscriminate examples of casual victims, including children and members of the untouchable community themselves, in order to impress others dwelling at a safe distance who possibly deserve severer condemnation.

Though we cannot point to any period of human history that is free from iniquities of the darkest kind, we still find citadels of malevolence that remain unshaken; factories that cruelly thrive upon the poverty and ignorance of famished cultivators. It only shows that the law of gravitation does not in the least respond to the stupendous load of callousness that accumulates till the moral foundations of our society begin to show dangerous cracks and civilizations are undermined.

What is truly tragic is the fact that the argument Mahatma Gandhi used, by exploiting an event of cosmic disturbance, far better suits the psychology of his opponents than his own; and it would not have surprised me if they had taken the opportunity of holding him and his followers responsible for the visitation of divine anger. As for us, we feel perfectly secure in the faith that our own sins and errors, however enormous, have not got enough force to drag down the structure of Creation to ruin.

We who are immensely grateful to Mahatma Gandhi for inducing by his wonderful inspiration freedom from fear and feebleness in the minds of our countrymen, feel profoundly hurt when any words from his mouth may emphasize elements of unreason which is the fundamental source of all blind powers that drive us against freedom and self respect.

5 February 1934

56. PROTEST AGAINST THE NAZIS

Dear Friend,

I thank you for drawing my attention to your address on 'Civilization's Debt to Asia,' published in *Israel's Messenger,* April, 1934.

To me racial hatred in any form is a creed of barbarism and I cannot recognize the value of any cause in whose name nations and peoples indulge their gluttony of violence. We in India are striving to safeguard our growing spirit of nationalism from this dangerous perversion of racial hatred, and when I see Western nations building their faith on this barbarism and making elaborate preparations for a scientific slaughter, I cannot help feeling proud of my people who, poor as they are and persecuted, yet are unwilling to win human rights through brutish ways. It revives my faith in the undying spirit of the East.

As regards the Hitler regime in Germany, we read different versions of it. And certainly it cannot be denied that the German people were goaded to many acts of desperate folly by the humiliations imposed on them by the victorious nations of the War. Nevertheless, if the brutalities we read of are authentic, then no civilized conscience can allow compromise with them. The insults offered to my friend Einstein have shocked me to the point of torturing my faith in modern civilization. I can only draw consolation from the hope that it was an unhappy act done in a drunken mood and not the sober choice of a people so gifted as the Germans.

All my life I have cried against blindness of prejudice that divides man from man and called upon my fellowmen all over the globe to stretch their hands in a common endeavour to realize the nobility of the human in each one of us. Today when this most enduring heritage from the truly great ones of all races, is being assaulted by the aggressive communalism of the Blacks and the fanatic materialistic idealism of the Reds on the other, I once again raise my humble voice of protest and warning, however feeble it may have grown with age. In our frantic despair to save the community let us not crush the free individual on the steps of whose sublime heresies humanity has ever been rising upwards.

August 1934

57. MY IDEALS WITH REGARD TO THE SREEBHAVANA

First of all the Sreebhavana should form itself into a perfect social unit composed of students, the Superintendent and the other officials and not merely remain an aggregate of individuals for some education purpose.

It is to be remembered that the Sreebhavana is not a final creation of any particular individual or of any group of persons. Those who are its inmates are to contribute their life to it and make it living. It should be their own creation—every moment of its growth. Let them endow it with 'sweetness and light', order, grace, cleanliness, and feel proud of its personality, which should reflect their own corporate being.

This is my earnest desire that those who are connected with the Sreebhavana should shoulder its responsibility, keeping the ideals of Santiniketan *ashrama* in their mind. In fact, this sharing of responsibility is an important item of education and the surest means of developing self-respect.

Girls in our *ashrama* can demand a reasonable amount of liberty in their everyday life. But true liberty is everywhere based upon severe discipline of responsibility. It may be lazily more comfortable to be ruled from outside than to take up the burden of freedom about our own management.

Since the establishment of the *ashrama,* it has ever been my wish that students should own their obligations in guiding, helping, and keeping each other straight, and preventing individuals from going into excesses which may bring discredit upon them all. In other words, I have always hoped that there should be the foundation of real *swaraj* in the student-life of the ashrama. Those who have no moral control over themselves are, from the very nature, sure to be subjected to compulsion from outside.

The degree of indifference showed by students in realizing the dignity of their responsibility in spite of their opportunity has been the degree of failure in self-rule in the *ashrama.*

I hope the girls of Sreebhavana will take advantage of this freedom of self-government and offer a permanent principle of conduct to the whole *ashrama.*

It is extremely desirable for the students' commonwealth that a set of rules of common behaviour should develop quite spontaneously and from within. This spirit of self-regulation should ever enjoy a free flow and lead to the fulfilment of our best hopes and endeavours. This success will depend entirely upon the goodwill and co-operation of the girls and not upon any set of fixed code of laws.

II

It is needless to say that our girls should have perfect manners in their behaviour towards each other and in their dealings with outsiders. It is ugly to be unmannerly and particularly for women it is unpardonable.

In every civilized community people have their forms of greeting; when girls meet the first time in the day, they should get used to observing the traditional form of courtesy to one another,—which is *namaskara.* The same salutation should be extended to guests. Needless to say, I expect them to get up from their seats and properly salute their teachers when meeting them. When there are newcomers in the hostel, they should not remain indifferent, but enquire after their wants and help them in every way possible. A new student should never feel that she has come in the midst of an inhospitable crowd. In the behaviour of older students among themselves there should be manifestations of friendliness and comradeship born of close association and co-operation.

Moderation in behaviour, in social communication, in expressions of emotion, is an essential part of good manners. We should remember that boisterousness must never be mistaken for exuberance of spirit. Good manners should be an outcome of good nature which reveals itself by willingly respecting others' legitimate claims, even going out of one's way to look to their convenience. It is positively objectionable to be noisy in the neighbourhood when some one is studying, to disturb one who wants to go to bed when it is due time and to enter somebody else's room without permission, ransacking her things, making her bed untidy, looking into her papers or letters, taking away books or articles of use. To get addicted to the pernicious habit of enjoying and circulating scandals and mischievous gossip breeds in one's character a vulgarity of a malignant type which must be completely eradicated from our nature.

Cleanliness and orderliness should never be neglected. There are some who seem to take pride in displaying slovenliness as a protest against indulgence in luxury. But well-dressed tidiness and foppishness do not belong to the same class. Attractiveness in one's dress may show a high quality of aesthetic sense and go hand in hand with a beautiful spirit of simplicity. It necessarily need not be for ostentation but for taking trouble to offer our respect for others. If we are careless in our dress when meeting people, we rudely show that we do not care for them.

Orderliness and tidiness are not only comfortable for ourselves but they reveal a spirit of hospitality to others and therefore become a duty which should scrupulously be observed in the arrangement of furniture, and the general care of the rooms and their surroundings. We naturally associate woman's presence with beauty and cleanliness in her home, these being an expression of her innate love of purity and her desire to please.

Where a number of persons are thrown together, we have to abide by certain unanimity of behaviour for the comfort and convenience of all. It is desirable that obedience to rules of decency and efficiency should be spontaneous, for it is truly uncivilized to violate those rules which are for common welfare. We should leave our beds in the morning at the scheduled time, perform our morning toilet, join the *Baitalik* in clean clothes, go and have our meals at the dining room in perfect order, maintain proper discipline in the class and on the playfield, be considerate and serviceable to each other at festive parties or picnics, enjoy walks in the evenings and after dusk return to the Hostel for study or music or entertainment. We should perform such daily round of tasks and diversions in a perfect spirit of grace never giving occasion to conflicts and confusions.

1934

58. COMMUNAL AWARD: TO MADAN MOHAN MALVIYA

My Dear Panditji,

I got your communication regarding the proposed Nationalist Conference in due time but could not reply to it earlier as we were celebrating the Rain Festival in the *Ashrama* and had number of guests from Calcutta and other places.

You all know that I have always disapproved of the Communal Award and I hope that our leaders will join their forces to save from its paralysing grip the political integrity of our nation. But not being a politician myself I shrink from taking part in a movement which I fear may create dissension in our ranks and strengthen the hands of our opponents. The responsibility is too great for me to identify myself with any particular party which is fighting for the cause.

My Dear Panditji,

I address this to Mahomedans as well as Hindus with the most sincere desire for the good of all sections of the community,

I urge that Hindus and Mahomedans should sit together dispassionately to consider the Communal Award and its implications to arrive at an agreed solution of the communal problem. It is needless to point out that self-government cannot be based on communal divisions, and separate electorate. No responsible system of government can be possible without mutual understanding of our communities and united representations at legislatures. We must concentrate all our forces to evolve a better understanding and co-operation between different sections of our people and thus lay a solid foundation for social and political reconstruction of our Motherland. I deprecate all expressions of angry feelings and most strongly appeal to Hindus and Musalmans to avoid saying and doing anything that may increase communal tension and further postpone the understanding between our communities without which there can be no peaceful progress in our country.

18 August 1934

59. FAREWELL TO ABDUL GHAFAR KHAN

We have you here with us only for a short period but we will not measure the worth of the event by the standard of time. Those really great, whose hearts are for all, who belong to all the lands of the world, transcend also the bounds of movements; they are for all time. Believe me, the memory of this short visit of yours to the *Ashrama* will ever remain fresh in our hearts.

Truth is the very foundation of your life, and I am sure that you radiate its influence all around you. We have realized this too, that all our efforts are everyday being frustrated for lack of this devotion to truth. You have come to this land whose unhappy being is shattered into fragments, in order to fulfil the purpose of providence to save her from the poison of fratricidal hatred which she is drugging herself to self-destruction. I have not the slightest doubts that you have been able to stimulate the hearts of our folk here with some of that great force of character which is your own. Pray accept the grateful homage of all of us.

This is our earnest prayer that you be long spared to help this land sick unto death towards vigorous health and truth.

15 September 1934

60. MY YOUNG FRIENDS

My Young Friends,

Let me assure you that the child within me is still actively alive. I cannot prove it by addressing you from this higher platform and solemnly posing as a distinguished visitor, frightening you into proper behaviour. But take it from me that if I had the opportunity to find my place in your midst I could easily share your life and your dreams. Do not be deceived by my grey exterior but keep your judgment in suspense till you are able to read my writings which contain spontaneous records of my confessions. There you will find expressions of a mind which refuses to grow old and callous in its touch with the great world to which we have been born. No doubt I am compelled to perform serious duties that help me to maintain my prestige of a mature age among the community of the grown-ups, but the best part of my activity has the inconsequential character of a mere play, fashioning structure of phantasy with airy nothings. It is in answer to the messages which come directly to my naked heart from the colourful playground of creation, wherever crowd fleeting images, the play things of the Eternal, in the blue of the sky and the green of the earth.

I have often received garlands from my fellow beings in recognition of some service or other which they consider as useful, but I have felt every day of my life, mother Nature crowning me with her morning light and kissing me with her fragrantly tender breeze, not because I have done anything valuable but because I have loved her. I have lived in this great world not only as a member of a society or of a group but as a light-hearted vagabond, free to roam or rest in the immense courtyard of this brown earth, chequered with lights and shadows. I have lived into the mystery of its being. You must not despise me because I may know less mathematics than you do, but I have come to the secret of existence not through any analytical mazes of exploration, but as a child approaching its mother's chamber. Because of this I stand close to you, the young hearts whom my heart recognizes as its fellow voyagers in the open road of light and life. This is by way of my introduction to you as a poet in which capacity I may claim my entry into the pure-blooded aristocracy of the child. I know you do not fully understand my works, but you may safely ignore them for they do not in any way affect you in your examination result. Yet I feel certain that this much you have realized from my talk that I have tried to approach you as your friend and not as your instructor and this pure friendliness of mine may continue to offer you companionship in my literary works when you grow older. Other distinguished visitors will come to you in future in the guise of advisers relentlessly taking up a great deal more time than I have done and then you will remember me gratefully for the merciful manner in which I have treated you in this address of mine which is remarkably short considering the occasion that has claimed it.

December 1934

61. A LETTER TO AN ENGLISH FRIEND

Dear Friend,

What you have said in your letter about certain opinions expressed by some of our young professors does, no doubt, represent the mental attitude of some of the young generation of modern India. It is a mentality bred of utter despair, a bitterness generated in a closed atmosphere of a narrow prospect of life. Mostly they are men of keen intellect, confident of their own attainments who find it hard to forget that they have lost their best opportunities and have been deprived of their life's fulfilment. They harbour a futile anger against their destiny and seek an outlet for their brooding vengefulness by hurling defiance at those ideals which men have held as sacred. They have readily accepted the teaching of some modern pundits of the West, that religion offers refuge to the cowards and supplies opiate to the mind that is helplessly compelled to suffer.

You have hinted in your letter about constructive programme, but you must know that those persons are extremely rare who have the genius to construct anything worth building, in an environment where things have to be begun from the very beginning, very often with meagre means and in unsympathetic circumstances. The burden of poverty in our country has been cruelly heavy and widespread, the training to fight it is absent, and on the top of it the depression of spirit that causes inertia finds its shelter in a body whose vitality has been run down owing to the want of nourishment and the consequent series of illnesses amidst surroundings devoid of proper medical help. It hurts me very deeply to find the best of our young minds indulging in a militant form of cynicism borrowed from the West, the cynicism which is all the more virulent because of its blankly negative character, destitute of all true vision. Because they have grown callously incapable of the deeper enjoyment of spiritual life they helplessly become addicted to cheap political sensationalism. I understand them, I suffer for them and I can never keep myself away from their wounded selves. I can only nourish a pathetic hope in my mind that in the end the wisdom which is of our own soil will find its way into their life, and if my own inspiration fails them I shall ever blame my own feeble power.

The boys with whom you had a talk are college students newly come who have not yet been naturalised in our *ashrama*. They are immature in mind; their education imperfect. Like all young men of similar stage they like to talk loud in order to hide their deficiency in language and feign scepticism because they are lacking in all thoughts; and they believe that by denying all time-honoured notions of truth they prove their own superiority. This must be a passing phase which a number of them, I hope, will outgrow and the rest of them will go on flaunting a livery of the smart only because they are incurably foolish.

1934

62. ISHOPANISHAT

(TO MAHADEV DESAI)

Dear Mahadeo,

First, let me make a confession—I have lost your letter—or very likely I took such a special care of it that it is not available even to me. However, I remember you asked me in your letter to explain to you the talk I had with you about *Ishopanishat.* For some time I have been extremely busy and therefore I have no choice but to be brief.

Ishopanishat has, from human point of view, divided truth into two aspects: one dealing with life and another with immortality. The characteristic note of this *Upanishat* is in the emptiness it lays upon the importance of both these aspects, none of which should be separated from the other. Avidya, which is the cult of the finite, deals with life—and according to *Ishopanishat* man should strive to live his full term of life in order to perform his *Karma.* For human beings, life is not merely a physiological progress, but it is fulfilment of his *Karma.* True *Karma* is not a series of activities generated by blind impulse of instincts or appetites. *Karma,* which gives meaning to our life, cannot be performed in ignorance or loss of truth—physical and moral. When through the help of *avidya,* the science of the finite, our rational and moral life reaches its fulfilment, then it is saved. The life lived in pursuance of mere animal needs, guided by a superficial and empirical knowledge of this world, is death for man. On the contrary, the life that has perfected through enlightened *Karma,* which is not fixed forms of ritualism, or unthinking conformity to customs, but which represents in its varied activities Man's reason, and will, and power of aesthetic enjoyment, lays the path towards the spiritual realization of the infinite. For the infinite is nothing negative,—it is not an emptiness that can be reached through an absolute elimination of the finite, but in it the finite has its ultimate meaning. And therefore according to *Ishopanishat avidya* and *vidya* both have to be perfected and harmonised. The cult of the finite exclusively pursued leads us to no final goal and yet it gives us something which is concrete, but the cult of the infinite excluding the finite is an abstraction, it is an illimitable abyss of nihilism. The East in the modern time has been beaten in the race of life, because it has neglected to cultivate the science of the finite, and the West is being driven into conflict of passions and unmeaning multiplication of things because it has lost its respect for the cult of the infinite. The salvation of humanity lies in the meeting of the East and West in a perfect harmony of truth.

1935

63. RAMCHANDRA SHARMA UNDERTAKES FAST: TAGORE'S APPEAL

I know fully well that my entreaties to those who have so far turned a deaf ear to the message preached through the impending death of this great soul, would go in vain. Despite that I would once again beseech my countrymen not to let the memory of this stern refusal to the call of this noble soul remain as a perpetual blot in the annals of our motherland. Wherever else this kind-hearted man has staked his life before the present attempt for the votaries of the deities concerned, they had not allowed him to die. If it should now be Bengal's turn to compel Pandit Ramchandra to embrace death by persisting in the utterly callous attitude towards this movement, then for that act of sheer inhumanity the entire nation shall repent heavily—there is no escape from that. I have nothing to say but to send up earnest prayers to God Almighty to so ordain things that the door for avoiding this grim tragedy may not be irrevocably banged yet.

1935

64. 'A MESSAGE OF CONDOLENCE'

Dear Vidyavati,

I do not know how adequately to impart my experience to you. I shall simply speak to you of an incident full of the most poignant sorrow of my life. My youngest son, beautiful in appearance and lovable in character, was about sixteen when he was invited to spend his vacation with a boy friend of his in Monghyr. I hastened to his side when I suddenly received a telegram in Calcutta, informing me of a serious attack of illness causing grave anxiety to his host who was a doctor. The boy lingered for three days after my arrival, trying repeatedly to assure me that he was free from all physical sufferings. When his last moment was about to come I was sitting alone in the dark in an adjoining room, praying intently for his passing away to his next stage of existence in perfect peace and well-being. At a particular point of time my mind seemed to float in a sky where there was neither darkness nor light, but a profound depth of calm, a boundless sea of consciousness without a ripple or murmur. I saw the vision of my son lying in the heart of the Infinite and I was about to cry to my friend, who was nursing the boy in the next room, that the child was safe, that he had found his liberation. I felt like a father who had sent his son across the sea, relieved to learn of his safe arrival and success in finding his place. I felt at once that the physical nearness of our dear ones to ourselves is not the final meaning of their protection. It is merely a means of satisfaction to our own selves and not necessarily the best that could be wished for them. I believe that the love which is true can help the departed spirit in crossing the boundaries of earthly life and finding its spiritual destination. And therefore it should be our sacred duty to direct that love of ours, through concentration of will, towards winning for them their best fulfilment and never to waste it in futile desire for our own consolation. Of course, all bereavements naturally bring sufferings, but let us through them find freedom and joy by realizing that they are our sacrifices which we dedicate for the salvation of our beloved ones, and that by our own emancipation we bring emancipation to them also.

With heartfelt sympathy and blessings,

27 December 1935

65. TO INDIAN NATIONAL CONGRESS

To The President, Indian National Congress, Bombay

My warmest greetings on the happy occasion of Golden Jubilee Celebrations. The destiny of India has chosen for its ally the power of soul and not that of muscle. And she is to raise the history of man from the muddy level of physical conflicts to a higher moral altitude.

27 December 1935

66. THE RICE WE EAT

When a people's diet takes a vicious path of its own impoverishment, it causes a graver mischief than any act of cruelty inflicted by an alien power. Such has unfortunately been the case in our province. Rice has been our staple food from which we have for generations received a great part of our health, strength, energy and intelligence. But curiously enough, especially among the upper class of our community, a fatal epidemic of foolishness has become prevalent which allows this principal food-stuff of ours to be depleted of its precious nourishing element. Rice mills are menacingly spreading fast extending throughout the province an unholy alliance with malaria and other flag-bearers of death robbing the whole people of its vitality through a constant weakening of its nourishment. We not only boil away an essential amount of nutrition from our daily ration of rice but also use elaborate machinery to polish off its skin which contains its most vital gift. This is a self-imposed form of famine deliberately welcomed by a people who had already been suffering from the scarcity of milk and that of ghee of a non-poisonous kind. One of the consequent diseases in the form of beri-beri has specially chosen its victims from the Bengalis, who still remain indifferent to its lesson. There had been, I am told, some proposal to check the progress of this fatal evil through the intervention of legislature. I am glad that it failed, for the people must not be treated like eternal babies carefully protected by its appointed nurses from its own utter stillness. It is only for ourselves to exercise our intelligence for choosing our food which must be wholesome and sustaining. It is for the people themselves to realize that in the long run it is not cheaper to substitute the callous force of machinery for the indigenous rice-huller, oil press and grind stone for crushing the wheat. Physical vigour born of healthy meals is valuable, not only for itself but for its power of enhancing one's earning capacity. Then again, we have to take into account the immense importance of our rural economic life whose course has been cruelly obstructed by the iron monster robbing our village women of some of their natural means of livelihood and the labouring class of its right to gather its simple living out of the gleanings from the people's own green field of life. It has gone on for long, this tampering with the time-honoured irrigation of living, in this country causing large desert tracks of privation in our villages. Would it be too much to expect a body of volunteers in Bengal to form a league whose members should take a solemn vow to use *dhenki*-hulled rice for their meals not allowing its nourishment to be stupidly thrown away by wasteful cooking? Could they not realize that it is the perpetuation of a national calamity to which most of us is daily helping by instituting in our homes an insiduous method of suicide?

28 December 1935

67. MESSAGE TO WORLD PEACE CONGRESS

If peace is to be anything more than the mere absence of war, it must be founded on the strength of the just and not on the weariness of the weak. The groan of peace in Abyssinia is no less ghastly than the howl of war in Spain. If then we are to strive for that true peace, in which the satisfaction of one people is not built on the frustration of another, then the average peace-loving citizen of the successful nations of today must extricate himself from the obvious anomaly of wishing for peace whilst sharing in the spoils of war,—which exposes his wish to the charge of mere pretence. He must not let himself be bribed on the promise of prosperity and honour and call it patriotism. We cannot have peace until we deserve it by paying its full price—which is, that the strong must cease to be greedy and the weak must learn to be bold.

1936

68. NEW EDUCATION FELLOWSHIP

Though my frail health deprives me of the privilege of being present in the midst of this gathering, I have great pleasure in welcoming you all on this occasion, which is distinguished by the presence of our guests from overseas. I am particularly happy to note the international character of this conference, for though each country may have its particular problems claiming particular solutions, true education, like all great arts, must have its basis in principles that condition human development everywhere. It may be my bias as an artist, but education seems to me essentially an art whose problem we solve not by discussing systems but by discovering creative sources of inspiration. When this source is a human one it dwells in a teacher who is ever a student and therefore through whom a perennial intellectual eagerness acts as a dynamic force spreading in its surroundings a disinterested impulse for knowledge. Those who have garnered for good their stock-in-trade as school masters and shut their minds against the growing harvest of truth can only reproduce their lessons as gramophone records, repeating with dull accuracy stale passages from second-hand stores. They burden the mind but seldom nourish it. Teachers should be ideal comrades of those whom they teach and through the course of teaching, their own minds should be stirred in sympathy with the stirring of the young minds. The joy of imbibing lessons oneself ought to find its true expression in infusing it in others. When we see such a living enthusiasm lacking in those who act as guides to their pupils, who are ready to raise to them ruling rods from a distance but not offer them the helping hand by their side, as too often is the case, they should be reminded that they have chosen a wrong vocation and should for the sake of humanity change it without delay for that of a jail warden. A genuine sympathy and respect for the students creates an atmosphere of freedom in the classes which is indispensable to the commerce of culture which is named education.

Another stream of inspiration ever flowing towards us comes from the heart of mother nature when she is generous in her gift of light and sky, in the colourful pageantry of her seasons. I can never forget the misery which I suffered as a boy when I was daily deprived of human sympathy within the school walls and nature's ministration of beauty around them. Young minds gradually forget their need of these vitamins of life and are taught to rely upon some substitute fare of lessons considered to be principal elements in the muscle building of the intellect. I believe that it is imperatively necessary that all important educational institutions should be founded in those places where nature reveals her eternal majesty of beauty and grandeur according to which our places of pilgrimage have generally been chosen in India. Consecration of our life waits to be received from nature's own hand and it should accompany our training of heart, mind and imagination, a training which is not only for the production of timber of a high market value, if mind could be compared to a tree, but for exhibiting the wealth of its flowers which contributes to the joy of creation, often without our noticing it.

Another necessary factor of education is the environment of national mind. But unfortunately we have not had the opportunity of cultivating it in India for over a century and such a privation can never be compensated for by the establishment of law and order, which our government has so often boasted of, and which is merely an imposition from outside, superficial in its genuineness. In the olden days in India there was a uniformity of culture, having its guardians and centres of distribution in different places which may be called university towns. Like as in the organ of the heart, the life blood of the common culture was generated and kept pure in these places where great scholars gathered and owned their sacred responsibility to the society to offer their learning freely to those who came to claim it. Today our few universities are like oases in the heart of a vast desert of illiteracy, whose gifts are for a few, producing a language and mental diet that remain foreign to the multitude. Such a meagre education, product of very narrow reservation plots, often has reactionary symptoms upon the nature of those who are classed as the educated, the strong gravitational pull of their surroundings violently dragging them back into the dark cell of medieval unreason. Such an education can never attain its depth of reality and when our foreign critics laugh at some imperfect manifestation of our minds, very often turning it into a propaganda for humiliating us before the world, they seem to be blissfully ignorant of their own responsibility for such a tragically stupid result.

Nor may we underrate the great influence exercised on the child's mind by the values that prevail in the society in which he is born and brought up. If these values be perverted, no sort or amount of formal education can save the child from their destructive effect. For these values affect the mind as subtly and surely as the physical climate on the body. Good education of children is not possible unless good ideals govern the society. Methods of education may be modern and scientific but they will only chain and debase the mind more effectively if the purposes they serve are ignoble. Educationists therefore must remain more or less helpless in an age where collective greed is glorified as patriotism and inhuman butchery is made the measure of heroism.

I have taken the liberty of drawing your attention to the universal principles that must govern the value of education as an art and determine its success for good or ill. As regards the particular problems that relate to this country I leave them for your mature deliberations, which I shall read with great pleasure. My own ideas regarding these problem I have emphasised so often before my countrymen that I am reluctant to reiterate what have come to be regarded, as mere platitudes. And platitudes indeed all ideas tend to become unless worked out in some living form. I am therefore glad that some of you will be coming after the conference to our *ashrama* at Santiniketan where I may be able to show you how I have struggled for the last thirty years to create for our children an appropriate atmosphere, giving it the principal place in our programme of teaching. For atmosphere there must be for developing the sensitiveness of soul, for affording mind its true freedom of sympathy.

Now that Mahatma Gandhi has taken up the cause of mass education in earnest we may be sure of great results in the near future. Already great interest has been roused in the country and controversy provoked over the question whether education can be made self supporting. Before you too are likewise provoked to violent agreement or disagreement with the proposal I would remind you that Gandhiji's genius is essentially practical, which means that his practice is immeasurably superior to his theory. As the scheme stands on paper, it seems to assume that material utility, rather than development of personality, is the end of education, that while education in the true sense of the word may be still available for a chosen few who can afford to pay for it, the utmost that the masses can have is to be trained to view the world they live in the perspective of the particular craft they are to employ for their livelihood. It is true that as things are even that is much more than what the masses are actually getting but it is nevertheless unfortunate that even in our ideal scheme, education should be doled out in insufficient rations to the poor, while the feast remains reserved for the rich. I cannot congratulate a society or a nation that calmly excludes play from the curriculum of the majority of its children's education and gives in its stead a vested interest to the teachers in the market value of the pupils' labour. But these defects seem such only on paper, for no man loves the children of the poor more than the Mahatma, and we may be sure that when the scheme is actually worked out by him we shall discover in it only one more testimony to the genius of this practical sage whose deeds surpass his word.

February 1936

69. THE ENGLISH IN INDIA

The British Empire is pluming itself on its generosity in making over some part of the machinery of the Government of India into our hands. What is distressing me is that the poisonous element mixed in the boon offered to us will continue to work noxiously for an indefinite time to come. It will ever keep inflamed the communal passions in Bengal, threatening her peace, which is an essential environment for all economic, social and cultural progress. The Moslems are apparently failing to realize that an unbalanced politics will never serve their own interest for long, that the communal split amounts to cutting at the root of national life.

You know, and I have never tried to keep it secret from anyone, that of all the Western peoples who have direct dealings with alien races I respect most the British people. Many things have recently happened in our country to wound us to the quick, in the doing of which British agents were concerned, but of which it is forbidden to speak. These have embittered the hearts of our countrymen at large though the punishment has fallen only on our youths. In spite of it all, I still say that it will not do to isolate such events when coming to our own judgment of the British people.

There are other great nations in Europe who exercise dominion over foreign peoples. And we cannot but have a sigh of relief whenever we recall that is not they who are our rulers. What I am writing to you now, and the freedom with which our representatives in the Legislatures expatiate on the shortcomings of the Government, would not have been possible under the domination of any other European nation which holds subject races under its autocratic grip. We admire the United States from a distance, because we have no relations with her. But, apart from her inhuman treatment of the Negroes, the instances of rank injustice perpetrated by her highest courts of law are such as do not fortunately belong to our normal experience in India.

When our rulers are annoyed, however contrary they may act for the time to their true national character they cannot altogether get rid of all sense of shame. For, in the nation to which they belong they have noble personalities who by that very fact are its truest representatives to whose judgment they cannot but defer although they try to come when irritated, close to the blood-and-iron methods with some superficial modifications. Nevertheless they cannot come down to the point of saying "We shall do just as we like"—as the Badshahs and Nawabs of old used to say, as some of our ruling chiefs of to-day would like to say and as the Fascist nations of Europe are actuals saying. Here, when we complain of the frightful conditions prevailing in the Andamans, then, even to such weaklings as we are, they are impelled seriously to report with benevolence beaming from their faces that the Andamans are as beautifully perfect from the moral and physical point of view as could be desired for the condemned. Had those Englishmen whose practice departs widely from English ideals been capable of openly insulting those ideals how few of the speakers in our legislative bodies would have remained outside that "penal paradise"?

I have seen many great Englishmen. They never hesitate to stand up against wrong whether done by others or by their own countrymen. These may not be statesmen, for statesmen are not usually to be reckoned as true representatives of the nation. If the persons wielding political power in England had been able to ignore the silent judgment of the great minds in their country they might have succeeded in levelling to the dust all the best canons of humanity—as has been done in Germany and Italy, and as might have been done in England if the new-fledged Fascists there had their way. In that case the Andamans would have been fully populated and the key of the speeches in our Legislatures pitched several tones lower—as in the case of Germany and Italy.

I must admit that my admiration of British character, in so far as that character is reflected in the governing of India, with its penal system, whipping, and solitary cell does not come to much more than a comparative statement. It is inhuman enough for us, as you must have found from the narrative of Jawaharlal's prison experience and also from numerous instances of political prisoners, in the prime of their youth, coming out to die after a few years of gaol, miserably broken down in health and spirit. And it is but meagre consolation to us to think that it could even have been worse according to the present standard of civilization that prevails in a large part of the West.

Some of our countrymen are annoyed with me and ask: If you have such high respect for the British people why do you not hanker for a perpetuation of their rule? My reply is that thus to be drawn into the widespread net of a foreign Imperialism can never be good for India. It would have been otherwise had this Empire connoted an undivided body-politic. But the conditions prevailing in the cowsheds of a dairyman are not to be compared with those obtaining in his homestead. In the former the question is one of the ample production of milk and of getting burdens cheaply carried. If its occupants display their horns in asserting their self-determination no time is lost in bringing home to them their true position.

The chronic want of food and water, the lack of sanitation and medical help, the neglect of means of communication, the poverty of educational provision, the all-pervading spirit of depression that I have myself seen to prevail in our villages after over a hundred years of British rule make me despair of its beneficence. It is almost a crime to talk of Soviet Russia in this country, and yet I cannot but refer to the contrast it presents. I must confess to the envy with which my admiration was mixed to see the extraordinary enthusiasm and skill with which the measures for producing food, providing education, fighting against disease were being pushed forward in their vast territories. There is no separating line of mistrust or insulting distinctions between Soviet Europe and Soviet Asia. I am only comparing the state of things obtaining there and here as I have actually seen them. And I state my conclusion that what is responsible for our condition in the so-called British Empire is the yawning gulf between its dominant and subjugated sections.

On the other hand, it has to be recognized that there is an inevitableness in the fate that has overtaken Hindu India. We have divided and subdivided ourselves into mincemeat, not fit to live but only to be swallowed. Never up to now has our disjointed society been able to ward off any threatening evil. We are a suicidal race, ourselves keeping wide open for ages, with marvellous ingenuity, gaps that we are forbidden to cross under penalty and cracks that are considered to be too sacred to be repaired because of their antiquity.

October 1936

70. SPANISH CIVIL WAR

TO THE CONSCIENCE OF HUMANITY

In Spain, the world civilization is being menaced and trampled under foot. Against the democratic government of the Spanish people Franco has raised the standard of revolt. International Fascism is pouring men and money in aid of the rebels. Moors and foreign legionaries are sweeping over the beautiful plains of Spain; trailing behind them death, hunger and desolation.

Madrid, the proud centre of culture and art is in flames. Her priceless treasures of art are being bombed by the rebels. Even hospitals and crèches are not spared. Women and children are murdered, made homeless, and destitute.

The devastating tide of International Fascism must be checked. In Spain this inhuman recrudescence of obscurantism, of racial prejudice, of rapine and glorification of war must be given the final rebuff. Civilization must be saved from its being swamped by barbarism.

At this hour of the supreme trial and suffering of the Spanish people, *I appeal to the conscience of humanity.*

"Help the peoples' front in Spain, help the Government of the people, cry in million voices 'Halt' to reaction come in your millions to the aid of democracy, to the succour of civilization and culture."

March 1937

71. APPEAL TO THE UNITED PARTY OF SIND

Office acceptance is only an outward temptation and practically the Hindus must realize this before hankering after offices.

Sind owes a debt to me and I have claims. We are today living in strange circumstances and it is sad that Sind is betraying the country. Sind may have Hindu-Muslim frictions, but you must realize that you are being duped by the glitter being shown to you. Office is sure to entangle us and we must rise above this. Urgency of time requires that we should rise above this. Otherwise, it will be betrayal of the country if we succumbed. Every Indian should be aware of the present political situation in the country so that he might not be duped into the temptation of office and won over.

Sind is playing into the hands of the powers that be in as much as every M.L.A. appears to hanker after jobs. Evidently the right people are not there.

April 1937

72. IN DEFENCE OF THE WORKERS ON STRIKE

It has deeply grieved me to learn of the suffering of hundreds of thousands of jute workers who have struck work since February last. This is causing misery not only to the workers themselves but also to their women and children. The demands for higher wages and for more humane conditions of work are just and reasonable. In every democratic country of the West, the Government looks after the welfare of the people. May we not expect that the Ministers under the new constitution would take-up this question affecting the lives of hundreds of thousands of workers and their families immediately and see that justice is done to them? Humanity demands that those who bear the burden of the society should be protected and looked after by the society itself. To give this strike a communal turn by stirring up ugly communal passions should be condemned by every right-thinking man.

I appeal to my countrymen to help the jute-workers and their helpless women and children in this period of their suffering and distress.

29 April 1937

73. ON INDIA

I love India, not because I cultivate the idolatry of geography, not because I have had the chance to be born in her soil, but because she has saved through tumultuous ages the living words that have issued from the illuminated consciousness of her great sons—*Satyam, Jnanam, Anantam Brahma,* Brahma is truth, Brahma is wisdom, Brahma is infinite; *Santam, Sivam, Advaitam,* peace is in Brahma, goodness in Brahma, and the unity of all beings.

Brahma-nishtho grhasthah syat tatvajnana-prakurvita
yad yad karma prakurvita tad Brahmani samarpayet

The householder shall have his life established in Brahma, shall pursue the deeper truth of all things and in all activities of life dedicate his works to the Eternal Being.

Thus we have come to know that what India truly seeks is not a peace which is in negation, or in some mechanical adjustment, but that which is in *Sivam,* in goodness; which is in *Advaitam,* in the truth of perfect union; that India does not enjoin her children to cease from *karma,* but to perform their *karma,* in the presence of the Eternal, with the pure knowledge of the spiritual meaning of existence; that this is the true prayer of Mother India;

Ya eko-varno bahudha saktiyogat varnan anekan nihitartho dadhati
vichaiti chante visvamadau sa no buddhya subhaya samyunaktu

He who is one, who is above all colour distinctions, who dispenses the inherent needs of men of all colours, who comprehends all things from their beginning to the end, let Him unite us to one another with the wisdom which is the wisdom of goodness.

1937

74. APPEAL FOR ANDAMAN PRISONERS

On the continent of Europe they have their Devil's Island, (French Penal Settlement), their Lipari (Italian Penal Settlement), their Concentration Camps (in Germany and Russia) and other specially built halls for the primitive exhibition of humanity, but in England they have no such unhallowed places for the intensification of suffering by wrenching away prisoners from their own soil. When to our dismay, we find that an infringement of their own rule has been made possible exclusively for the subject races, the insult of their distinction humiliate all of us, and I offer my protest in the name of my country.

It is more than a week since about 200 political prisoners have gone on hunger-strike in the Andamans. The news of the hunger-strike was withheld from us for a long time. This callous indifference to public sentiment is a sad reminder of our national helplessness. In England or in any other democratic country government would not dare keep a fact of such national importance as this hunger-strike secret for such a long time.

The political prisoners have demanded repatriation to India from the Andamans. Their demand is just and modest. When the power is not responsible to the people of this country, it is only natural that the people will be apprehensive of the treatment that is meted out to political prisoners exiled in an island thousands of miles away from India and demand that these political prisoners should be kept in India where at least some kind of popular control can be exercised to soften the inhuman rigour of prison life in India.

It appears that the Government of India have shifted their own responsibilities regarding the question of repatriation of the Andaman prisoners on to the shoulders of the Bengal Government. Moreover, the Government of India have rejected the petition of the political prisoners on the plea of their inability to consider the collective petition of all prisoners.

Once again the heartless inflexibility of the Government machinery has triumphed over its sense of humanity and justice.

In those Provinces of India where the representatives of the people have taken up the reins of administration, political prisoners have been unconditionally released and all encroachment on the civil liberty of the people has been removed.

It is only in the Province of Bengal that hundreds of boys are detained without trial. The Press is now and then gagged to remind us of the power that is not answerable to the will of the people of this country, and the civil liberty that the people of Bengal enjoy has become as unreal as a mirage in the desert.

We all know that once before in the past during another hunger-strike amongst the political prisoners in the Andamans, three young lives were lost. Two of them were the direct victims of the cruel system of forced feeding. Shall we and the Bengal Government allow the same tragedy to occur in a larger number this time once again?

I appeal to the Bengal Government to line up with the Governments of Bombay, Madras and the Central Provinces and to treat with broad-minded sympathy and humanity the case of political prisoners and detenus.

The pitiless method of punishment that still persists in most parts of the world in their penal system is enough to condemn human civilization, but of late an aggravated spirit of vindictiveness has suddenly grown in virulence in some of the Western countries in their dealings with political victims. India has not altogether escaped in her government from manifesting in some degree such Fascistic infection which has scant respect for the law and for the legitimate claim of human freedom.

And, the gloom of despair has spread from hundreds of stricken homes over this unfortunate province when men and women of tender age and made to suffer an indefinite period of detention without trial, undergoing various modes of penalty, physical and psychological.

On this present occasion I am requested by my countrymen to lend my voice in asking our rulers, not for any radical change in the administration of the law, which, no doubt is sorely needed but for some mitigation in its severity.

3 August 1937

(Personal and Confidential)

Dear Sir John Anderson,

I feel greatly relieved to learn from Dr. Amiya Chakravorty, who had an interview with you on the 14th inst., that you and your Government are taking the earliest opportunity of bringing about a satisfactory settlement with regard to the Andaman prisoners. It is needless to emphasize that the matter is fraught with grave consequences and I am afraid, if no generous gesture is forthcoming from the Government, the situation might be too embittered for ever restoring a normal atmosphere in the Province. I have sent just now the following cable to the prisoners:

Earnestly Appeal To You To Call Off Hunger Strike (Stop) Your Case Taken Up By The Whole Nation (Stop) Feel Restoration Of Atmosphere Favourable For Discussion Will Be Greatly Helpful.

And I am also writing to Mahatma Gandhi and Pandit Nehru, whose words would have great consideration with the prisoners to issue similar appeal to them. I quite realize that the calling off of the fast would considerably lessen the tension in the country and restore an atmosphere more suitable for a dispassionate discussion. I have every hope that our request would be honoured by the prisoners and the Government will also generously review the whole situation.

Dr. Chakravorty tells me that a scheme of repatriation has been already accepted by the Government and that you are also considering the question of release of detenus. I feel very strongly on these matters on humanitarian grounds and we should like Great Britain to take the lead in abolishing the system of maintaining penal settlements for political prisoners, entirely cut-off from humanising contacts with society and we trust that in India the reform of prisons will follow the advanced technique now being adopted by a modern country.

16 August 1937

75. IN RESPONSE TO RASBEHARI BOSE'S APPEAL

'WHO AM I TO RECALL SUCH RIGHTEOUS PROTEST'

Dear Rasbehari,

Your cable has caused me many restless hours. For, it hurts me very much to have to ignore your appeal. I wish you had asked for my co-operation in a cause against which my spirit did not protest. I know in making this appeal you counted on my great regard for the Japanese, for I along with the rest of Asia did once admire and look up to Japan and did once fondly hope that in Japan Asia had at last discovered its challenge to the West, that Japan's new strength would be consecrated in safeguarding the culture of the East against alien interests, but Japan has not taken long to betray that rising hope and repudiate all that seemed significant in her wonderful and to us symbolic awakening and has now become itself a worse menace to the defenceless peoples of the East.

Worst than its economic exploitation, worse indeed than its geographical aggression, is this daily perpetration of pitiless massacres and its unashamed championship of its inhumanity. Countries have been conquered before in history and seen in wider perspective. There is nothing very inhuman or shocking in a virile race overstepping the dilapidated fences built by the previous victories of an earlier race and until science had made man's inhumanity so effective, such fighting like all life seemed only half cruel, all that is changed and today when one nation invades another its wrong is not only that of mere imperialist ambition but of human butchery more indiscriminate than any plague and if one outraged conscience all over the world cries out against such a wrong, who am I to recall such righteous protest.

This protest has not been engineered by any single individual. It is as spontaneous and heartfelt as the admiration that the peoples of the East felt for Japan thirty years ago I should be powerless to check it even if I dared to attempt it. You must, therefore, forgive me that I am unable to oblige you and believe me when I say that I have great sympathy with my countrymen in Japan as indeed I have with the Japanese themselves, but the cry that comes from China of broken hearts and heads and broken bones is far too piercing and awful.

11 October 1937

76. VANDE MATARAM

An unfortunate controversy is raging round the question of the suitability of Vande Mataram as national song. In offering my own opinion about it, I am reminded that the privilege of originally setting its first stanza to the tune was mine, when the author was still alive, and that I was the first person to sing it before a gathering at an early session of the Calcutta Congress.

To me, the spirit of tenderness and devotion expressed in its first portion and the emphasis it gave to the beautiful and beneficent aspects of our Motherland made a special appeal, so much so that I found no difficulty in dissociating it from the rest of the poem and from those portions of the book of which it is part, with all the sentiments of which, brought up as I was in this monotheistic ideals of my father, I could have no sympathy.

It first caught on as an appropriate National Anthem at the poignant period of our strenuous struggle for asserting the people's will against the decree of separation hurled upon our province by the ruling power. Subsequent developments, during which Vande Mataram became a national slogan, cannot, in view of the stupendous sacrifices of some of the best of our youths, be likely ignored at a moment, when it has once again become necessary to give expression to our triumphant confidence in the victory of our cause.

I freely concede that the whole of Bankim's Vande Mataram poem, read together with its context, is liable to be interpreted in ways that might wound Muslim susceptibilities but a national song, though derived from it, which has spontaneously come to consist only of the first two stanzas of the original poem and need not remind us every time of the whole of it, much less of the story with which it was accidentally associated. It has acquired a separate individuality and an inspiring significance of its own, in which I see nothing to offend any sect or community.

30 October 1937

77. APPEAL TO JOURNALISTS

In this most critical period of the history of our province, when problems of tremendous difficulty are loudly challenging us, I earnestly appeal to the editors of our journals to be extremely careful in avoiding the temptation of constantly giving exaggerated emphasis to popular weaknesses—those that work against the binding force in the fruit-bearing soil of our national being.

Innumerable channels of self depreciation, along which we are carrying on our daily traffic in mutual revilement, are creating deeper mischief in the internal constitution of our body-politic than the manoeuvring of those outsiders who pile up a world-opinion against us with the dexterous use of half-truths and facts distorted into a caricature.

Evidently, the more we are being pushed through a combination of evil forces into the background from all places of honour, the more virulent is becoming the fury of mutual debasement in Bengal, where the demand for the stinking stuff of calumny is copiously met with, not only through the puny publications of the poisonous mushroom type, but often journals belonging to a higher distinction. Under their constant fusillade of vilifications, and their underground mining operations institutions split up in factions, and reputations are light-heartedly dragged in the mud. In almost every department of life an exhibition is going on in Bengal of the unhealthy instinct that encourages malignant pleasure in discrediting all persons and pursuits that have reached any degree of prominence, headless of the fact that by doing it we discredit our own country before the world; that by dimming the lighted spots in our society through the smoke-screen of slander, we only prove the innate obscurity of our own nation's mind.

This is the reason why Bengal though rich in imagination and intelligence is woefully deficient in institutions that could only be based upon mutual trust and co-operation and on an unfaltering loyalty to a common cause. These symptoms are specially to be dreaded when some amount of responsibility is placed in our hands for guiding our political destiny,—the responsibility which will depend for its fulfilment upon 'Sweetness and light', upon the magnanimity of heart and on a strict adherence to truth, justice and forbearance of spirit.

25 December 1937

78. JAGADISH CHANDRA BOSE

I

Years ago, when Jagadish Chandra, in his militant exuberance of youthfulness, was contemptuously defying all obstacles to the progress of his endeavour, I came into intimate contact with him, and became infected with his vigorous hopefulness. There was every chance of his frightening me away into a respectful distance, making me aware of the airy nothingness of my own imaginings. But to my relief, I found in him a dreamer, and it seemed to me, what surely was a half-truth, that it was more his magical instinct than the probing of his reason which startled out secrets of nature before sudden flashes of his imagination. In this I felt our mutual affinity but at the same time our difference, for to my mind he appeared to be the poet of the world of facts that waited to be proved by the scientist for their final triumph, whereas my own world of visions had their value not in their absolute probability, but in their significance of delightfulness. All the same, I believe that a part of my nature is logical which not only enjoys making playthings of facts, but seeks pleasure in an analytical view of objective reality. I remember often having been assured by my friend that I only lacked the opportunity of training to be a scientist but not the temperament. Thus in the prime of my youth I was strangely attracted by the personality of this remarkable man and found his mind sensitively alert in the poetical atmosphere of enjoyment which belonged to me.

At this time he was busy detecting in the behaviour of the non-living some hidden impulses of life, This aroused a keen enthusiasm in me who had ever been familiar with the utterance of the Upanishad which proclaims that whatever there is in this moving world vibrates with life. Afterwards he shifted his enquiries from the field of physics to the biological realm of plants. With the marvellously sensitive instruments which he invented he magnified the inaudible whisperings of vegetable life, which seemed to him somewhat similar in language to the message of our own nerves. My mind was overcome with joy at the idea of the unity of the heart-beats of the universe, and I felt sure that the pulsating light which palpitates in the stars has its electric kinship in the life that throbs in my own veins. I knew that this was not science, but my mind trembled with the hope that the opening message had already been declared and final evidences were in preparation.

At last when Jagadish Chandra sailed across the sea to place the results of his researches before the questioning scrutiny of the West, my heart expanded with an undoubting expectation of our country's claim to a world-recognition being accepted and at the prospect of a wide establishment of a wonderful truth which is native to our oriental attitude of mind. With what little lay in my power I helped him in his adventure but, fortunately, since then no more help was needed either in companionship or in other ways from a man like me who was too heavily burdened with his own responsibilities. His fame spread rapidly and material contributions from all sides showered upon his schemes, which centralized at last in the Bose Institute. I fervently hope that the Spirit of Science will find its lasting shrine in this place and the aspiration of the great master will remain a living force in its heart, making it a perpetual memorial worthy of him.

This tribute of mine to the memory of Jagadish will appear inadequately feeble, especially in contrast to the repeated magnification of his name in my writings both in prose and verse at the time when his fame was not luminously apparent above the horizon and when, I am sure, my fellowship and unfaltering faith in his genius did hearten and help him. But my struggling health, which has lately been wrenched back from the grip of death, is incompetent for most of my important tasks and also the singing hope that began its first soaring in immensity has completed its journey in its terminus.

1937

II

When by some fortunate chance I came into an intimate contact with Sir Jagadish, he was in the prime of his youth and I was very nearly of his age. At that moment his mind seemed entranced with a vision of the living creatures' fundamental kinship with the world of the unconscious. He was busy in employing his marvellous inventiveness in coaxing mute Nature to yield her hidden language. The response which he received through skilful questioning revealed to him glimpses of the mystery of an existence that concealed its meaning underneath a contradiction of its appearance. I had the rare privilege of sharing the daily delight of his constant surprises. I believe, poets inherit the primeval age in their temperament when things in their infant simplicity revealed a common feature. Somehow these lovers of *Maya* feel the joy of their being spread all over the creation, which makes them indulge in seeking the analogy of the living in things that appear lifeless. Such an attitude of mind may not in all cases be based upon any definite belief, animistic or pantheistic; it may be merely a make-believe, as we notice in children's play, which owes its origin to the lurking tendency in our subconscious mind to ascribe life-energy to all activities in the natural world. I was made familiar from my boyhood with the Upanishad which, in its primitive intuition, proclaims that whatever there is in this world vibrates with life, the life that is one in the infinite.

This might have been the reason of the eager enthusiasm with which I expected that the idea of the boundless community of life in the world was on the verge of a final sanction from the logic of scientific verification. Being allowed to follow the Master's footsteps in the privacy of his pursuit, even though as a mere picker of his casual hints, I had my daily feast of wonders. At this early stage of his adventure when obstacles were powerfully numerous and jealousy largely predominated over appreciation, friendly companionship and sympathy must have had some needful value for him even one who to maintain intellectual communion with him lacked special competency. Yet I can proudly claim to have helped him in some of his immediate needs and occasional hours of despondency in those days of an inadequate recognition and feeble support that he received from the public.

In the background of that distant memory of mine, I find not the slightest gleam of a vision of the enormous success that could before long combine scientific renown with a vast material means adequate enough to build this Institute, one of the very few richly endowed mediums in India for bestowing the benediction of science upon his countrymen. In fact, it makes me laugh at myself today to read, in some of my old letters, my effort to encourage him with the likelihood of filling the gaps in his funds when my own resources were precariously limited to persuading friends who were foolish enough to have faith in me. Still it is comically sweet to think of the proud magnificence in my assurance fitfully accompanied by contribution absurdly poor compared to the ceaseless flow of tribute that, later on, he could attract by his own magnetic personality and also by the general confidence he widely aroused in his genius. But I repeat again, it was sweet to have dreamed impracticable dreams and to have done however little it was possible, as it proves a courage of joy in the faith in greatness which itself is a bounteous gift to one's own mind.

However ill-equipped as I was by the deficiency in my training and by the poet's idiosyncrasy to be a fit companion to a man of science at a luminous period of his self-revelation, I was still accepted as his close friend and, possibly because of the contrariety in our natural vocations, I was able to offer some stimulation to his urge of fulfilment. Not having the necessary amount of vanity in my constitution, it had been the subject of constant wonder in my mind.

Since then time passed quickly, maturing the fruits of our expectation. During this period of his fast-growing triumph, I was modest enough to feel less and less the urgency of my comradeship in his journey towards the goal, which was no longer arduous or beset with uncertainty. And yet I can rightfully claim the credit for strengthening in some measure his trust in his own destiny, by adding to it my own unwavering faith, at that painfully hesitant moment of fortune during the dubious dawn of his career, when even persons of meagre resources might have some important use.

Victory is the inalienable claim of all genuine power having the might of attraction that naturally exploits all kindred elements on its path and moulds them into an image of glory. And such an image is this Institute, which represents the Master's lifelong endeavour taking a permanent shape in the form of a centre for the inspiration of similar endeavours.

However, the early association of mine with the Master's first great challenge of genius to his fate, whose path at that time did not run smooth, belongs for me to a remote period of a history in which I feel myself hazily indistinct. And this made me seriously waver to accept the invitation for taking an honoured seat at a ceremonial meeting in this institution. The presumptuousness of youth made me absurdly proud to imagine that my companionship was growing into an organic part in the history that was being evolved before my eyes, and, in that belief I did try to hearten the hero, which was a part of my vanity. But foolish youth does not last for ever, and I have had time to come to realize my limitation. Anyhow it is quite obvious, that I am a mere poet carrying on my *sadhana* in the temple of language, the most capricious deity who is apt to ignore her responsibility to logic, often losing herself in the nebulous region of fantasy. Our oriental custom is to bring proper gifts to sacred shrines, but my gift of words for this occasion cannot but be out of place among the records of memorable proceedings of a learned society.

Fortunately there are some few men among us, who can claim fellowship with the aristocracy in the realm of science, and can be expected to make splendid this ceremony with the wealth of their thoughts. I can only bless this institution from that obscure distance where the multitude of the uncared-for generations of this country have helplessly drifted to the pitiless toil of primitive land-tilling. I offer my salutation to the illustrious founder of this Institute, humbly sitting by those who are deprived of a sufficiency of that knowledge which only can save them from the desolating menace of scientific devilry and from the continual drainage of the resources of life, and I appeal to this Institute to bring our call to science herself to rescue the world from the clutches of the marauders who betray her noble mission into an unmitigated savagery.

1937

79. THE BRITISH CONSTITUTION IN INDIA

To The Editor of the Manchester Guardian

Sir,

My English friends have done me the honour of inviting my opinion on what, for want of a better term, is being called the "New Constitution for India". Let me first of all make clear that an entire misapprehension is widely prevalent in the West which presupposes that the federation, now about to be imposed at the centre, will represent something not very far short of complete autonomy. Japan has been making wide use of that word in China. Let us hope that Englishmen will not be content to follow her example by employing it in India in a similar manner.

For let me ask the simple and obvious question: How can a country have autonomy whose people are for the most part disarmed, deprived of control over four-fifths of their national purse, and allowed to have nothing to do with their own external affairs? I am sure the British would despise themselves if they had to tolerate even any distant analogy of this, or some caricature of freedom offered by niggardly benevolence, in their own homes.

But our rulers are likely to protest that they have nothing but pity and love for us, and that they are painfully enduring the extra burden of governing us only to discharge their sacred duty by maintaining law and order. If some of us are impudent enough to refer them to the balance-sheet of their extended rule and point out that it discloses an unbroken continuity of poverty, ignorance, enfeebled life-force, with a stead deterioration in the value of our human capital, we are likely to be severely reprimanded. Yet it is not at all difficult for anybody to calculate the amount of positive benefit conferred upon us by our Government if he takes care to study the amount of expenditure allotted to education, sanitation, and economic improvement compared with the population of India and then examines its parallel in Japan.

I want to tell the British people quite plainly: So long as you hold us in your grip, you can never have either our trust or our friendship. We know that, in your own homes, you have many kindly virtues and are admirable for your sense of fair play and human justice. Perhaps for that very reason you find it difficult to understand how the same English people out here can betray your best traditions. But then you have to remember that possession of empire always corrupts, and it has corrupted you.

I am sure that the sensitive minds among you are already feeling that you have gained your Imperial prestige at too heavy a price, that the greatness of the end you have achieved is being fast destroyed by the Nemesis you have provoked in violating the best part of your nature while achieving it. And I believe you realize that the burden of surfeited Empire has dragged you down to that degree of weakness which makes you too timid to be ready adequately to deal with miscreant nations that are defiantly marching against political decency and your own interest and dignity. Those thoughtful and brave individuals among you who are eager to disown the precarious prestige of an Empire founded upon force, are yet far too few in number and their resources are too meagre to retard effectively the gathering impetus of the blind rush of power to a self-destructive end.

If you ask my personal opinion, I hardly imagine that catastrophe can now be avoided, since the only event in which all the powers of Europe are engaged with furious and frenzied zeal seems to be that of paving the path for mutual annihilation. Yet in spite of this I have the hope that misfortune and suffering, if they became inevitable, will not exceed that limits of retribution and bring about a collapse of the entire European civilization; for there is much in that civilization that is noble and worthy of being cherished. But Fate itself works in blind fits and starts, and one never knows where the Nemesis will lead, if we keep on provoking it. Our own fate in India is still linked up with yours, and though the downfall of your Imperial structure may mean a release of our people from its helpless dependence there are great aspirations and hopes which we share in common with many noble spirits in your own land and long to see fulfilled. They and we stand united against the deadening and unreasoning elements among your own people as well as amongst ours. It is not that the Indian people stand sworn to enmity against the British People, but that awakened India in common with awakened Britain is opposed to those blind and sinister powers which are traitors to both.

As regards the new Constitution, it is really not worth troubling about as it stands. It was made by politicians and bureaucrats, who, even as they were framing it were sending some of our best men and women to prison, mainly without trial. It therefore embodies all their narrow caution and miserly mistrust.

No! It is not through such an artificial structure that any final good can come to us. The future lies in our learning to ally ourselves with those humane forces in the world, wherever found, which are seeking to end altogether the exploitation of man by man and nation by nation.—Yours, etc.

28 February 1938

80. TO THE PEOPLE OF CHINA

I

Your neighbouring nation which is largely indebted to you for the gift of your cultural wealth and therefore should naturally cultivate your comradeship for its own ultimate benefit, has suddenly developed a virulent infection of imperialistic rapacity imported from the West and turned the great chance of building the bulwark of a noble destiny in the East into a dismal disaster. Its loud bluster of power, its ruthless orgy of indiscriminate massacre of life, demolition of education centres, its callous defiance of all civilized codes of humanity has brought humiliation upon the modern spirit of Asia that is struggling to find its honoured place in the forefront of modern age. It is all the more unfortunate because some of the proud powers of the west, tottering under the burden of their bloated property, are timidly condoning the blood-sodden politics of the standard-bearers of their own highly reputed civilization, humbly bending their knees at the altar of indecent success that has blasted some time-honoured citadel of sacred human rights.

At this desperate age of moral upset it is only natural for us to hope that the continent which has produced the two greatest men, Buddha and Christ, in the whole course of human events, must still fulfil its responsibility to maintain the purest expression of character in the teeth of the scientific effrontery of the evil genius of man. Has not that expectation already shown its first luminous streak of fulfilment in the person of Gandhi in a historical horizon obscured by centuries of indignity? However, Japan has cynically refused its own great possibility, its noble heritage of 'bushido' and has offered a most painful disillusionment to us in an unholy adventure through which even some apparent success of hers is sure to bend down to the dust, loaded with a fatal burden of failure.

Our only consolation lies in the hope that the deliberate aggression of violence that has assailed your country will bear a sublime meaning in the heroic suffering it causes in a promise of the birth of a new soul of the nation. You are the only great people in the world who never had the snobbishness of extolling the military power as one of the glorious characteristics of national spirit, and when the same brute force of militarism with its hideous efficiency has overtaken your country we pray with all our heart that you may come out of this trial once again to be able to justify your trust in the true heroism of higher humanity in this cowardly world ready to prove traitor to its own best ideals. Even if a mere physical success be immediately missed by you yet your moral gain will never be lost and the seeds of victory that are being sown through this terrible struggle in the depth of your being will over and over again prove their deathlessness.

July 1938

II

Dear Friend,

China is great. Every day you are proving it at the cost of an incredible suffering and sacrifice. The heroism your people are displaying is epic in quality. I feel sure whatever may happen your victory will ever remain resplendent in the moral field of human endeavour.

26 December 1939

81. 'FASCISM' OF THE STATE OF TRAVANCORE

Along with the whole country I have felt grievously hurt that an enlightened Indian state like Travancore should have initiated a regime of fascism with its technique of shooting, denial of elementary of rights of freedom and a deliberate denial of elementary rights of freedom and a deliberate persecution of the Congressmen. Whatever the provocation or the nature of dispute, the methods that have been pursued to exert authority are without justification. At a time when India is moving towards a new era of freedom it is essential that the state should feel a sense of responsibility for giving shape to a humane civilization and not prove their unfitness by allying themselves with forces that threaten the existence of civilized society.

October 1938

82. LETTERS TO CZECHOSLOVAKIA

I

Dear Friend,

I feel so keenly about the suffering of your people as if I was one of them. For what has happened in your country is not a mere local misfortune which may at the best claim our sympathy, it is a tragic revelation that the destiny of all those principles of humanity for which the peoples of the West turned martyrs for three centuries rests in the hands of cowardly guardians who are selling it to save their own skins. It turns one cynical to see the democratic peoples betraying their kind when even the bullies stand by each other.

I feel so humiliated and so helpless when I contemplate all this, humiliated to see all the values, which have given whatever worth modern civilization has, betrayed one by one, and helpless that we are powerless to prevent it. Our country is itself a victim of these wrongs. My words have no power to stay the onslaught of the maniacs, nor even the power to arrest the desertion of those who erstwhile pretended to be the saviours of humanity. I can only remind those who are not yet wholly demented that when men turn beasts they sooner or later tear each other.

As for your own country, I can only hope that though abandoned and robbed, it will maintain its native integrity and falling back upon its own inalienable resources will recreate a richer national life than before.

I am sending you a copy of my English rendering of a recent poem of mine, yet unpublished, in which my outraged sentiment has found its expression. You may use it as you like, though it will also be published in the November issue of the *Visvabharati Quarterly*. If you like I can also send you the Bengali original.

With best wishes and kind regards.

15 October 1938

II

BETRAYAL OF CZECHOSLOVAKIA

My Dear Lesny,

It was sad to read in your letter all the news about the great betrayal of your magnificent people at the hands of England and France. I met Mr. Nehru a few days back. He was in Central Europe at the time of the tragic happenings and he gave me a graphic description of the woes of the mutilation of Czechoslovakia. But it is there and you have but to submit to destiny. Let me only hope, your brave people will not lose heart and you will not fail to rebuild once again your own future.

14 February 1939

83. TAGORE AND NOGUCHI

41 Sakurrayama, Nakano, Tokyo
July 23, 1938

Dear Rabindranath

When I visited you at Shantiniketan a few years ago, you were troubled with the Ethiopian question, and vehemently condemned Italy. Retiring into your guest chamber that night, I wondered whether you would say the same thing on Japan, if she were equally situated like Italy. I perfectly agreed with your opinion and admired your courage of speaking, when in Tokyo, 1916, you censured the westernization of Japan from a public platform. Not answering back to your words, the intellectual people of my country were conscious of its possible consequence, for, not only staying as an unpleasant spectacle, the westernization had every chance for becoming anything awful.

But if you take the present war in China for the criminal outcome of Japan's surrender to the West, you are wrong, because, not being a slaughtering madness, it is, I believe, the inevitable means, terrible it is though, for establishing a new great world in the Asiatic continent, where the "principle of live-and-let-live" has to be realized. Believe me, it is the war of

"Asia for Asia". With a crusader's determination and with a sense of sacrifice that belongs to a martyr, our young soldiers go to the front. Their minds are light and happy, the war is not for conquest, but the correction of mistaken idea of China, I mean Kuomingtung government, and for uplifting her simple and ignorant masses to better life and wisdom. Borrowing from other countries neither money nor blood, Japan is undertaking this tremendous work single-handed and alone. I do not know why we cannot be praised by your countrymen. But we are terribly blamed by them, as it seems, for our heroism and aim.

Sometime ago the Chinese army defeated in Huntung province by Hwangho River, had cut from desperate madness several places of the river bank; not keeping in check the advancing Japanese army, it only made thirty hundred thousand people drown in the flood and one hundred thousand village houses destroyed. Defending the welfare of its own kinsmen or killing them,—which is the object of the Chinese army, I wonder? It is strange that such an atrocious inhuman conduct ever known in the world history did not become in the West a target of condemnation. Oh where are your humanitarians who profess to be a guardian of humanity? Are they deaf and blind? Besides the Chinese soldiers, miserably paid and poorly clothed, are a habitual criminal of robbery, and then an everlasting menace to the honest hardworking people who cling to the ground. Therefore the Japanese soldiers are followed by them with the paper flags of the Rising Sun in their hands; to a soldierly work we have to add one more endeavour in the relief work of them. You can imagine how expensive is this war for Japan. Putting expenditure out of the question, we are determined to use up our last cent for the final victory that would ensure in the future a great peace of many hundred years.

I received the other day a letter from my western friend, denouncing the world that went to Hell. I replied him, saying: "Oh my friend, you should cover your ears, when a war bugle rings too wild. Shut your eyes against a picture of your martial cousins becoming a fish salad! Be patient my friend, for a war is only spasmodic matter that cannot last long, but will adjust one's condition better in the end. You are a coward if you are afraid of it. Nothing worthy will be done unless you pass through a severe trial. And the peace that follows after a war is most important." For the peace we Japanese are ready to exhaust our resources of money and blood.

Today we are called under the flag of "Service-making", each person of the country doing his own bit for the realization of idealism. There was no time as today in the whole history of Japan, when all the people, from the Emperor to a rag-picker in the street, consolidated together with one mind. And there is no more foolish supposition as that our financial bankruptcy is a thing settled if the war drags on. Since the best part of the Chinese continent is already with us in friendly terms, we are not fighting with the whole of China. Our enemy is only the Kuomingtung government, a miserable puppet of the West. If Chiang Kai-shek wishes a long war, we are quite ready for it. Five years? Ten years? Twenty years? As long as he desires, my friend. Now one year has passed since the first bullet was exchanged between China and Japan; but with a fresh mind as if it sees that the war has just begun, we are now looking the event in the face. After the fall of Hankow, the Kuomingtung government will retire to a remote place of her country; but until the western countries change their attitude towards China, we will keep up fighting with fists or wisdom.

The Japanese poverty is widely advertised in the West, though I do not know how it was started. Japan is poor beyond doubt,—well, according to the measure you wish to apply to. But I think that the Japanese poverty is a fabricated story as much as richness of China. There is no country in the world like Japan, where money is equally divided among the people. Supposing that we are poor, I will say that we are trained to stand the pain of poverty. Japan is very strong in adversity.

But you will be surprised to know that the postal saving of people comes up now to five thousand million *yen,* responding to the government's propaganda of economy. For going on, surmounting every difficulty that the war brings in, we are saving every cent and even making good use of waste scraps. Since the war began, we grew spiritually strong and true ten times more than before. There is nothing hard to accomplish to a young man. Yes, Japan is the land of young men. According to nature's law, the old has to retire while the young advances. Behold, the sun is arising, be gone all the sickly bats and dirty vermins! Cursed be one's intrigue and empty pride that sin against nature's rule and justice.

China could very well avoid the war, of course, if Chiang Kai-shek was more sensible with insight. Listening to an irresponsible third party of the west a long way off, thinking too highly of his own strength, he turned at last his own country, as she is today, into a ruined desert to which fifty years would not be enough for recovery. He never happened to think for a moment that the friendship of western countries was but a trick of their monetary interest itself in his country. And it is too late now for Chiang to reproach them for the faithlessness of their words of promise.

For a long time we had been watching with doubt at Chiang's programme, the consolidation of the country, because the Chinese history had no period when the country was unified in the real meaning, and the subjugation of various war-lords under his flag was nothing. Until all the people took an oath of co-operation with him, we thought, his programme was no more than a table talk. Being hasty and thoughtless, Chiang began to popularize the anti-Japanese movement among the students who were pigmy politicians in some meaning because he deemed it to be a method for the speedy realization of his program; but he never thought that he was erring from the Oriental ethics that preached on one's friendship with the neighbours. Seeing that his propagation had too great effect on his young followers, he had no way to keep in check their wild jingoism, and then finally made his country roll down along the slope of destruction. Chiang is a living example who sold his country to the west for nothing, and smashed his skin with the crime of westernization. Dear Rabindranath, what will you say about this Chiang Kai-shek?

Dear poet, today we have to turn our deaf ears towards a lesson of freedom that may come from America, because the people there already ceased to practice it. The ledger-book diplomacy of England is too well known through the world. I am old enough to know from experience that no man is better than others, while one country being no more worse than others. Though I admit that Japan is today ruled by militarism, natural to the actual condition of the country, I am glad that enough freedom of speaking and acting is allowed to one like myself. Japan is fairly liberal in spite of the war time. So I can say without fear to be looked up that those service-crazy people are drunken, and that a thing in the world, great and true, because of its connection with the future, only comes from one who hates to be a common human unit, stepping aside so that he can unite himself with Eternity. I believe that such a one who withdraws into a snail's shell for the quest of life's hopeful future, will be in the end be a true patriot, worthy of his own nation. Therefore I am able not to disagree the name of poet, and to try to live up to the words of Browning who made the Grammarian exclaim:

"Leave Now for dogs and apes! Man has Forever."

Yours very sincerely,
Yone Noguchi

Uttarayan, Santiniketan, Bengal
September 1, 1938

Dear Noguchi,

I am profoundly surprised by the letter that you have written to me neither its temper nor its contents harmonise with the spirit of Japan which I learnt to admire in your writings and came to love through my personal contacts with you. It is sad to think that the passion of collective militarism may on occasion helplessly overwhelm even the creative artist, that genuine intellectual power should be led to offer its dignity and truth to be sacrificed at the shrine of the dark gods of war.

You seem to agree with me in your condemnation of the massacre of Ethiopia by Fascist Italy but you would reserve the murderous attack on Chinese millions for judgment under a different category. But surely judgments are based on principle, and no amount of special pleading can change the fact that in launching a ravening war on Chinese humanity, with all the deadly methods learnt from the West Japan is infringing every moral principle on which civilization is based. You claim that Japan's situation was unique, forgetting that military situations are always unique, and that pious war-lords, convinced of peculiarly individual justification for their atrocities have never failed to arrange for special alliances with divinity for annihilation and torture on a large scale.

Humanity, in spite of its many failures, has believed in a fundamental moral structure of society. When you speak, therefore, of "the inevitable means, terrible it is though, for establishing a new great world in the Asiatic continent"—signifying, I suppose, the bombing on Chinese women and children and the desecration of ancient temples and Universities as a means of saving China for Asia—you are ascribing to humanity a way of life which is not even inevitable among the animals and would certainly not apply to the East, in spite of her occasional aberrations. You are building your conception of an Asia which would be raised on a tower of skulls. I have, as you rightly point out, believed in the message of Asia, but I never dreamt that this message could be identified with deeds which brought exaltation to the heart of Tamer Lane at his terrible efficiency in manslaughter. When I protested against "Westernisation" in my lectures in Japan, I contrasted the rapacious Imperialism which some of the *Nations* of Europe were cultivating with the ideal of perfection preached by Buddha and Christ, with the great heritage of culture and good neighbourliness that went to the making of Asiatic and other civilizations. I felt it to be my duty to warn the land of Bushido, of great Art and traditions of noble heroism, that this phase of scientific savagery which victimised Western humanity and had led their helpless masses to a moral cannibalism was never to be imitated by a virile people who had entered upon a glorious renascence and had every promise of a creative future before them. The doctrine of "Asia for Asia" which you enunciate in your letter, as an instrument of political blackmail, has all the virtues of the lesser Europe which I repudiate and nothing of the larger humanity that makes us one across the barriers of political labels and divisions. I was amused to read the recent statement of a Tokyo politician that the military alliance of Japan with Italy and Germany was made for "highly spiritual and moral reasons" and "had no materialistic considerations behind them". Quite so. What is not amusing is that artists and thinkers should echo such remarkable sentiments that translate military swagger into spiritual bravado. In the West, even in the critical days of war-madness, there is never any dearth of great spirits who can raise their voice above the din of battle and defy their ours war-mongers in the name of humanity. Such men have suffered, but never betrayed the conscience of their peoples which they represented. Asia will not be westernised if she can learn from such men: I still believe that there are such souls in Japan though we do not hear of them in those newspapers that are compelled at the cost of their extinction to reproduce their military master's voice.

"The betrayal of intellectuals" of which the great French writer spoke after the European war, is a dangerous symptom of our Age. You speak of the savings of the poor people of Japan, their silent sacrifice and suffering and take pride in betraying that this pathetic sacrifice is being exploited for gun running and invasion of a neighbour's hearth and home, that human wealth of greatness is pillaged for inhuman purposes. Propaganda, I know, has been reduced to a fine art, and it is almost impossible for people in non-democratic countries to resist hourly doses of poison, but one had imagined that at least the men of intellect and imagination would themselves retain their gift of independent judgement. Evidently such is not always the case; behind sophisticated arguments seem to lie a mentality of perverted nationalism which makes the "intellectuals" of today go blustering about their "ideologies" dragooning their own "masses" into paths of dissolution. I have known your people and I hate to believe that they could deliberately participate in the organized drugging of Chinese men and women by opium and heroin, but they do not know; in the meanwhile, representatives of Japanese culture in China are busy practising their craft on the multitudes caught in the grip of an organization of a wholesale human pollution. Proofs of such forcible drugging in Manchukuo and China have been adduced by unimpeachable authorities. But from Japan there has come no protest, not even from her poets.

Holding such opinions as many of your intellectuals do, I am not surprised that they are left "free" by your Government to express themselves. I hope they enjoy their freedom. Retiring from such freedom into "a snail's shell" in order to savour the bliss of meditation "on life's hopeful future", appears to me to be an unnecessary act, even though you advice Japanese artists to do so by way of change. I cannot accept such separation between an artist's function and his moral conscience. The luxury of enjoying special favouritism by virtue of identity with a Government which is engaged in demolition, in its neighbourhood, of all salient bases of life, and of escaping, at the same time, from any direct responsibility by a philosophy of escapism, seems to me to be another authentic symptom of the modern intellectual's betrayal of humanity. Unfortunately the rest of the world is almost cowardly in any adequate expression of its judgment owing to ugly possibilities that it may be hatching for its own future and those who are bent upon doing mischief are left alone to defile their history and blacken their reputation for all time to come. But such impunity in the long run bodes disaster, like unconsciousness of disease in its painless progress of ravage.

I speak with utter sorrow for your people; your letter has hurt me to the depths of my being. I know that one day the disillusionment of your people will be complete, and through laborious centuries they will have to clear the debris of their civilization wrought to ruin by their own war-lords run amok. They will realize that the aggressive war on China is insignificant as compared to the destruction of the inner spirit of chivalry of Japan which is proceeding with a ferocious severity. China is unconquerable, her civilization, under the dauntless leadership of Chiang Kai-Shek, is displaying marvellous resources; the desperate loyalty of her peoples, united as never before, is creating a new age for that land. Caught unprepared by a gigantic machinery of war, hurled upon her peoples, China is holding her own; no temporary defeats can ever crush her fully aroused spirit. Faced by the borrowed science of Japanese militarism which is crudely western in character, China's stand reveals an inherently superior moral stature. And today I understand more than ever before the meaning of the enthusiasm with which the big-hearted Japanese thinker Okakura assured me that *China is great.*

You do not realize that you are glorifying your neighbour at your own cost. But these are considerations on another plane: the sorrow remains that Japan, in the words of Madame Chiang Kai-Shek which you must have read in the *Spectator,* is creating so many ghosts. Ghosts of immemorial works of Chinese art, of irreplaceable Chinese institutions, of great peace-loving communities drugged, tortured, and destroyed. "Who will lay the ghosts?" she asks. Japanese and Chinese people, let us hope, will join hands together, in no distant future, in wiping off memories of a bitter past. True Asian humanity will be reborn. Poets will raise their song and be unashamed, one believes, to declare their faith again in a human destiny which cannot admit of a scientific mass production of fratricide.

Yours sincerely,
Rabindranath Tagore

P.S.—I find that you have already released your letter to the Press; I take it that you want me to publish my answer in the same manner.

41 Sakurayama, Nakano, Tokyo
October 2, 1938

Dear Tagore,

Your eloquent letter, dated Sept. 1st was duly received. I am glad that the letter inspired me to write you once more.

No one in Japan denies the greatness of China,—I mean the Chinese people. China of the olden times was great with philosophy, literature and art—particularly in the T'ang dynasty. Under Chinese influence Japan started to build up her own civilization. But I do not know why we should not oppose the misguided government of China for the old debt we owe her people. And nobody in Japan ever dreams that we can conquer China. What Japan is doing in China, it is only, as I already said, to correct the mistaken idea of Chiang Kai-Shek; on this object Japan is staking her all. If Chiang conies to senses and extends his friendly hands for the future of both the countries, China and Japan, the war will be stopped at once.

I am glad that you still admire Kakuzo Okakura with enthusiasm as a thinker. If he lives today, I believe that he will say the same thing as I do. Betraying your trust, many Chinese soldiers in the front surrender to our Japanese force, and join with us in the cry, "Down with Chiang Kai-Shek!" Where is Chinese loyalty to him?

Having no proper organ of expression, Japanese opinion is published only seldom in the West; and real fact is always hidden and often camouflaged by cleverness of the Chinese who are a born propagandist. They are strong in foreign languages, and their tongues never fail. While the Japanese are always reticent, even when situation demands their explanation. From the experiences of many centuries, the Chinese have cultivated an art of speaking, for they had been put under such a condition that divided their country to various antagonistic divisions; and being always encroached by the Western countries, they depended on diplomacy to turn a thing to their advantage. Admitting that China completely defeated Japan in foreign publicity, it is sad that she often goes too far, and plays trickery. For one instance I will call your attention to the reproduced picture from a Chinese paper on page 247 of the *Modern Review* for last August, as a living specimen of "Japanese Atrocities in China: Execution of a Chinese Civilians." So awful pictures they are,—awful enough to make ten thousand enemies of Japan in a foreign country. But the pictures are nothing but a Chinese invention, simple and plain, because the people in the scenes are all Chinese, slaughterers and all. Besides any one with commonsense would know, if he stops for a moment, that it is impossible to take such a picture as these at the front. Really I cannot understand how your friend-editor of the *Modern Review* happened to published them.

It is one's right to weave a dream at the distance, and to create an object of sympathy at the expense of China. Believe me that I am second to none in understanding the Chinese masses who are patient and diligent, clinging to the ground. But it seems that you are not acquainted with the China of corruption and bribery, and of war lords who put money in a foreign bank when their country is at stake. So long as the country is controlled by such polluted people, the Chinese have only a little chance to create a new age in their land. They have to learn first of all the meaning of honesty and sacrifice before dreaming it. But for this new age in Asia, Japan is engaging in the war, hoping to obtain a good result and mutual benefit that follow the swords. We must have a neighbouring country, strong and true, which is glad to cooperate with us in our work of reconstructing Asia in the new way. That is only what we expect from China.

Japan's militarism is a tremendous affair no doubt. But if you condemn Japan, because of it, you are failing to notice that Chiang's China is a far more great military country than Japan. China is now mobilizing seven or eight million soldiers armed with European weapons. From cowardice or being ignorant of the reason why they had to fight, the Chinese soldiers are so inspirited in the front. But for this unavailability you cannot forgive Chiang's militarism, if your denial is absolute and true. For the last twenty years Chiang had been trying to arm his country under the western advisers; and these western advisers were mostly from Italy and Germany, the countries of which you are so impatient. And it should be attributed to their advice that he started war; though it is too late to blame the countries that formally provided him with military knowledge, it is never too late for him to know that the western countries are not worthy of trust. There is no country in the world, that comes to rescue the other at her own expense. If you are a real sympathizer of China, you should come along with your program what she had to do, not passing idly with your condemnation of Japan's militarism. And if you have to condemn militarism, that condemnation should be equally divided between China and Japan.

It is true that when two quarrel, both are in the wrong. And when fighting is over, both the parties will be put perhaps in the mental situation of one who is crying over spilt milk. War is atrocious,—particularly when it is performed in a gigantic way as in China today. I hope that you will let me apply your accusation of Japanese atrocity to China, just as it is. Seeing no atrocity in China, you are speaking about her as an innocent country. I expected something impartial from a poet.

I have to think *(sic)* you that you called my attention to the "Modern intellectual's betrayal of humanity", whatever it be. One can talk any amount of idealism, apart from in reality, if he wishes, and take the pleasure of one belonging to no country. But sharing patriotism equally with the others, we are trying to acquit the duty of our birthright, and believe that it is never too late to talk Heaven when immediate matter of the earth is well arranged.

Supposing that we accept your advice to become a vanguard of humanity according to your prescription, and supposing that we leave China to her own will, and save ourselves from being a "betrayal of the intellectuals", who will promise us with the safety of Japanese spirit that we cultivated with pairs of thousand years, under the threat of communism across a fence? We don't want to barter our home land for an empty name of intellectuals. No, you mustn't talk nonsense! God forbid!

Admitting, that militarism is criminal, I think that, if your humanity makes life a mutilated mud-fish, its crime would never be smaller than the other. I spent my whole life admiring beauty and truth, with one hope to lift life to a dignity, more vigorous and noble; from this reason, I knelt before the Kalighat, Calcutta, because Kali's smeared face in madness, with three wild eyes, promised me with a forthcoming peace. And also at Elephanta Island; near Bombay, I learned from the Three-headed Siva a lesson of destruction as inevitable truth of life. Then I wrote:

> "Thy slaughter's sword is never so unkind as it appears.
> Creation is great, but destroying is still greater,
> Because up from the ashes new Wonder take its flight."

But if you command me to obey the meekness of humanity under all the circumstances, you are forgetting what your old

Hindu philosophy taught you. I say this not only for my purpose, because such reflection is important for any country.

I wonder who reported to you that we are killing innocent people and bombing on their unprotected towns. Far from it, we are trying to do our best for helping them, because we have so much to depend on them for cooperation in the future, and because Bushido command us to limit punishment to a thing which only deserves it. It was an apt measure of our Japanese soldiers that the famous cave temples of the 5th century in North China were saved from savage rapacity of the defeated Shinese (*sic*) soldiers in flight. Except Madame Chiang with frustrated brain, no one has seen the "ghosts of Chinese institutions and art, destroyed". And if those institutions and art, admitting that they are immemorial and irreplaceable, had been ever destroyed, it is but the crazy work of Chinese soldiers, because they want to leave a desert to Japan. You ought to know better since you are acquainted with so many Japanese, whether or not we are qualified to do anything barbarous.

I believe that you are versed in Bushido. In olden times soldiery was lifted in Japan to a status equally high as that of art and morality. I have no doubt that our soldiers will not betray the tradition. If there is difference in Japanese militarism from that of the West, it is because the former is not without moral element. Who only sees its destroying power is blind to its other power in preservation. Its human aspect is never known in the foreign countries, because they shut their eyes to it. Japan is still as unknown existence in the West. Having so many things to displease you, Japanese militarism has still something that will please you, if you come to know more about it. It is an excusable existence for the present condition of Japan. But I will leave the full explanation of it to some later occasion.

Believe me that I am never an eulogist of Japanese militarism, because I have many differences with it. But I cannot help accepting as a Japanese what Japan is doing now under the circumstances, because I see no other way to show our minds to China. Of course when China stops fighting, and we receive her friendly hands, neither grudge nor ill feeling will remain in our minds. Perhaps with some sense of repentance, we will then proceed together on the great work of reconstructing the new world in Asia.

I often draw in my mind a possible man who can talk from a high domain and act as a peace-maker. You might write General Chiang, I hope, and tell him about the foolishness of fighting in the presence of a great work that is waiting. And I am sorry that against the high-pitched nature of your letter, mine is low-toned and faltering, because as a Japanese subject I belong to one of the responsible parties of the conflict.

Finally one word more. What I fear most is the present atmosphere in India, that tends to wilfully blacken Japan to alienate her from your country. I have so many friends there, whose beautiful nature does not harmonise with it. My last experiences in your country taught me how to love and respect her. Besides there are in Japan so many admirers of your countrymen with your noble self as the first.

Yours sincerely,
Yone Noguchi

Uttarayana, Santiniketan, Bengal
October 27, 1938

Dear Noguchi,

I thank you for taking the trouble to write to me again. I have also read with interest your letter addressed to the Editor, *Amrita Bazar Patrika*, and published in that journal.* It makes the meaning of your letter to me more clear.

---

* The following is the text of the letter referred to:

Dear Editor,

Dr. Tagore's reply to my letter was a disappointment, to use his words, hurted me to the depths of my being. Now I am conscious that language is an ineffective instrument to carry one's real meaning. When I wanted an impartial criticism he gave me something of prejudiced bravado under the beautiful name of humanity. Just for a handful of dream, and for an intellectual's ribbon to stick in his coat, he has lost a high office to correct the mistaken idea of reality.

It seems to us that when Dr. Tagore called the doctrine of "Asia for Asia" a political blackmail, he relinquished his patriotism to boast

I am flattered that you still consider it worthwhile to take such pains to convert me to your point of view, and I am really sorry that I am unable to come to my senses, as you have been pleased to wish it. It seems to me that it is futile for either of us to try to convince the other since your faith in the infallible right of Japan to bully other Asiatic nations into line with your Government's policy is not shared by me, and my faith that patriotism which claims the right to bring to the altar of its country the sacrifice of *other* people's rights and happiness will endanger rather than strengthen the foundation of any great civilization, is sneered at by you as the "quiescence of a spiritual vagabond".

If you can convince the Chinese that your armies are bombing their cities and rendering their women and children homeless beggars—those of them that are not transformed into "mutilated mud-fish" to borrow one of your own phrases—, if you can convince these victims that they are only being subjected to a benevolent treatment which will in the end "save" their nation, it will no longer be necessary for you to convince us of your country's noble intentions. Your righteous indignation

---

quiescence of a spiritual vagabond, and wilfully supporting the Chinese side, is encouraging Soviet Russia, not to mention the other Western countries. I meant my letter to him to be a plea for the understanding of Japan's viewpoint, which, in spite of its many failures, is honest. I wonder whether it is a poet's privilege to give one whipping before listening to his words. When I dwelled on the saving of the people of Japan at the present time of conflict, he denounced it as their government's exploitation "for gun running and invasion of a neighbour's hearth and home". But when he does not use the same language towards his friend China his partiality is something monstrous. And I wonder where is his former heart which made us Japanese love him and honour him. But still we are patient, believing that he will come to senses and take a neutral dignity fitting to a prophet who does not depart from fair judgment.

Living in a country far from your country, I do not know where Dr. Tagore's reply appeared in print. Believing that you are known to his letter, I hope that you will see way to print this letter of mine in your esteemed paper.

Yours sincerely,
Yone Noguchi

against the "polluted people" who are burning their own cities and art-treasures (and presumably bombing their own citizens) to malign your soldiers, reminds me of Napoleon's noble wrath when he marched into a deserted Moscow and watched its palaces in flames. I should have expected from you who are a poet at least that much of imagination to feel, to what inhuman despair a people must be reduced to willingly burn their own handiwork of years', indeed centuries', labour. And even as a good nationalist, do you seriously believe that the mountain of bleeding corpses and the wilderness of bombed and burnt cities that is every day widening between your two countries, is making it easier for your two peoples to stretch your hands in a clasp of ever-lasting good will?

You complain that while the Chinese, being "dishonest", are spreading their malicious propaganda, your people, being "honest", are reticent. Do you not know, my friend, that there is no propaganda like good and noble deeds, and that if such deeds be yours, you need fear no "trickery" of your victims? Nor need you fear the bogey of communism if there is no exploitation of the poor among your own people and the workers feel that they are justly treated.

I must thank you for explaining to me the meaning of our Indian philosophy and pointing out that the proper interpretation of Kali and Shiva must compel our approval of Japan's "dance of death" in China. I wish you had drawn a moral from a religion more familiar to you and appealed to the Buddha for your justification. But I forget that your priests and artists have already made sure of that, for I saw in a recent issue of "The Osaka Mainichi and The Tokyo Nichi Nichi" (16th September, 1938) a picture of a new colossal image of Buddha erected to bless the massacre of your neighbours.

You must forgive me if my words sound bitter. Believe me, it is sorrow and shame, not anger, that prompt me to write to you. I suffer intensely not only because the reports of Chinese suffering batter against my heart, but because I can no longer point out with pride the example of a great Japan. It is true that there are no better standards prevalent anywhere else and that the so-called civilized peoples of the West are proving equally barbarous and even less "worthy of trust". If you refer me to them, I have nothing to say. What I should have liked is to be able to refer them to you. I shall say nothing of my own people, for it is vain to boast until one has succeeded in sustaining one's principles to the end.

I am quite conscious of the honour you do me in asking me to act as a peace-maker. Were it in any way possible for me to bring you two peoples together and see you freed from this death-struggle and pledged to the great common "work of reconstructing the new world in Asia", I would regard the sacrifice of my life in the cause a proud privilege. But I have no power save that of moral persuasion, which you have so eloquently ridiculed. You who want me to be impartial, how can you expect me to appeal to Chiang Kai-Shek to give up resisting until the aggressors have first given up their aggression? Do you know that last week when I received a pressing invitation from an old friend of mine in Japan to visit your country, I actually thought for a moment, foolish idealist as I am, that your people may really need my services to minister to the bleeding heart of Asia and to help extract from its riddled body the bullets of hatred? I wrote to my friend:

> "Though the present state of my health is hardly favourable for any strain of a long foreign journey, I should seriously consider your proposal if proper opportunity is given me to carry out my own mission while there, which is to do my best to establish a civilized relationship of national amity between two great peoples of Asia who are entangled in a desolating mutual destruction. But as I am doubtful whether the military authorities of Japan, which seem bent upon devastating China in order to gain their object will allow me the freedom to take my own course, I shall never forgive myself if I am tempted for any reason whatever to pay a friendly visit to Japan just at this unfortunate moment and thus cause a grave misunderstanding. You know I have a genuine love for the Japanese people and it is sure to hurt me too painfully to go and watch crowds of them being transported by their rulers to a neighbouring land to

perpetrate acts of inhumanity which will brand their name with a lasting stain in the history of Man."

After the letter was dispatched came the news of the fall of Canton and Hankow. The cripple, shorn of his power to strike, may collapse but to ask him to forget the memory of his mutilation as easily as you want me to, I must expect him to be an angel.

Wishing your people whom I love, not success, but remorse.

Yours sincerely,
Rabindranath Tagore

84. W.B. YEATS

Loss by death is not for Yeats. He had already reached classic heights of literature while alive. Today my mind goes back to the time when I first met Yeats, full of exuberant life and youthfulness. The same picture of the glowing genius of a magnificent personality will, I am sure, remain unfaded in memory of all time. I shall cherish to the end the fact that my life was linked with the memory of one of the rarest poets of modern Europe.

1939

85. BIHAR CO-OPERATIVE FEDERATION: 21ST CONFERENCE

The cooperative movement which is gradually gaining ground in our economic life, because it represents the highest truth of man —the truth of his unity, is also the only way that can lead to the true wealth of the people, the wealth born of the great meeting of individual wills. The huge megatherium of capitalism with its stupendous tail of bought up workers will naturally become extinct when individual men come to realize their own truth— not through the indecent exaggeration of their exclusive wealth but through a combination of their individuality founded upon mutual trust and undertaking.

Barbarism is exclusive, especially guarding its cave-dwellings of isolation. And the barbarians, the mistrustful of other; constantly ready with their bows and arrows, remain stunted in mind and poor in spirit. Likewise the isolated disproportion of exclusive wealth is barbarous. It will become civilized when it evolves the true fulfilment of its moral character, its power of co-operation and when it grows sincerely ashamed of its iniquitous greed and of the unseemly scrimmage of competition through which one gains profit at the cost of another's loss.

20 August 1939

86. A TRIBUTE TO MAHATMA GANDHI

Occasionally there appear in the arena of politics, makers of history, whose mental height is above the common level of humanity. They wield an instrument of power, which is almost physical in its compelling force and often relentless, exploiting the weakness in human nature—its greed, fear, or vanity. When Mahatma Gandhi came and opened up the path of freedom for India, he had no obvious medium of power in his hand, no overwhelming authority of coercion. The influence which emanated from his personality was ineffable, like music, like beauty. Its claim upon others was great because of its revelation of a spontaneous self-giving. This is the reason why our people have hardly ever laid emphasis upon his natural cleverness in manipulating recalcitrant facts. They have rather dwelt upon the truth which shines through his character in lucid simplicity. This is why, though his realm of activity lies in practical politics, peoples' minds have been struck by the analogy of his character with that of the great masters, whose spiritual inspiration comprehends and yet transcends all varied manifestations of humanity, and makes the face of worldliness turn to the light that comes from the eternal source of wisdom.

1939

87. EUROPEAN ORDER AND WORLD ORDER

I have read your letter and the P.E.P. pamphlet with profound interest—it does one good to know that all civilized thought and planning have not been submerged by war-passions. Your letter gives me new hope and is a confirmation of the spiritual integrity of the European civilization in which I have always believed—the wide-awake humanity of the West that diplomatic machinations can never crush. I can realize from your brochure on *(European Order And World Order)*, that the best minds of Europe are being put to a severe test, that they have the sanction of the peoples of Europe in trying to formulate a Federal Union which will unite the peoples in spite of the ring leaders of blind Nationalism, who, sitting safely in the citadels of power, send the youth of the land to destroy each other on the battlefield. In Europe, the real battle goes on—that between organized passion and unconquerable majesty of the human heart—and your peoples have the vitality to live through the struggle. I can't believe in the victory of any belligerent powers,—as belligerents they are doomed. I can hope for the triumph of the united peoples of Europe under some such system as you propose in your letter to Lord Halifax and in the programme sponsored by the P.E.P.

'But what about India? It does not need a defeatist to feel deeply anxious about the future of millions who with all their innate culture and their peaceful traditions are being simultaneously subjected to hunger, disease, exploitations foreign and indigenous, and the seething discontents of communalism. Our people do not posses the vitality that you have in Europe; and the crisis, even before this war started in the West, had become acute in India. Needless to say, interested groups led by ambition and outside instigation, are today using the communal motive for destructive political ends.'

February 1940

88. 'FREEDOM OF MIND'

Dear Nevinson,

I have read your circular letter with great interest and entirely associate myself with the freedom of mind which you advocate. As you know, by accepting Presidentship of the *Indian Council of Civil Liberties,* I have publicly associated myself with organized effort to further democratic ideals for our peoples. The European and the Far-Eastern Wars, as well as the complications in the Indian situation, have made our task more imperative.

My age and the work that I have been doing in this corner of Bengal where we have our Educational and Rural Development Centres, make it difficult for me to extend my activities in other fields. But I join you in your crusade for the liberty of the human spirit and share your hope that the Western Civilization will yet triumph over the ordeal that it has set for itself. In some ways it is even harder for India to pursue the path of freedom, not only our unnatural political situation which hampers free national expression but the legacies of mediaeval habits and thought will have to be overcome. It is, therefore, all the more necessary that leaders of thought in your country and ours should counteract the passions of the day and maintain close contact in our human endeavour.

February 1940

89. TELEGRAM TO ROOSEVELT

[*The draft of Tagore's telegram to President Franklin D. Roosevelt on the Fall of Paris during World War II*]

Today, we stand in awe before the fearfully destructive force that has so suddenly swept the world. Every moment I deplore the smallness of our means and the feebleness of our voice in India so utterly inadequate to stem in the least, the tide of evil that has menaced the permanence of civilization.

All our individual problems of politics to-day have merged into one supreme world politics which, I believe, is seeking the help of the United States of America as the last refuge of the spiritual man, and these few lines of mine merely convey my hope, even if unnecessary, that she will not fail in her mission to stand against this universal disaster that appears so imminent.

June 1940

90. BENGAL'S GREAT INHERITANCE

Bengal's great inheritance is her culture which can only be threatened by our own weakness, no external power can deprive us of freedom in the sacred shrine of learning or compel us to compromise our integrity by menace of fear or favour.

We are proud of our Bengali language, which must be preserved from harm and nourished by the devotion of our people; no sacrifice would be too great in the task of strengthening its foundation in the minds of our new generation at the educational institutions and outside.

Having devoted over 70 years of my life to the service of our mother-language and to the welfare of Bengal I have earned the right to make this appeal! My age and health prevent me from taking part in public affairs, but the danger which menaces the cultural existence of my own province has touched me profoundly and I cannot help sending these few words from my sick bed.

December 1940

91. MAN'S LOST HERITAGE

I am passing through a period of physical suffering. The doctors have forbidden me to think or to talk. All the same I cannot help it. The doctors do not know that along with physical agony, I am conscious of another pain which they cannot control. The failure of humanity in the West to preserve the worth of their civilization and the dignity of man which they had taken centuries to build up, weighs like a nightmare on my mind.

It seems clear to me that this failure is due to man's repudiation of moral values in the guidance of their national affairs and to their belief that every thing is determined by a physical chain of events which could be manipulated by man's cunning or might. The consequences of this belief are proving terrible to man. The first experiment in this diabolical faith was launched in Manchuria. What it has demonstrated is this: that though the poor and innocent people of China have suffered, those that were responsible for this suffering and for like suffering elsewhere, have all been drawn into this vortex. Those who built their power on moral cynicism are themselves proving its victims. The nemesis is daily growing more ruthless.

Even that great and proud power, which had no copunction in trampling on our rights, is now reduced to the tragic state of having to defend its own elementary right of existence against foreign menace. Despite our humiliation at its hands, it is not a sight which we can contemplate with ease. Rather we should take a lesson from its fate and beware of moral irresponsibility in the direction of our own national affairs.

We are in the habit of calling Chengiz Khan's hordes barbarians, but not even the terrible Mongols were guilty of such gross betrayal of Humanity as the so-called civilized nations of today are perpetrating before our very eyes. But in the very act of this condemnation one is arrested by one's sympathy for their sufferings. For their own peoples are paying the price of these wrongs.

My utmost sympathy goes out to the brave and innocent people of China who have suffered most and deserved least of this suffering. They have been the victims of a violence they never perpetrated on others, they have been dragged down into the pit of destruction which they did nothing to dig. I hope they will survive the wrong and will once more be enabled to build up a great civilization.

In the midst of this insane orgy of violence and destruction, I shall continue to hold fast to my faith in the final recovery of man's lost heritage of moral worth. Man is great. We who stand by him have the privilege of sharing disaster and defeat, but never the ignominy of betraying the great trust of humanity. I know that even in this demented world, there are individuals scattered all over who believe with me.

November 1940

92. WELCOME TO XU BEIHONG

We welcome you as a messenger of China's great culture; you have brought to us in India the gift of spiritual sympathy which, centuries ago, united our ancient humanities. China and India shared the dawn of a great Renaissance, and even in these days of political cataclysm the memoried light of that comradeship remains.

True rebirth of a civilization comes not from a deadly pursuit of power, which alienates and destroys, but from expression of its inner heart; such an expression, generous and ever renewing, brings neighbours together in the great adventure of mankind.

Here in Santiniketan we have striven to maintain that inner spirit of understanding, that integrity of work guided by ideals and linked with service of man, which, we believe Asia has to offer to civilization. You have come to us with the vision of art, with the sensitive appeal of truth which must triumph over rude shocks of circumstance; your visit will strengthen us, and bring our effort nearer to fulfilment. With great joy I look forward to an era of warm kinship between our neighbouring lands and to the assertion of historical forces in the East that will save us all from the encroaching darkness.

February 1940

93. MESSAGE TO 'FORWARD'

I have great faith in humanity. Like the sun it can be clouded, but never extinguished. I admit that at this time when guns are thundering all the world over, the baser elements appear predominant. The powerful are exulting at the number of their victims. They take the name of science to cultivate the schoolboy superstition that they have certain physical signs indicating their eternal right to rule, as the explosive force of the earthquake once might have claimed, with enough evidence, its never-ending sway over the destiny of this earth. But they in their turn will be disappointed.

Theirs is the cry of a past that is already exhausted, a past that has thrived upon the exclusive spirit of national individualism, which will no longer be able to keep the balance in its perpetual disharmony with its surroundings. Only those races will prosper who, for the sake of their own perfection and permanent safety, are ready to cultivate the spiritual magnanimity of mind that enables the soul of man to be realized in the heart of all races.

For men to come near to one another, and yet to continue to ignore the claims of humanity, is a sure process of suicide. We are waiting for the time when the spirit of the age will be incarnated in a complete human truth and the meeting of men will be translated into the Unity of Man.

February 1941

94. REPLY TO MISS RATHBONE

I have been deeply pained at Miss Rathbone's open letter to Indians. I do not know who Miss Rathbone is but I take it that she represents the mentality of the average 'well-intentioned' Britisher. Her letter is mainly addressed to Jawaharlal and I have no doubt that if that noble fighter of freedom's battle had not been gagged behind prison bars by Miss Rathbone's countrymen, he would have made a fitting and spirited reply to her gratuitous sermon. His enforced silence makes it necessary for me to voice my protest even from my sick bed. The lady has ill served the cause of her people by addressing so indiscreet, indeed impertinent, a challenge to our conscience. She is scandalised at our ingratitude,—that having 'drunk deeply at the wells of English thought' we should still have some thought left for our poor country's interests.

English thought, in so far as it is representative of the best traditions of western enlightenment, has indeed taught us much, but let me add, that those of our countrymen who have profited by it have done so despite the official British attempts to ill educate us. We might have achieved introduction to Western learning through any other European language. Have all the other peoples in the world waited for the British to bring them enlightenment? It is sheer insolent self-complacence on the part of our so-called English friends to assume that had they not 'taught' us we would still have remained in the dark ages. Through the official British channels of education in India have flowed to our children in schools not the best of English thought but its refuse, which has only deprived them of a wholesome repast at the table, of their own culture.

Assuming, however, that English language is the only channel left to us for 'enlightenment', all that 'drinking' deeply at its wells has come to us in 1931, even after a couple of centuries of British administration, only about one per cent of the population was found to be literate in English,—while in the USSR in 1932, after only fifteen years of Soviet administration, 98 per cent of the children were educated. (These figures are taken from *The Statesman's* year-Book, an English publication, not likely to err of the Russian side.) But even more necessary than the so-called culture are the bare elementary needs of existence, on which alone can any superstructure of enlightenment rest.

And what have the British, who held tight the purse strings of our nation for more than two centuries and exploited its resources, done for our poor people? I look around and see famished bodies crying for bread. I have seen women in villages dig up mud for a few drops of drinking water, for wells are even more scarce in Indian villages than schools.

I know that the population of England itself is today in danger of starvation and I sympathise with them, but when I see how the whole might of the British navy is engaged in convoying food vessels to the English shores and when I recollect that I have seen our people perish of hunger and not even a cartload of rice brought to their door from the neighbouring district, I cannot help contrasting the British at home with the British in India.

Shall we be then grateful to the British, if not for keeping fed, at least for preserving law and order?

I look around and see riots raging all over the country. When scores of Indian lives are lost, our property looted, our women dishonoured, the mighty British arm stir in no action, only the British voice is raised from overseas to chide us for unfitness to put our house in order.

Examples are not wanting in history when even fully armed warriors have shrunk before superior might and contingencies have arisen in the present war when even the bravest among the British, French and Greek soldiers have had to evacuate the battlefield in Europe because they were overwhelmed by superior armaments,—but when our poor, unarmed and helpless peasants, encumbered with crying babes, flee from homes unable to protect them from armed goondas, the British officials, perhaps smile in contempt at our cowardice!

Every British civilian in England is armed today for protecting his hearth and home against the enemy, but in India even lathi-training was forbidden by decree. Our people have been deliberately disarmed and emasculated in order to keep them perpetually cowed and at the mercy of their armed masters.

The British hate the Nazis for merely challenging their world-mastery and Miss Rathbone expects us to kiss the hand of her people in servility for having riveted chains on ours. A Government must be judged not by pretensions of its spokesman but by its actual and effective contribution to the well-being of the people.

It is not so much because the British are foreigners that they are unwelcome to us and have found no place in our hearts, as because, while pretending to be trustees of our welfare, they have betrayed the great trust and have sacrificed the happiness of millions in India to bloat the pockets of new capitalists at home.

I should have thought that the decent Britisher would at least keep silent at these wrongs and be grateful to us for our inaction, but that he should add insult to injury and pour salt over our wounds, passes all bounds of decency.

June 1941

B. On Books

THIRTY SONGS FROM THE PUNJAB AND KASHMIR

When I was given an opportunity of hearing Ratan Devi sing some Indian songs, I felt uneasy in my mind. I never could believe it possible for an Englishwoman to give us any music that could be hailed as Indian. I was almost certain that it was going to be something that defies all definitions, and that I was expected to sit listening to some of those contemptible tunes that a foreigner, without the power to discriminate and patience to learn, usually picks up in India.

I remembered the unlucky day in my early boyhood, when I was asked by some English ladies to sing. I happened to know a tune of a non-descript kind which had the reputation, with us, of being of Italian origin, and I confidently selected that one in the hope of its being readily appreciated by my audience. It produced an outburst of merriment, quite unexpected in its irrepressible suddenness, and I was emphatically assured that it might be anything but Italian.

Since then, if asked to sing before Europeans, I boldly took my chance and dealt with Indian songs of unexceptionable character. The result used to be less disastrous, but hardly more satisfactory. So I came to the conclusion that mere tunes cannot stand by themselves, and unless given with some idea of the musical system to which they belong lack all their luster and meaning. In recent times the attention of Europe has been drawn to all branches of Oriental arts, and I have witnessed the sight of Europeans listening to Indian music with deep interest. But all the same, it is always difficult to know if their appreciation is not altogether fantastic, and until you hear them sing or play, and thus come into the touch of their heart, you cannot realize their true feeling.

It is a well-known fact that history is prone to repeat its jokes; and while I was dreading lest it should again be my turn to be the victim of its second perpetration of the one I was subjected to years ago, only with slight variations this time, Ratan Devi began by singing a few European folk-songs with the piano accompaniment. They were delightful, and I prayed in my mind that she should end the evening as she had begun, with the music familiar to her. But fortunately for me, my prayer was not granted.

Ratan Devi left her piano and sat on the floor, squatting down in Indian fashion, and took up the *tambura* on her lap. After the first few notes my misgivings were completely dispelled. The tunes she sang were not of the cheap kind that can easily adapt itself to the uninformed taste of any hasty foreign traveller, satisfying his shallow curiosity. They were Behag, Kandra, Malkaus,—sung with all their richness of details, depth of modulations and exquisite feeling. The times that she observed were the usual difficult ones in Indian music, the cadence of which is never too obvious or the division of beats too emphatic. Neither tunes nor times were the least modified to make them simpler or to suit them to the European training of the singer.

Though the music was immaculately Indian, yet Ratan Devi's voice was her own, and it could not possibly be mistaken for that of any Indian *ustad*. In our country the execution of a song is considered to be of minor importance. India goes to the extreme of almost holding with contempt any finesse in singing, and our master singers never take the least trouble to make their voice and manner attractive. They are not ashamed if their gestures are violent, their top notes cracked and their bass notes unnatural. They take it to be their sole function to display their perfect mastery over all the intricacies of times and tunes, forms and formalities of the classic traditions. Those of the audience who have the human weakness to demand something more, who are not content with the presentation of a music with its richness of forms and play of power, but whose senses have to be satisfied as well, are held to be beneath the notice of any self-respecting artists. They think it to be the duty of the hireling musicians of dancing parties to cater for the enjoyment of fastidious dandies whose eyes and ears are apt to take offence at the least touch of roughness. Anyhow, the cultivation of the flawless perfection of the exterior has been severely neglected in India.

The ideal is otherwise in Europe. A stupendously vast amount of energy is constantly occupied in this country in perfecting outward details in everything, the least deviation from which takes away from the value of a thing much more than it deserves. Here the stage arrangement must be extravagantly perfect and the artist in the pride of the intrinsic merit of his art cannot afford to pay his respect to the public by appearing careless in the least detail of execution. As Europe is willing to pay a very high price for this, perhaps she has got her reward.

I at once realized this when I heard Ratan Devi sing. There was not a sign of effort in her beautiful voice, and not the least suggestion of the uncouthness we are accustomed to in our singers. The casket was as perfect as the gem.

Sometimes the meaning of a poem is better understood in a translation, not necessarily because it is more beautiful than the original, but as in the new setting the poem has to undergo a trial, it shines more brilliantly if it comes out triumphant. So it seemed to me that in Ratan Devi's singing our songs gained something in feeling and truth. Listening to her I felt more clearly than ever that our music is the music of cosmic emotion. It deals not primarily with the drama of the vicissitudes of human life. It does not give emphasis to the social enjoyment of men. In fact, in all our festivities the business of our music seems to me to bring to the heart of the crowded gathering the sense of the solitude and vastness that surround us on all sides. It is never its function to provide fuel for the flame of our gaiety, but to temper it and add to it a quality of depth and detachment. The truth of this becomes evident when one considers that *Sāhānā* is the *rāginī* specially used for the occasion of wedding festivals. It is not at all gay or frolicsome, but almost sad in its solemnity. Our *rāginīs* of springtide and rains, of midnight and daybreak, have the profound pathos of the all-pervading intimacy, yet immense aloofness of Nature.

Ratan Devi sang an *alap* in Kāndra, and I forgot for a moment that I was in a London drawing-room. My mind got itself transported in the magnificence of an eastern night, with its darkness, transparent, yet unfathomable, like the eyes of an

Indian maiden, and I seemed to be standing alone in the depth of its stillness and stars.

1913

TO THE NATION

The peoples are living beings. They have their distinct personalities. Therefore the French and the Germans, who not only live in close neighbourhood, but also contain in themselves in a large measure a racial similarity, have their individual differences that cannot be overlooked.

But the nations are not living beings, they are organizations of power. Their physical and mental aspects are monotonously the same everywhere. Their differences are merely the differences in degree of efficiency. When by some chance, through some cracks, the human personality sends up its own life shoots, the hard consistency of organization suffers, but the people finds its own manifestation. But where the subjugation of humanity by the machine is complete, there the Nation is triumphant. In the modern world the fight is going on between the living spirit of the people and the methods of Nation organizing. It is like the struggle that went on in Central Asia, between man's cultivated area of habitation and the continual encroachment of desert sands, till the human region of life and beauty was choked out of existence. When the spread of the higher ideals of humanity is not held as important, the hardening system of national efficiency grows in strength, and at least for some limited period of time it proudly proves itself to be the fittest to survive.

But it is the survival of that part of man which is the least living. And this is the reason why dead monotony is the sign of the spread of the Nation. The modern towns which present the physiognomy of this dominance of the Nation are everywhere the same from San Francisco to London from London to Tokyo, —they show no faces but merely masks.

The peoples, being living persons, must have their self-expression, and this leads to creations. These creations are literature, art, philosophy, social symbolism and ceremonials. They are different in different peoples, but they are not antagonistic. They are like different dishes in one common feast, adding richness to our enjoyment and understanding of truth. They are making the world of man fertile of life and variedly beautiful.

But the Nations do not create, they merely produce and destroy. Organizations of production are necessary—even the organizations of destruction may be so—but when actuated by greed and hatred they occupy the best part of our world, crowding into a corner the living man who creates, then the harmony is lost and human history runs at a breakneck speed towards fatal catastrophe.

Humanity, where it is living, is guided by inner ideals, but where it is dead organization it is impervious to them. For this organizing endeavour has no growth, but merely augmentation. Therefore its building process is external and it does not fully respond to our inner moral guidance. In this building we can pile up one stone brick upon another and cement them according to our latest scientific recipe. But its foundation is the living nature of man, which cannot suffer such dead weight to be indefinitely loaded upon its heart. Therefore at last, some apparently slight cause makes it move and heave and the huge structure resting upon it sways and cracks. Once it begins to come down we do not know how to stop it. It looks irrational and evil in its sudden course of disruption and mere spouting of moral maxims or prudent advices is unable to prevent the force of moral gravitation in its action of restoring balance.

The ideal of the social man is unselfishness, but the ideal of the nation is selfishness. Therefore, selfishness in the individual is condemned, but in the nation it is extolled. This leads to a hopeless moral blindness, confusing the religion of the people with the religion of the nation. Therefore we find men convinced of the superior claims of Christianity because Christian nations are in possession of the greater part of the world. It is like supporting a thief's religion by quoting the amount of his stolen property. Nations celebrate their successful massacre of men by thanking God in their churches. They forget that Thugs also ascribed their success in manslaughter to the favour of their goddess. But in the case of the latter their goddess frankly represented the principle of destruction. It was this criminal tribe's own murderous instinct deified; the instinct, not of one individual, but of the whole community, therefore held sacred. In the same manner in modern churches, selfishness, hatred, vanity and greed in their collective aspect of national instincts do not scruple to share the homage paid to God.

We must admit that evils there are in human nature and in spite of our faith in moral laws and training in self-control they come out in individual cases of unrighteousness. But they carry on their foreheads their own brand of infamy, and their very successes add to their monstrosity.

All through man's history there will be some who will suffer and others who will cause suffering—and the conquest of evil will never be a fully accomplished fact but a continuous process in our civilization, like the process of burning in a flame.

All creation is the harmony of the contradiction between the eternal ideal of perfection and the infinite incompleteness of realization. So long as the positive ideal of goodness keeps step with the negative incompleteness of attainment, so long as there is no absolute separation between them, we need not be afraid of suffering and loss.

Therefore in former ages when some particular people became turbulent and tried to rob others of their human rights, they sometimes achieved success in their adventures and sometimes failed, and it was nothing more than that. But when this idea of the Nation, which has achieved universal acceptance in the present day, tries to pass off the cult of selfishness as a moral duty simply because that selfishness is gigantic in stature, then it not only commits depredations but attacks the very vitals of humanity. It unconsciously generates in people's minds an attitude of defiance against moral law. For they are taught by repeated devices the lesson that the Nation is greater than the people, and yet this nation scatters to the winds every moral law that the people hold as sacred.

It has been said that a disease becomes most acutely critical when the brain is affected. For it is the brain which is constantly directing the siege against all disease forces. The spirit of national selfishness is that brain disease of a people, which, for the time being, shows itself in red eyes and clenched fists, in violence of talk and movements while all the time shattering its natural system of healing. It is the power of self-sacrifice, the moral faculty of sympathy and co-operation which is the guiding spirit of social vitality. Its function is to maintain a beneficent relation of harmony with its surroundings. But when it begins to ignore the moral law which is universal, and uses it only within the bounds of a narrow sphere, then its strength becomes like the strength of muscular convulsion, which not being a movement of harmonious health, hurts itself in the end.

What is worse, this moral aberration of peoples, decked with the showy title of patriotism, proudly walks abroad, passing itself off as a highly moral influence. Thus it has spread its inflammatory contagion all over the world, proclaiming its fever-flush to be the best sign of health. It is causing at the hearts of peoples, naturally inoffensive, a feeling of envy at not having their temperature as high as their delirious neighbours, and not being able to cause as much mischief as these others do, but merely having to suffer it.

I have often been asked by my Western friends how to cope with this evil which has attained such sinister strength and dimensions. In fact, I have often been blamed for merely giving warning but offering no alternative. Having been bred in the atmosphere of system-worship our mind has got into the habit of a superstitious reverence for system. Therefore when we suffer as a result of a particular system we believe that some other system will bring us better luck. We have forgotten this simple truth that all systems produce evil sooner or later when the psychology which is at the root of them is wrong. The system which is national today may assume the shape of international tomorrow, but so long as men have not forgotten their idolatry of the baser passions, so long as vanity and greed and jealousy can claim moral sacrifice from us when they assume bulkiness of dimensions, the new system will become a new instrument of suffering to man or at best will become ineffectual. And because we are trained to confound good system with moral goodness itself, every ruined system makes us distrustful of moral law.

Therefore, I do not put my faith in any new institution, but in the drainage of those stagnant moral pollutions which give rise to poisonous vapour. For this we are to look for individuals all over the world who must think clearly, feel nobly and act rightly and thus become the channels of universal moral truth. For this truth once introduced goes on with its own living creation, overcoming all hindrances. Our moral ideals do not work with chisels and hammers, but like living seeds in proper ground spread their roots in the soil and their branches in the sky without consulting architects for their plans. What is necessary is purity in thought, feeling and will, and the rest will follow.

This is the reason why, when I met Monsieur Richard in Japan, I became more reassured in my mind about the higher era of civilization than when I read about the big schemes which the politicians are formulating for ushering the age of peace into the world. It is not upon mere number or bulk that our salvation depends but upon the truth which can afford to look small. When gigantic forces of destruction were holding their orgies of fury I saw this solitary young Frenchman, unknown to fame,... face beaming with the lights of the new dawn and his voice vibrating with the message of new life, and I felt sure that the great Tomorrow has already come though not registered in the Calendar of the statesmen.

17 January 1917

THE WEB OF INDIAN LIFE

Indians, like all other peoples of the world, are naturally susceptible to flattery. But unfortunately they have been deprived of their share of it, even in wholesome measure, both by the Fates presiding at the making of their history as well as by the guests partaking of their salt. We have been declared inefficient in practical matters by our governors, foreign missionaries have created a vast literature proclaiming our moral obliquity, while casual visitors have expressed their opinion that we are particularly uninteresting to the intellectual mind of the West. Other peoples' estimate of our work is a great part of our world, and the most important other peoples in the present age being the Europeans, it has become tragic in its effect for us to be unable to evoke their appreciation. There was a time when India could touch the most sensitive part of Europe's mind by storming her imagination with a gorgeous vision of wealth. But cruel time has done its work and the golden illusion has vanished, leaving the ragged poverty of India open to public inspection, charitable or otherwise. Therefore epithets of a disparaging nature from the West find an easy target in India, bespattering her skin and piercing her vital parts. Epithets once given circulation die-hard, for they have their breeding-places in our mental laziness and in our natural readiness to believe that whatever is different from ourselves must be offensive. Men can live through and die happy in spite of disparagement, if it comes from critics with whom they have no dealings. But unfortunately our critics not only have the power to give us a bad name, but also to hang us. They play the part of Providence over three hundred millions of aliens whose language they hardly know, and with whom their acquaintance is of the surface. Therefore, the vast accumulation of calumny against India, continually growing and spreading over the earth, secretly and surely obstructs the element of heart from finding an entrance into our government.

One can never do justice from a mere sense of duty to those for whom one lacks respect. And human beings, as we are, justice is not the chief thing that we claim from our rulers. We need sympathy as well, in order to feel that we have human relationship with them and thus retain as much of our self-respect as may be possible.

For some time past a spirit of retaliation has taken possession of our literature and our social world. We have furiously begun to judge our judges, and the judgment comes from hearts sorely stricken with hopeless humiliation. And because our thoughts have an organ whose sound does not reach outside our country, or even the ears of our governors within its boundaries, their expression is growing in vehemence. The prejudice cultivated on the side of the powerful is no doubt dangerous for the weak, but it cannot be wise on the part of the strong to ignore that thorny crop grown on the opposite field. The upsetting of truth in the relationship of the ruler and the ruled can never be compensated by the power that lies in the grip of the mailed fist.

And this was the reason which made us deeply grateful to Sister Nivedita, that great-hearted Western woman, when she gave utterance to her criticism of Indian life. She had won her access to the inmost heart of our society by her supreme gift of sympathy. She did not come to us with the impertinent curiosity of a visitor, nor did she elevate herself on a special high perch with the idea that a bird's eye view is truer than the human view because of its superior aloofness. She lived our life and came to know us by becoming one of ourselves. She became so intimately familiar with our people that she had the rare opportunity of observing us unawares. As a race we have our special limitations and imperfections, and for a foreigner it does not require a high degree of keen-sightedness to detect them. We know for certain that these defects did not escape Nivedita's observation, but she did not stop there to generalize, as most other foreigners do. And because she had a comprehensive mind and extraordinary insight of love she could see the creative ideals at work behind our social forms and discover our soul that has living connexion with its past and is marching towards its fulfilment.

But Sister Nivedita, being an idealist, saw a great deal more than is usually seen by those foreigners who can only see things, but not truths. Therefore I have heard her being discredited by the authority of long experience, which is merely an experience of blindness carried through long years. And of these I have the same words to say which I said to those foreign residents of Japan, whose long experience itself was like a film obscuring the freshness of their sight, making them conscious of only some outer details, specially where they irritated their minds. Instead of looking on the picture side of the canvas, if they look on the blank side it will not give any more value to their view because of the prolonged period of their staring.

The mental sense, by the help of which we feel the spirit of a people, is like the sense of sight, or of touch—it is a natural gift. It finds its objects, not by analysis, but by direct apprehension. Those who have not this vision merely see events and facts, and not their inner association. Those who have no ear for music, hear sounds, but not the song. Therefore when, by reason of the mere lengthiness of their suffering, they threaten to establish the fact of the tune to be a noise, one need not be anxious about the reputation of the music. Very often it is the mistakes which require a longer time to develop their tangles, while the right answer comes promptly.

It is a truism to say that shadows accompany light. What you feel as the truth of a people, has its numberless contradictions, just as the single fact of the roundness of the earth is contradicted by the innumerable facts of its hills and hollows. Facts can easily be arranged and heaped up into loads of contradiction; yet men having faith in the reality of ideals hold firmly that the vision of truth does not depend upon its dimension, but upon its vitality. And Sister Nivedita has uttered the vital truths about Indian life.

21 October 1917

'A GREAT CHANNEL FOR COMMUNICATION'

The following anthology has its greatest interest in being a self-recording evidence of the earliest response that Bengal gave to the touch of the West. I think we can safely assess that she is the only country in the Orient which has shown any distinct indication of being thrilled by the voice of Europe as it came to her through literature. We are not concerned with a critical estimate of Bengal's earliest literary adventures in the perilous fields of a foreign tongue. But the important fact is this, that while there are other eastern countries captivated by the sight of the immense power and prosperity which Europe presented to us, Bengal has been stirred by the forces of new ideas breaking upon her from the western horizon. One of its earliest effects upon our students was to rouse them into an aggressive antagonism against orthodox conventions, irrespective of their merits. It was a sudden self-assertion of life after its repression for ages. This shock, which roused Bengal mainly came through literature, and a great part of her energy followed the same channel of literature for its expression.

The most memorable instance of the working of ideas in Bengal in the time of her early contact of mind with Europe has been Rammohun Roy's message of life to India,—a life centering in the spiritual idea of the all-pervading oneness of God, as inculcated in the Upanishads, and comprehending in its circumference all varieties of human activities from the moral down to the political. It was a call to move and fully to live, not from a blind love of movement, but as directed by an inner guidance coming from the heart of India's own wisdom.

Though the above instance does not directly touch the literary side of our life, yet I cite it to show that it was through her sensitiveness to ideas that Bengal has been deeply moved from the time of her first acquaintance with Europe. And ever since, the same formation of ideals has been going on through various stages of action and reaction. Those who have the talent and love for constructive work can show their productions in a palpable form and with a rapidity of results. But Idea works in the depth of life, bringing about fundamental changes in the very soil and seeds, and sprouts forth from the unseen in its own time in a living creative form. Its early energies are engaged and seem wasted in work of destruction, in explosions of discontent, in constant vacillation in choice, thus easily lending itself to the charge of volatility and indecision. But life has its side which is vigorously destructive and full of uncertainties and contradictions. The signs of perturbation so evident in Bengal, in her social and religious life, in her intellectual adjustments, only show that creative ideas are at work in the centre of her being. I trust I do not merely prove my patriotic bias by saying that, of all countries in the East, Bengal is most earnestly engaged in the exploration of life's ideal. All the great personalities she has produced in the modern time have presented to us according to their light, some ideal solution of life's inner problem. We are fully aware that this is not all that humanity requires, that there are other questions more immediately importunate which have to be answered if we must live; and there are signs that we are beginning actively to recognise this important fact. But all the same we must confess, that whatever it may have cost us, we have dealt more with the ideas that move our soul by kindling our imagination than with acquiring and arranging materials to help us in our struggle for existence. This led to an active conflict in Bengal between the Old and New a constant shifting of her outlooks upon life and unrest owing to her groping for something positive by which she can win for good her own true place in the world.

Our present age of renaissance began its career with an exaggerated faith in the foreign and the external to find out at last that life is a process of constant self-unfolding, whose impulse comes from the centre of its own being. In Bengal we meet with all the different stages of this development and therefore more than in other parts of India, it is here that love of imitation of the West runs to excess pompously proud of its tawdriness and incongruity. On the other hand in Bengal have been originated all the recent movements for the seeking of truth that is our national heritage. The West which at first drew us on to itself, has forcibly flung us back upon an intense consciousness of our personality. The breath of inspiration, coming from the West has kindled the original spark in us into a flame that lay smothered in the ashes of dead habits and rigidity of traditional forms. This has been illustrated by the course our literature has taken almost completely abandoning its earlier foreign bed, finding its natural channel in the mother tongue. The following collection of English poems written by Bengali authors also proves it, in which the earlier writings are timorously imitative while the later ones boldly burn with their own fire, daring to challenge time's judgment with their claim of immortality. I believe foreign readers, while reading this book, will find much to think of in the fact that Bengal's response through literature to the call of the West is something unique in the history of the modern East. It has a future, for it is quickened with life, and it carries within itself a hope that one day it will become a great channel for communication of ideas between the adventurous West and the East of the immemorial tranquility.

1918

THE ROBBERY OF THE SOIL

The standard of living in modern civilization has been raised far higher than the average level of our necessity. The strain which this entails serves at the outset to increase our physical and mental alertness. The claim upon our energy accelerates growth. This in its turn produces activity that expresses itself by raising life's standard still higher.

When this standard attains a degree that is a great deal above the normal it encourages the passion of greed. The temptation of an inordinately high level of living, which was once confined only to a small section of the community, becomes widespread. The burden is sure to prove fatal to the civilization which puts no restraint upon the emulation of self-indulgence.

In the geography of our economic world the ups and downs produced by inequalities of fortune are healthy only within a moderate range. In a country divided by the constant interruption of steep mountains no great civilization is possible because in such places the natural flow of communication is always difficult. Like mountains, large fortunes and the enjoyment of luxury are also high walls of segregation; they produce worse divisions in society than any physical barriers.

Where life's simple wealth does not become too exclusive and owners of individual property find no great difficulty in acknowledging their communal responsibility. In fact wealth can even become the best channel for social communication. In former days in India public opinion levied heavy taxes upon wealth and most of the public works of the country were voluntarily contributed by the rich. The water supply, medical help, education and amusement were naturally maintained by men of property through a spontaneous sense of mutual obligation. This was made possible because the limits set to the individual right of self-indulgence were narrow and surplus wealth easily followed the channel of social responsibility. In such a society civilization was supported by strong pillars of property, and wealth gave opportunity to the fortunate for self-sacrifice.

But, with the rise of the standard of living, property changes its aspect. It shuts the gate of hospitality which is the best means of social communication. Its owners display their wealth in an extravagance which is self-centred. This creates envy and irreconcilable class division. In other words property becomes anti-social.

Because property itself, with what is called material progress, has become intensely individualistic, the method of gaining it has become a matter of science and not of social ethics. Property and its acquisition break social bonds and drain the life sap of the community. The unscrupulousness involved plays havoc the world over and generates a force that can coax or coerce peoples to deeds of injustice and of wholesale horror.

The forest fire feeds upon the living world from which it springs till it exhausts itself completely along with its fuel. When a passion like greed breaks loose from the fence of social control it acts like that fire, feeding upon the life of society. The end is annihilation. It has ever been the object of the spiritual training of man to fight those passions that are anti-social and to keep them chained. But lately abnormal temptation has set them free and they are fiercely devouring all that is affording them fuel.

There are always insects in our harvest field which, in spite of their robbery, tend to leave a sufficient surplus for the tillers of the soil, so that it does not pay us to try to exterminate them altogether. But when some pest, that has an enormous power of self multiplication, attacks our total food crop we must consider this a great calamity. In human society, in normal circumstances, there are many causes that make for wastage, yet it does not cost us much to ignore them. But today the blight that has fallen upon our social life and its resources is disastrous because it is not restricted within reasonable limits. This is an epidemic of voracity that has infected the total area of civilization. We all claim our right, and freedom, to be extravagant in our enjoyment if we can afford it. Not to be able to waste as much upon myself as my rich neighbour does merely proves a poverty in myself of which I am ashamed, and against which my women folk, and other parasites, naturally cherish their own grievance. Ours is a society in which, through its tyrannical standard of respectability, all the members are goading each other to spoil themselves to the utmost limit of their capacity. There is a continual screwing up of the ideal level of convenience and comfort, the increase in which is proportionately less than the energy it consumes. The very shriek of advertisement itself, which constantly accompanies the progress of unlimited production, involves the squandering of an immense quantity of material and of life force which merely helps to swell the sweepings of time. Civilization today caters for a whole population of gluttons. An intemperance, which could safely have been tolerated in a few, has spread its contagion to the multitude. This universal greed, which now infects us all, is the cause of every kind of meanness, of cruelty and of lies in politics and commerce, and vitiates the whole human atmosphere. A civilization, which has attained such an unnatural appetite, must, for its continuing existence, depend upon numberless victims. These are being sought in those parts of the world where human flesh is cheap. In Asia and Africa a bartering goes on through which the future hope and happiness of entire peoples is sold for the sake of providing some fastidious fashion with an endless supply of respectable rubbish.

The consequence of such a material and moral drain is made evident when one studies the condition manifested in the grossness of our cities and the physical and mental anaemia of the villages almost everywhere in the world. For cities inevitably have become important. The city represents energy and materials concentrated for the satisfaction of an exaggerated appetite, and this concentration is considered to be a symptom of civilization. The devouring process of such an abnormality cannot be carried on unless certain parts of the social body conspire and organize to feed upon the whole. This is suicidal; but, before a gradual degeneracy ends in death, the disproportionate enlargement of the particular portion looks formidably great. It conceals the starved pallor of the entire body. The illusion of wealth becomes evident because certain portions grow large on their robbery of the whole.

A living relationship, in a physical or in a social body, depends upon sympathetic collaboration and helpfulness between the various individual organs or members. When a perfect balance of interchange begins to operate, a consciousness of unity develops that is no longer easy to obstruct. The resulting health or wealth are both secondary to this sense of unity which is the ultimate end and aim, and a creation in its own right. Whenever some sectarian ambition for power establishes a dominating position in life's republic, the sense of unity, which can only be generated and maintained by a perfect rhythm of reciprocity between the parts is bound to be disturbed. In a society where the greed of an individual or of a group is allowed to grow uncontrolled, and is encouraged or even applauded by the populace, democracy, as it is termed in the West, cannot be truly realized. In such an atmosphere a constant struggle goes on among individuals to capture public organizations for the satisfaction of their own personal ambition. Thus democracy becomes like an elephant whose one purpose in life is to give joy rides to the clever and to the rich. The organs of information and expression, through which opinions are manufactured, and the machinery of administration, are openly or secretly manipulated by the prosperous few, by those who have been compared to the camel which can never pass through the needle's eye, that narrow gate that leads to the kingdom of ideals. Such a society necessarily becomes inhospitable, suspicious, and callous towards those who preach their faith in ideals, in spiritual freedom. In such a society people become intoxicated by the constant stimulation of what they are told is progress, like the man for whom wine has a greater attraction than food.

Villages are like woman. In their keep is the cradle of the race. They are nearer to nature than the towns and are therefore in closer touch with the fountain of life. They have the atmosphere which possesses a natural power of healing. Like woman they provide people with their elemental needs, with food and joy, with the simple poetry of life and with those ceremonies of beauty which the village spontaneously produces and in which she finds delight. But when constant strain is put upon her through the extortionate claims of ambition, when her resources are exploited through the excessive stimulus of temptation, then she becomes poor in life. Her mind becomes dull and uncreative; and, from her time-honoured position as the wedded partner of the city, she is degraded to that of maid-servant. The city, in its intense egotism and pride, remains blissfully unconscious of the devastation it is continuously spreading within the village, the source and origin of its own life, health and joy.

True happiness is not at all expensive. It depends upon that natural spring of beauty and of life, harmony of relationship. Ambition pursues its own path of self-seeking by breaking this bond of harmony, digging gaps, creating dissension. Selfish ambition feels no hesitation in trampling under foot the whole harvest field, which is for all, in order to snatch away in haste that portion which it craves. Being wasteful it remains disruptive of social life and the greatest enemy of civilization.

In India we had a family system of our own, large and complex, each family a miniature society in itself. I do not wish to discuss the question of its desirability, but its rapid decay in the present day clearly points out the nature and process of the principle of destruction which is at work in modern civilization. When life was simple, needs normal, when selfish passions were under control, such a domestic life was perfectly natural and truly productive of happiness. The family resources were sufficient for all. Claims from one or more individuals of that family were never excessive. But such a group can never survive if the personal ambition of a single member begins separately to clamour for a great deal more than is absolutely necessary for him. When the determination to augment private possession, and to enjoy exclusive advantage, runs ahead of the common good and of general happiness, the bond of harmony, which is the bond of creation, must give way and brothers must separate nay even become enemies.

This passion of greed that rages in the heart of our present civilization, like a volcanic flame of fire, is constantly struggling to erupt in individual bloatedness. Such eruptions must disturb man's creative mind. The flow of production which gushes from the cracks rent in society gives the impression of a hugely indefinite gain. We forget that the spirit of creation can only evolve out of our own inner abundance and so add to our true wealth. A sudden increase in the flow of production of things tends to consume our resources and requires us to build new storehouses. Our needs, therefore, which stimulate this increasing flow, must begin to observe the limitation of normal demand. If we go on stoking our demands into bigger and bigger flames the conflagration that results will no doubt, dazzle our sight, but its splendour will leave on the debit side only a black heap of charred remains. When our wants are moderate, the rations we each claim do not exhaust the common store of nature and the pace of their restoration does not fall hopelessly behind that of our consumption. This moderation leaves us leisure to cultivate happiness, that happiness which is the artist soul of the human world, and which can create beauty of form and rhythm of life. But man today forgets that the divinity within him is revealed by the halo of this happiness. The Germany of the period of Goethe was considered to be poverty-stricken by the Germany of the period of Bismarck. Possibly the standard of civilization, illuminated by the mind of Plato or by the life of the Emperor Asoka, is underrated by the proud children of modern times who compare former days with the present age of progress, an age dominated by millionaires, diplomats and war lords. Many things that are of common use today were absolutely lacking in those days. But are the people that lived then to be pitied by the young of our day who enjoy so much more from the printing press but so much less from the mind?

I often imagine that the moon, being smaller in size than the earth, produced the condition for life to be born on her soil earlier than was possible on the soil of her companion. Once she too perhaps had her constant festival of colour, of music and of movement; her store-house was perpetually replenished with food for her children. Then in course of time some race was born to her that was gifted with a furious energy of intelligence, and that began greedily to devour its own surroundings. It produced beings who, because of the excess of their animal spirit, coupled with intellect and imagination, failed to realize that the mere process of addition did not create fulfilment; that mere size of acquisition did not produce happiness; that greater velocity of movement did not necessarily constitute progress and that change could only have meaning in relation to some clear ideal of completeness. Through machinery of tremendous power this race made such an addition to their natural capacity for gathering and holding, that their career of plunder entirely outstripped nature's power for recuperation. Their profit makers dug big holes in the stored capital of the planet. They created wants which were unnatural and provision for these wants was forcibly extracted from nature. When they had reduced the limited store of material in their immediate surroundings they proceeded to wage furious wars among their different sections, each wanting his own special allotment of the lion's share. In their scramble for the right of self-indulgence they laughed at moral law and took it to be a sign of superiority to be ruthless in the satisfaction each of his own desire. They exhausted the water, cut down the trees, reduced the surface of the planet to a desert, riddled with enormous pits, and made its interior a rifled pocket, emptied of its valuables. At last one day the moon, like a fruit whose pulp had been completely eaten by the insects which it had sheltered, became a hollow shell, a universal grave for the voracious creatures who insisted upon consuming the world into which they had been born. In other words, they behaved exactly in the way human beings of today are behaving upon this earth, fast exhausting their store of sustenance, not because they must live their normal life, but because they wish to live at a pitch of monstrous excess. Mother Earth has enough for the healthy appetite of her children and something extra for rare cases of abnormality. But she has not nearly sufficient for the sudden growth of a whole world of spoiled and pampered children.

Man has been digging holes into the very foundations not only of his livelihood but of his life. He is now feeding upon his own body. The reckless waste of humanity which ambition produces is best seen in the villages where the light of life is gradually being dimmed, the joy of existence dulled, and the natural bonds of social communion are being snapped every day. It should be our mission to restore the full circulation of life's blood into these martyred limbs of society; to bring to the villagers health and knowledge; a wealth of space in which to live, a wealth of time in which to work, to rest and enjoy mutual respect which will give them dignity; sympathy which will make them realize their kinship with the world of men and not merely their position of subservience.

Streams, lakes and oceans are there on this earth. They exist not for the hoarding of water exclusively each within its own area. They send up the vapour which forms into clouds and helps in a wide distribution of water. Cities have a special function in maintaining wealth and knowledge in concentrated forms of opulence, but this should not be for their own exclusive sake; they should not magnify themselves, but should enrich the entire society. They should be like the lamp post, for the light it supports must transcend its own limits. Such a relationship of mutual benefit between the city and the village remains strong only so long as the spirit of co-operation and self-sacrifice is a living ideal in society as a whole. When some universal temptation overcomes this ideal when some selfish passion finds ascendancy then a gap is formed and widened between them. The mutual relationship between city and village becomes that of exploiter and victim. This is a form of perversity in which the body becomes its own enemy. The termination is death.

We have started in India, in connection with Visva-Bharati, a kind of village work the mission of which is to retard this process of race suicide. If I try to give you details of the work the effort will look small. But we are not afraid of this appearance of smallness, for we have confidence in life. We know that if, as a seed, smallness represents the truth that is in us, it will overcome opposition and conquer space and time. According to us the poverty problem is not so important. It is the problem of unhappiness that is the great problem. The search for wealth which is the synonym for the production and collection of things can make use of men ruthlessly can crush life out of the earth and for a time can flourish. Happiness may not compete with wealth in its list of needed materials, but it is final, it is creative therefore it has its own source of riches within itself. Our object is to try to flood the choked bed of village life with streams of happiness. For this the scholars, the poets, the musicians, the artists as well as the scientists have to collaborate have to offer their contribution. Otherwise they live like parasites, sucking life from the country people, and giving nothing back to them. Such exploitation gradually exhausts the soil of life, the soil which needs constant replenishing by the return of life to it through the completion of the cycle of receiving and giving back.

The writer of the following paper, who was in charge of the rural work in Visva-Bharati, forcibly drew our attention to this subject and made it clear to us that the civilization which allows its one part to exploit the rest without making any return is merely cheating itself into bankruptcy. It is like the foolish young man, who suddenly inheriting his father's business, steals his own capital and spends it in a magnificent display of extravagance. He dazzles the imagination of the onlookers, he gains applause from his associates in his dissipation, he becomes the most envied man in his neighbourhood till the morning when he wakes up, in surprise, to a state of complete indigence. Most of us who try to deal with the poverty problem think of nothing else but of a greater intensive effort of production, forgetting that this only means a greater exhaustion of materials as well as of humanity, and this means giving a still better opportunity for profit to the few at the cost of the many. But it is food which nourishes and not money. It is fullness of life which makes us happy and not fullness of purse. Multiplying materials intensifies the inequality between those who have and those who have not. This is the worst wound from which the social body can suffer. It is a wound through which the body is bled to death!

1922

ZOROASTRIAN HYMNS

The most important of all outstanding facts of Iranian history is the religious reform brought about by Zarathushtra. He was the first man we know who gave a definitely moral character and direction to religion, and at the same time preached the doctrine of monotheism, which offered an eternal foundation of reality of goodness as an ideal of perfection. All religions of the primitive type try to keep men bound with regulations of external observances. These, no doubt, have the hypnotic effect of vaguely suggesting a realm of right and wrong; but the dimness of their light produces phantasms leaving men to aberrations. Zarathushtra was the greatest of all the pioneer prophets who showed the path of freedom to men, the freedom of moral choice, the freedom from blind obedience to unmeaning injunctions, freedom from the multiplicity of shrines which draw our worship away from the single-minded chastity of devotion. To most of us it sounds like a truism today when we are told that the moral goodness of a deed comes from the goodness of intention. But it is a truth which once came to a man like a revelation of light in the darkness and has not yet reached all the obscure corners of humanity. There are men we still see around us who fearfully follow, hoping thereby to gain merit, the path of blind formalisms, which have no living moral source in the mind. This will make us understand the greatness of Zarathushtra. Though surrounded by believers in magical rites, he proclaimed in those dark days of unreason, that religion has its truth in its moral significance, not in external practices of imaginary value; that it is to uphold man in his life of good thoughts, good words and good deeds.

The outer expression of truth reaches its white light of simplicity through its inner realization. True simplicity is the physiognomy of perfection. In the primitive stage of spiritual growth, when man is dimly aware of the mystery of the infinite in his life and the world, when he does not fully know the inward character of his relationship with this truth, his first feeling is either that of dread or of a greed of gain. This drives him into wild exaggeration in worship, into frenzied convulsion of ceremonialism. But in Zarathushtra's teachings, which are best reflected in his Gathas, we have hardly any mention of the ritualism of worship. Conduct and its moral motives, such as Vohumano, Asha and Aramaiti, have received almost the sole attention in them.

The orthodox Persian form of worship in ancient Iran included animal sacrifices and offering of *haoma* to the *daevas*. That all this should be discountenanced by Zarathushtra not only shows his courage, but the strength of his realization of the Supreme Being as Spirit. We are told that it has been mentioned by Plutarch: 'Zarathushtra taught the Persians to sacrifice to Ahura Mazda "vows and thanksgivings".' The distance between faith in the efficacy of blood-stained magical rites and cultivation of moral and spiritual deals as the true form of worship is immense. It is amazing to see how Zarathushtra was the first among men who crossed this distance with a certainty of realization which imparted such a fervour of faith in his life and his words. The truth which filled his mind was not a thing borrowed from books or received from teachers. He did not come to it by following a prescribed path of tradition. It flashed upon him as an illumination of his entire life, almost like a communication to his personal self, and he proclaimed the utmost immediacy of his knowledge in these words:

> When I conceived of Thee, O Mazda, as the very First and the Last, as the most Adorable One, as the Father of Good Thought, as the Creator of Truth and Right, as the Lord Judge of our actions in life, then I made a place for Thee in my very eyes.—Yasna, 31–8. (Translation by D.J. Irani)

It was the direct stirring of his soul which made him say:

> Thus do I announce the Greatest of all. I weave my songs of praise for Him through Truth, helpful and beneficent to all that live. Let Ahura Mazda listen to them with His Holy Spirit, for the Good Mind instructed me to adore Him; by His Wisdom let Him teach me about what is best.—Yasna, 45–6.

The truth which is not reached through the analytical process of reasoning, and does not depend for proof on some corroboration of outward facts, or the prevalent faith and practice of the people—the truth, which comes like an inspiration out of context with its surroundings, brings with it an assurance that it has been sent from a divine source of wisdom; that the individual who has received it is specially chosen and therefore has his responsibility as the messenger of God. Zarathushtra felt this sacredness of his mission and believed himself to be the direct medium of communication of Divine Truth.

So long as man deals with his God as the dispenser of benefits to the worshipper, who knows the secret of propitiating him, he tries to keep him for his own self or for the tribe to which he belongs. But directly the moral or spiritual nature of God is apprehended, this knowledge is thrown open to all humanity; and then the idea of God, which once gave unity only to a special people, transcends limitations of race and gathers together all human beings within one spiritual circle of union. Zarathushtra was the first prophet who emancipated religion from the exclusive narrowness of the tribal God, the God of a chosen people, and offered it to the universal man. This is a great fact in the history of religion. The Master said, when the enlightenment came to him:

> Verily I believe Thee, O Ahura Mazda, to be the Supreme Benevolent Providence, when Sraosha came to me with the Good Mind, when first I received and became wise with Thy words! And though the task be difficult, though woe may come to me, I shall proclaim to all mankind Thy message, which Thou declarest to be the best.—Yasna, 43–11.

He prays to Mazda:

> This I ask Thee, tell me truly, O Ahura, the religion that is best for all mankind—the religion, based on truth, which should prosper all that is mine, the religion which establishes our actions in order and justice by the Divine Songs of Perfect Piety, which has, for its intelligent desire of desires, the desire for Thee, O Mazda!—Yasna, 44–10.

With the undoubted assurance and hope of one who has got a direct vision of Truth he speaks to the world:

> Hearken unto me, Ye, who come from far and near! Listen, for I shall speak forth now; ponder well over all things, weigh my words with care and clear thought. Never shall the false teacher destroy this world for a second time; for his tongue stands mute, his creed exposed.—Yasna, 45–1.

I think it can be said without doubt that such a high conception of religion, uttered in such a clear note of affirmation, with a sure conviction that it is a truth of the ultimate ideal of perfection which must be revealed to all humanity, even at the cost of martyrdom, is unique in the history of religion belonging to such a remote dawn of civilization.

There was a time when along with other Aryan peoples the Persians also worshipped the elemental gods of nature, on whose favour they depended for the good things of life. But such favour was not to be won by any moral duty performed or by any service of love. In fact, it was the crude beginning of the scientific spirit trying to unlock the hidden sources of power in nature. But through it all there must have been some current of deeper desire which constantly contradicted the cult of power and indicated a world of inner good infinitely more precious than material gain. Its voice was not strong at first, nor was it heeded by the majority of the people; but its influence, like the life within the seed, was silently working. Then comes the great teacher; and in his life and mind the hidden fire of truth suddenly bursts out in a flame. The best in the people works for long obscure ages in hints and whispers till it finds its voice, which can never again be silenced. For that voice becomes the voice of mankind, no longer confined to a particular time or people. It works across intervals of silence and oblivion, depression and defeat, and comes out again and again with its conquering call. It is a call to the fighter—the fighter against untruth—against all that lures away man's spirit from its high mission of freedom into the meshes of materialism. And Zarathushtra's voice is still a living voice, not a mere matter of academic interest for historical scholars who deal with the dead facts of the past. It is not a voice which is only to guide a small community of men in the daily details of their life. For have we not seen that Zarathushtra was the first of all teachers who, in his religious teachings, sent his words to all human races across the distance of space and time? He was not like a man who by some chance of friction had lighted a lamp, and knowing that it could not be shared by all, secured it with a miser's care for his own domestic use. But he was the watcher in the night, who stood on the lonely peak facing the East and broke out singing the poems of light to the sleeping world when the sun came out on the brim of the horizon. He declared that the sun of truth is for all, that its light is to unite the far and the near. Such a message always arouses the antagonism of those whose habits have become nocturnal, whose vested interest is in the darkness. And there was a bitter fight in the lifetime of the prophet between his followers and others who were addicted to the ceremonies that had tradition on their side and not truth.

We are told that 'Zarathushtra was descended from a kingly family', and also that the first converts to his doctrines were of the ruling caste. But the priesthood, 'the Kavis and the Karapans, often succeeded in bringing the rulers over to their side'. So we find that, in this fight, the princes of the land divided themselves into two opposite parties, as we find in India in the Kurukshetra war. 'With the princes have the Kavis and the Karapans united, in order to corrupt man by their evil deeds.' Among the princes that stood against Zarathushtra, as his enemies, the mighty Bendva might be included, who is mentioned in Yasna, xlix, 1-2. From the context we may surmise that he stood on the side of the infidels. A family or a race of princely blood were probably the Grehma (Yasna, xxxii, 12-14). Regarding them it is said that they 'having allied with the Kavis and the Karapans, have established their power in order to overpower the prophet and his partisans. In fact, the opposition between the pious and the impious, the believers and the unbelievers, seem very often to have led to open combat. The prophet prays to Ahura that he may grant victory to his own, when both the armies rush together in combat, whereby they can cause defeat among the wicked, and procure for them strife and trouble.'

There is evidence in our Indian legends that in ancient India also there have been fights between the representatives of the orthodox faith and the Kshatriyas, who, owing to their own special vocation, had a comparative freedom of mind about the religion of external observances. The proofs are strong enough to lead us to believe that the monotheistic religious movement had its origin and principal support in the kingly caste of those days, though a great number of them fought to oppose it.

I have discussed in another place the growth in ancient India of the moral and spiritual element in her religion which had accompanied the Indian Aryan people from the time of the Indo-Iranian age, showing how the struggle with its antagonistic force has continued all through the history of India. I have shown how the revolution which accompanied the teachings of Zarathushtra, breaking out into severe fights, had its close analogy in the religious revolution in India whose ideals are still preserved in the Bhagavadgita.

It is interesting to note that the growth of the same ideal in the same race in different geographical situations has produced results that, in spite of their unity, have some aspect of difference. The Iranian monotheism is more ethical, while the Indian is more metaphysical in its character. Such a difference in their respective spiritual developments was owing, no doubt, to the more active vigour of life in the old Persians and the contemplative quietude of mind in the Indians. This distinction in the latter arises in a great measure out of the climatic conditions of the country, the easy fertility of the soil and the great stretch of plains in Northern India affording no constant obstacles in physical nature to be daily overcome by man, while the climate of Persia is more bracing and the surface of the soil more rugged. The Zoroastrian ideal has accepted the challenge of the principle of evil and has enlisted itself in the fight on the side of Ahura Mazda, the great, the good, the wise. In India, although the ethical side is not absent, the emphasis has been more strongly laid on subjective realization through a stoical suppression of desire, and the attainment of a perfect equanimity of mind by cultivating indifference to all causes of joy and sorrow. Here the idea, over which the minds of men brooded for ages, in an introspective intensity of silence, was that man as a spiritual being had to realize the truth by breaking through his sheath of self. All the desires and feelings that limit has being are keeping him shut in from the region of spiritual freedom.

In man the spirit of creation is waiting to find its ultimate release in an ineffable illumination of Truth. The aspiration of India is for attaining the infinite in the spirit of man. On the other hand, as I have said before, the ideal of Zoroastrian Persia is distinctly ethical. It sends its call to men to work together with the Eternal Spirit of Good in spreading and maintaining Kshatra, the Kingdom of Righteousness, against all attacks of evil. This ideal gives us our place as collaborators with God in distributing His blessings over the world.

> Clear is this all to the man of wisdom as to the man who carefully thinks; he who upholds Truth with all the might of his power, he who upholds Truth the utmost in his word and deed, he, indeed, is thy most valued helper, O Mazda Ahura!—Yasna, 31–22

It is, in fact, of supreme moment to us that the human world is in an incessant state of war between that which will save us and that which will drag us into the abyss of disaster. Our one hope lies in the fact that Ahura Mazda is on our side if we choose the right course. The law of warfare is severe in its character; it allows no compromise. 'None of you,' says Zarathushtra, 'shall find the doctrine and precepts of the wicked; because thereby he will bring grief and death in his house and village, in his land and people! No, grip your sword and cut them down!'—Yasna, xxxi, 18.

Such a relentless attitude of fight reminds us of the Old Testament spirit. The active heroic aspect of this religion reflects the character of the people themselves, who later on spread their conquests far and wide and built up great empires by the might of their sword. They accepted this world in all seriousness. They had zest in life and confidence in their own strength. They belonged to the western half of Asia, and their great influence travelled through the neighbouring civilization of India and towards the Western Continent. Their ideal was the ideal of the fighter. By the force of their will and deed of sacrifice they were to conquer *haurvatat,* welfare in this world, and *ameratat,* immortality in the other. This is the best ideal of the West, the great truth of fight. For Paradise has to be gained through conquest. That sacred task is for the heroes, who are to take the right side in the battle and the right weapons.

1924

THE CASE FOR INDIA

We have recently heard a proposal to segregate the Indian population in some Christian Commonwealth of South Africa. It is a plan to smother their self-respect under the cover of political untouchability.

India has been suffering from such segregation of her personality for a long period of foreign subjection. She is exiled in a dimness of insignificance. Not only is she ostracized by her rulers from human relationships with themselves, but under a prolonged primitive condition of indecorous indigence she is ignored by the community of nations. This is the worst calamity that can happen to any country when before the modern lidless gaze of publicity all peoples are exposed to each other's view. If India were completely concealed and forgotten she could bear it much more easily than now when she is pilloried before the world public in her unkempt poverty, illiteracy, fierce stupidity of fanaticism and all variety of ragged wretchedness which inevitably follows the lack of education and negligence from an unsympathetic overlordship.

It is easy to be unjust to those whose existence is blurred by privations of all kinds, who are made inexpressive, inarticulate. There can be no question that the minds of the vast masses in India remain muffled under an appalling ignorance and destitution, and this remediable fact is too often exploited in order to classify them as eternal victims to others whose prosperity must be maintained by a perpetual parasitism upon these repressed races. I have more than once had the occasion to notice an outburst of irritation even from some Americans at the idea of India ever dreaming of political severance of British connection. It costs them nothing to think that we Indians are innately and immutably different from themselves and that it would be annoyingly absurd for us to aspire after the same human rights for which they once had fought against their own brothers. Such an attitude of contempt we helplessly bear through our suppressed opportunity of self-expression, because we have been forced too long to dwell fettered in an oppressively narrow cell of closed prospects.

I do not wish to go into details about the elementary needs of our people which it is the moral obligation of a civilized government to provide, the needs of adequate education, sanitation, medical help and economic well-being. I take this opportunity merely to emphasize the greatest of all our needs, which is to remind ourselves and others that this universal degradation in India is not inevitably founded upon an inborn incapacity of the race. The dark facts of our bankruptcy are evident to any casual visitor, but the truth which is permanent in the spirit of the people must be explored in the history of our past. A critical search should be made to find out the nature of the accidents that are responsible for the present condition of the country which once had the dangerous reputation of a fabulous wealth attracting round her treasure-house adventurers from distant shores.

This is what Will Durant has taken the trouble to attempt in his book *The Case for India*. Once when travelling meant real trouble strange countries gradually yielded themselves to be properly known. The comfortable method of touring today is like hastily gorging one's meals without mastication, ignoring the necessary process of taste and digestion. Geographical experiences have become thinned into shadow pictures and the modern means of publicity have enabled the purveyors of superficial unrealities to ply their trade with too great ease.

But our author has taken the trouble to know. The miserable condition of the country he has seen with his own eyes; but, what is rare with most tourists, he has explored the history of our misfortune. Will Durant has treated us with the respect due to human beings, acknowledging our right to serious consideration. This has come to me as a surprise, for such courtesy is extremely rare today to those people who have not the power to make themselves obnoxious. When I was young, we had a romantic vision of the West, which still revealed its soul in the last glow of the illumination of the French revolution. It was the chivalrous West which trained the enthusiasm of its knights errant ready to take upon themselves the cause of the oppressed, of those who suffered from the miserliness of their fate. And we felt certain that the special mission of the Western civilization was to bring emancipation of all kinds to all races in the world. Though the West came to our share as a cunning tradesman, it brought with it also the voice of Burke and a literature whose background was majestic and which claimed justice for all humanity. The atmosphere of that century was generous with the young hope of man. But the tradesman has triumphed at last and the spirit of chivalry loudly laughed to extinction. From this inhospitable age of the overgrown national worldliness, which everywhere outside Soviet Russia is in idolatrous awe of material power we have long ceased to expect justice, we of an alien continent brought to the altar of power as sacrifice. And I repeat once again that I was surprised when I noticed in Will Durant's book a poignant note of pain at the suffering and indignity of the people who are not his kindred, an indignant desire to be just to the defeated race whose own voice is low within the solitary cell of its obscurity. I know that the author will have a small chance of reward in popularity from his readers and his book may even run the risk of being proscribed to us, not having the indecency to deal with an unwholesome calumny against the people who are already humiliated by their own evil fortune. But he, I am sure, has his noble compensation in upholding the best tradition of the West in its championship of freedom and fair play. I am specially thankful to him for the service he has rendered to the English nation by largely quoting from its own members the condemnation of British policy where it has cruelly betrayed its responsibility to India; for after my recent disillusionment I sadly need confirmation of the faith I still wish to maintain in the raw magnanimity of soul in those who are the true representatives of this great race.

1931

VOICELESS INDIA

In her *Voiceless India,* Miss Emerson has amply proved that she has her own natural right of a sensitive mind to come to a people who happen to be foreign to her and in judging whom she has done herself justice. The bond of kinship that prevails within a community not only protects it from wanton cruelty and injustice from inside but is the natural nerve channel through which we directly feel our own race in its entirety. But the stranger from outside can easily be unjust, owing to the fact that he has not to pay for his conduct in his own feeling and be checked by that deeper sensibility which goes directly beyond the miscellany of facts into the heart of a living unity. And for the sake of his own benefit and others' safety he must bring with him his inner light of imagination, so that he may feel truth and not merely know facts. It is fully evident that Miss Emerson is gifted with this rare faculty, that she has realized a complete vision of an alien life by making it her own.

It is a very hard trial for a Western woman to have to spend long lonely months in an environment where most things conspire to hurt the modern taste and standard of living. The author of this book did not choose the comfortable method of picking up information from behind a lavish bureaucratic hospitality, under a revolving electric fan, and in an atmosphere of ready-made official opinions. For the materials of the present book she did not move about among the upper circle of the modern sophisticated India where communication was through her own language and tendencies of mind were not wholly unfamiliar to her. She boldly took it upon herself unaided to enter a region of our life, all but unexplored by the Western tourists, which had the one great advantage, in spite of its difficulties, that it offered no other path open to the writer but that of sharing the life of the people. In fact, in this adventure of hers she followed the examples of the true born travellers of the golden age of travelling when the pilgrims across the seas and mountains did not carry with them their own mental and physical habits—the barricading aloofness of their own race and culture.

And I can easily imagine what the author had to pay for her experience, not in money but in a part of her life itself. The constant toll that a pitiless climate exacts from our vitality for the barest privilege of living, the mean tyrannies of the tropics that often cause desperate discomforts and, what is worse, a perpetual state of subconscious irritation in our mind, are enough provocation for a foreigner to make him unreasonably vengeful in his judgment and language. There is no sign of that in Miss Emerson's writings, not even of a temptation to be superciliously funny at any awkwardness of the simple village folk among whom she lived. These villages had no allurements of the romantic India, incomprehensibly mystic in her ritualism, or ineffably grand in her relics and ruins. The background of life they had was dull and drab, with no lurid fascination of vice so important for making its detailed descriptions gratifying to some readers in their search for a vicarious enjoyment under the cover of moral indignation. All this has given an opportunity to disclose the personality of the writer herself, not only through the intellectual sanity displayed in this book, but, what is more precious, in her depth of human sympathy.

She never idealised, not even for the sake of literary flourishes, any aspects of the village life to which she was so intimately close. She never minimised the primitive crudities of its features, things that were stupid, ungainly, superstitious, or even evil in their moral ugliness, but her narration, in spite of its unmitigated truth, never hurts, because all through it runs the gracious touch of the woman, the pure instinct of sympathy which, while it bares and handles the sores, is yet tender to them. And these unfortunate Indian villages, deserted by their own capable men, neglected with scant notice by their politicians, cruelly ignored by their government, dumbly suffering unspeakable miseries, putting all the blame upon their inexorable fate, bent down to the dust by the load of indignities, deprived of education, sanitary or medical help, living upon a pitifully meagre ration of food that has hardly any nutrition, and a scant supply of water full of microbic menace—they need a true woman's heart to give them voice, for they are like children in their utter helplessness disowned by their parents.

What Miss Emerson has discovered concerning the poverty of the Indian village, causing it to sink down under the weight of a land tax too heavy to be borne, has been openly acknowledged, to their credit, by a small band of Indian civilians who have been obliged to administer the system which they saw actually crushing the poor. Sir William Hunter said many years ago: 'The Government assessment does not leave enough food to the cultivator to support himself and his family throughout the year.' Sir Henry Cotton and Sir William Wedderburn, both high officials, have confessed the same unpalatable truth. More recently still, Mr. C.J. O'Donnel, who held in his own day one of the chief administrative positions in the Government of India, has declared: "It makes little difference to three hundred million Indian peasants what the Simon Commission may recommend, but I fear that the *ryot* will remain 'the most pathetic figure in the British Empire'; for 'his masters have ever been unjust to him, and Christendom will have one more failure to its discredit'."

I feel personally grateful to Miss Emerson for the masterly picture she has drawn of our pathetic village life, so vivid and yet sober in its colour—the honest colour of truth; for I myself have spent some part of my youth in its neighbourhood and have made it my mission with all my inadequate individual resources to befriend them who are friendless, who are eternal tenants in an extortionate world having nothing of their own.

1930

CHRIST

Dear Charlie,

I have read your book on Christ. It made me think. The mode of self-expression in a Christian life is in love which works, in that of a Hindu it is in love which contemplates, enjoys the spiritual emotion as an end in itself. The attitude of mind that realizes the superhuman in a human setting has rendered a great service to civilization, just as its perversion has been the cause of an awful and widespread mischief. You know, how all through my life, my idea of the divine has concentrated in Man the Eternal and I find that in your own religious experience. You have the same idea centred in a concrete historic personality. Evidently it strongly helps you in the realization of perfection in your life and it must be a source of unfailing consolation to you to be able to feel in your constant love a divine comradeship in Christ. The mental and physical energy stored up for ages in your western constitution urges you to activities that are saved from aberration when they are related to a living centre of Truth. Instances of heroic devotion and unselfish sacrifice springing from that source are most valuable for us in order to keep us firm in the faith in the abiding truth in the immortal. And I know you have been of help to your fellow beings not merely for some individual benefits that you may have rendered them but for a direct inspiration that gives us certainly of the ultimate greatness of Man.

With love.

1932

REBEL INDIA

'Rebel India' is an eminently honest book which can only be written by a type of Englishman with whom we are least familiar in India. I cannot doubt that there must be a number of such men among those who have made it their task to rule this country or are employed here in various other capacities. I only wish, for the sake of their own nation, that such individuals could be clearly discerned by us through the unhuman atmosphere which densely envelops them, blurring their features into a herd uniformity.

During my last visit in England I was assured by a responsible member of Parliament that the Englishman may be wanting in imagination, but it should never be doubted that he is honest. I am sure he was right, but it is necessary, specially in the present moment, that this fact should be completely evident to us who can hardly have opportunity of studying this people in their natural environment. It is needless to say that the quality of honesty undergoes its hardest trial where self-interest is concerned not merely that of an individual but of one's own nation. The tremendous pressure of expediency in the cause of nationalism too often effects deviation of character from the moral orbit which an honourable man follows in all other calls of life even at the risk of hurt and loss.

Generally speaking, the background of an Englishman's activities in India in his pursuit of personal gain or administration of the country, intimately represents his national self-interest, which very often does not coincide with the vital interest of the land of his exile. Lacking most other incentives and outlets for his energy in the direction of a great social life, multitudinous in its ideals and claims, he intensely cultivates an imperialistic worldliness which can never be honest and just in its relation to those whom it must exploit for its maintenance. Every individual Englishman in India, be he a planter, station master, shop assistant, dentist or hotel keeper, head clerk of a merchant office, whatever may be his character, culture and capacity, cannot help being strongly obsessed by a sense of almost personal ownership with regard to India. As an Englishman he meets everywhere in this country with special concession and consideration to which he is not accustomed among his own people and which he can never naturally claim for any uncommon gift of his own. Everything in India every moment encourages in him a dangerously exaggerated consciousness of superiority and of political overlordship merely owing to the accident of his birth. No wonder that it completely damages the mind and character of the average man who belongs to the vast majority of the mediocre. It was in 1878 that I first came to England, and I remember how I was often told by my English friends that the retired Anglo-Indians as a rule were intolerable. Evidently in those days the normal type of Englishman was fundamentally different from those who had eaten India's salt for any length of time. But in the meanwhile India has been taking her revenge and gradually saturating the atmosphere of English character with the noxious exhalations that rise from unresisting humiliation of humanity.

And, therefore, what surprises me in this book is the perfect honesty of the author in his description and discussion of things he has noticed during his tour in India, the unpleasant sights and happenings that were not creditable to his own people.

The unnatural relation of the race of the rulers to that of the ruled, representing the subjection of an entire country made profitable to an entire nation living aloof across an enormous distance, must kill moral probity because it kills human sympathy.

Very few individuals can be expected to resist the moral contamination which such imperialistic parasitism must engender and nowhere is the tragedy of fine minds succumbing to the insidious poison of racial arrogance made more evident than amongst the Englishman in India whose self-lowered prestige must at all costs be preserved by military power. One waits in vain therefore for a voice of protest from this privileged community against the unsympathetic treatment that is being meted out in their name and with their cognizance to a people whom they know to be defenceless and whose most pitifully human claims must needs be ignored by the impersonal spirit of law and order. Moral integrity with regard to its hapless victims is an unnecessary item in the make up of a commercial policy whose ambition is to reap dividends with the maximum of speed and comfort.

'Rebel India', I repeat, is an honest book. Reading it I feel encouraged to hope that individual Englishman in our land will emulate his attitude of sober judgment and, no matter how inconvenient it may be to do so, dare face facts as they really are today in India.

1933

PREFACE TO 'DELIVERANCE'

The early epoch of Bengali prose suggests its parallel in the beginning of the biological age on this earth when its animal creations were cumbersome in their gait, lacking in a rhythm submissive to life. Though the time is not remote, yet it seems to us belonging almost to a pre-historic period of evolution when Bengali prose painfully struggled on with its a dynamic grammar and vocabulary containing words that were mostly inert and colourless. Our own growing intimacy with the modern European mind and its manner of expression reacted upon our language giving it more and more freedom of movement and pliancy in its functions. During a remarkably rapid course of self-discovery it has developed the courage to be able to cross the orthodox enclosure of a pseudoclassical form of literature rigid in its ceremonialism. This freedom has brought our fiction close to the everyday life of the people, a large section of which was formerly shunned as untouchable in our domain of culture. The latest of the leaders who, through this path of liberation, has guided Bengali novels nearer to the spirit of modern world literature is Saratchandra Chatterji. He has imparted a new power to our language and in his stories has shed the light of a fresh vision upon the too familiar region of Bengal's heart, revealing the living significance of the obscure trifles in people's personality. He has achieved the best reward of a novelist: he has completely won the hearts of Bengali readers.

1940

WHEN PEACOCKS CALLED

In an age of fratricide, aided by intellectual dehumanization in large areas of the world, it is difficult to restore the calm air so necessary for the realization of great human ideals. Hilda Seligman has chosen in her book to reveal the organization side of a great humanism, which came with King Asoka of India. My good thoughts go with the author in her venture to present ancient India through its message which has a perennially modern significance.

1940

1949

CONVERSATIONS AND INTERVIEWS

MARGUERITE WILKINSON AND TAGORE

'I have heard that your poems are often sung, and chanted by the people of your country', said I, 'that is true, is it not?'

'Yes', he (Tagore) said, 'it is true. Our people love poetry. I know villagers in my neighbourhood, who after their day's work in the field, gather under the stars before some hut and sing in chorus till midnight devotional songs belonging to the best lyrical literature of their language.'

'If the people enjoy singing your poems is it because they are like folk poetry?'

'Some of my poems are like folk poetry,' said Dr. Tagore, 'but some are in the romantic style and some in the classical style.'

'The music that goes with them is your own music, is it not?'

'Yes.'

'Can you tell me something about it?'

'It is difficult to do that because it is not at all like your Western music. When I first went to England I was taken to hear a great singer—she had been in opera. I could not understand why people found her singing beautiful. To me it was strange—imitative—I did not like it. But I said to myself, "If so many people think it is beautiful, and such intelligent people, I will try to understand." And so I studied the Western music and I have found much to admire in it. But your people will not study our music. When they come to India and do not like it at once they will not try to understand....'

I could readily believe that the Americans with money enough to travel to India would not be the ones to stop and study the music or art of Bengal long and faithfully. Our intolerance, where it existed in this connection, might readily be the result of the pressure of our practical occidental lives upon us, or of our breathless haste. Just why English musicians should not be interested in Indian music I do not know.

'When you make a poem and music for it do you make the verbal and musical melodies together? Or does the music come first, so that you fit words to it, or the words, so that you fit music to them?'

'Sometimes I make the words first and then put music with them later. Sometimes I make a melody first and then put words with it. Sometimes the music is subordinated to the words. Sometimes the words are subordinated to music.'

'How does this method affect your rhythms?'

'They are always changed. Anything new added always changes what was before. It is like colour added to the lines of a picture. When you add melody to words the rhythm is changed.'

'Yet you do not change the emotional key—a love song remains in the same mood, or a lament for a dead friend retains the spirit of sorrow even when the new element is added.'

Dr. Tagore gave assent at once.

'The new thing that is added—it is not alien,' he said.

'You believe, then, that either in a poem or in a song, rhythm always means something, is always intimately related to the emotion expressed?'

Dr. Tagore seemed to think that rhythm would have no value otherwise.

'Where', I asked him, 'do the poets of your country find their rhythms? Do they get them out of rhetorics?'

He laughed gently and shook his head.

'Before me', he said, 'they went much to the rhetorics. I have set them free.'

'Where do your own rhythms come from?'

'From the subconscious' he said, 'like a spring bubbling out of the earth.'

'Will you tell me something of the kinds of rhythm you have in your language!'

'We have many kinds of rhythm, a great rhythmical variety. Our words have no individual idiosyncrasies, no accent of their own to be respected, as English words have. In that our language is more like French. Many rhythmical bars that are rare or quite impossible in English are common with us. We have a four-syllable bar and five-syllable bar.'

'Where does the verse-accent come?'

'On the first syllable, usually. It is like the ebbing away of the breath, a bar of one of these rhythms—the full breath at the beginning—then the renewal at the beginning of the next bar.'

Dr. Tagore then kindly recited a few lines from one of his poems written with four-syllable to the bar. The rhythmical effect was very beautiful. While he was reciting I noticed that his finger, lying on the table, beat the time of the rests at the end of the line. Evidently the poets of Bengal know that time is time in silence just as much as in sound. At this moment we were interrupted and I went away with the memory of that gently wavering rhythm, 'like the ebbing away of the breath', but clearly marked from bar to bar and line to line, wishing that I could have heard many more of these poems in the language which I did not understand, yet found so clearly musical.

1921

BENEDETTO CROCE AND TAGORE

Poet: I am sorry to have troubled you to have come to Rome, but I could not leave Italy without seeing you. I would have been ashamed to have returned to India without meeting you. I did not know you were in Naples, otherwise I would certainly have seen you there.

Croce: The pleasure is all mine in having been able to come to see you. You do not know how much I admire your poetry. Not only for its thoughts, but for its sober form—as we Italians call it—its classical form. This is quite different from our ideas of oriental poetry which we usually think of as steeped in fancies.

Poet: And I am an admirer of your philosophy and your literary criticism. Your "Poetry and not-Poetry," which I read in English translation, appeared to me as a very concise and yet full treatment of the subject.

Croce: My idea of divinity is similar to yours: God is not a being amongst beings, but the Being of Beings.

Poet: That is exactly my idea.

Croce: Not to divide the world into two water-tight compartments: material and spiritual, but to see the working of the spirit in the totality of the two,—the idea has found expression in your thoughts: in a perfect form.

Poet: I believe your Italian mind is synthetic; you see things in their integral aspect.

Croce: Italian genius is something mid-way between the French and the German. It possesses the analytic subtlety of the French, and also the comprehensive character, which is sometimes apt to become confused, of the German. The Italian mentality seeks to reach profundity, but at the same time demands clearness.

Poet: This is a great asset. If this is so, then your country is the fit place for a synthesis of Western Science and Eastern Philosophy. We look at Italy as a country where something new in the field of culture is developing, and we want to grasp it and take it back with us.

Croce: That is true. During the twenty years before the war, there was a new cultural movement in Italy. The confusion caused by the world war has, to a certain extent, arrested this development. But I think this temporary suspension, rather than damaging it, may have beneficial results. The scattered seeds will bury themselves in the ground and will render good fruit in the future.

Poet: The Western civilization, for which we had one time great reverence, is showing a tendency to give great reverence to the things that are of the outside world. This is a unilateral development and is causing the loss of a good deal of the prestige which it had in the East. The development of elements which have reference to the inner life is also necessary.

Croce: Yes, it is true, but the external things must not be rejected. They cannot be isolated, they must be permitted by idealism. The most difficult thing is to unite the Oriental and the Occidental attitudes of mind: to look upon ideas as facts and upon facts as ideas.

Poet: In the Visva-Bharati in India we are trying to form a centre where the greatest minds of this age can come and meet. I would be happy if you would come once and join us.

Croce: I sincerely hope it will be possible some day. In the meantime let me take the liberty of sending you my works, but at present I do not wish to trouble you any longer.

1926

ROMAIN ROLLAND AND TAGORE

I. VILLENEUVE

The talk turned to Goethe and European literature of the 18th century. Rolland was speaking enthusiastically about Weimar. He said that in order to catch the spirit of Goethe, one must go to Weimar which retained something of the harmony of Goethe's spirit. Goethe had lived in other places but the inward significance of his life could not be appreciated without visiting Weimar.

Rolland then began speaking about the music of the 18th century. He asked: 'Have you heard anything of Gluck? He lived in the 18th century. Among modern European composers he has the largest amount of what I may call the Greek feeling, retaining in music only what was serene and beautiful, and eliminating with austere severity everything that was superfluous. Before him European music was something like medieval Gothic architecture. It possessed great exuberance of spirit, but was apt to get lost in a mass of details. The reform accomplished by Gluck at the end of the 18th century, just before the outbreak of the French Revolution, was coming back to pure line and pure form. He was a German, or rather a Bohemian, who lived much in France where he was well appreciated.'

Tagore: I have always felt the immense power of your European music. I love Beethoven and also Bach. I must confess, it takes a good deal of time to understand and thoroughly appreciate the idiom of your music. As a young boy I heard European music being played on the piano; much of it I found attractive, but I could not enter fully into the spirit of the thing. Do the different countries of Europe have peculiar features of their own in their music? For example, has Italian music any special characteristics? Is the general spirit different from that of German music?

Rolland: Very different indeed. A good deal of modern European music had originally come from Italy but became completely changed in its development. In the south the music has more beauty, but as you go to the north it becomes more and more complex. In the old Italian music of the 16th century you find delicate lines and shades, and the beauty of melody is prominent; in the north there is more emotion. Among modern composers Puccini has great gifts but lacks in taste, and I think modern Italian music is rather spoiled and extravagant. In old Italy the composer and poet were both seeking for purity.

After some more discussion about music, Tagore said: 'I want to ask you a question. The purpose of art is not to give expression to emotion but to use it for the creation of significant form. Literature is not the direct expression of any emotion. Emotion only supplies the occasion which makes it possible to bring forth the creative act. A Grecian urn is not the representation of any particular emotion which is at all important: but it gives form to some definite urge of the artist's mind. In European music I find, however, that an attempt is sometimes made to give expression to particular emotions. Is this desirable? Should not music also use emotion as material only, and not as an end in itself?'

Rolland: A great musician must always use emotion as substance out of which beautiful forms are created. But in Europe musicians have had such an abundance of good material that they tended to over-emphasise the emotional aspects. A great musician must have poise, for without it his work perishes.

Tagore: Take the opera *Il Traviata.* Is it not too definite? Does it not try to describe everything in too definite terms?

Rolland: Yes, it is a defect of our music, especially since the beginning of the 19th century, after the romantic work of Beethoven was written and particularly after Wagner.

Tagore: In India we have the other extreme. The singer often takes too much liberty with the music. In pictures and in literature the outward form is fixed, at music requires for its interpretation the human voice; even in instrumental music you have the human hand which is very flexible. The singer must therefore be a true artist and not merely an artisan. In India the composer has to depend a great deal on the finger to make the music complete by his rendering, but unfortunately the singer often overshadows the composer by his own variations.

Rolland: This was also the state of affairs in Europe at the time of Handel. In old Italian music, interpretation was left to the singers, the composers always leaving many things indefinite. In the popular comedies of Italy the music given by the composer was simply a kind of sketch. The player improvised, filled in, and often sang extempore, sometimes to the accompaniment of the composer. Every time both songs and music were different, and a good deal has naturally vanished.

Tagore: That is a characteristic of music, much of it vanishes. A good deal depends on the singer; its medium is a living channel.

Rolland: In those days singers were terrible tyrants, especially in the south. In the north we had greater precision; the northern tradition is to have things as definite as possible.

Tagore: Yes, that also is necessary. Your modern music is now well organized and harmony keeps the music pure, free from adulteration and counterfeits, as the currency of a country is kept pure by the mints.

Rolland: But don't you think it is only music which is petrified that can be kept pure in this way? Music which is living cannot be kept completely unchanged.

After some time Tagore said: 'You know, I am not merely a writer of verse; I am keenly interested in music and I myself compose songs. I have always felt puzzled why there are such great differences in musical form in different countries. Surely music should be more universal than other forms of art, for its vehicle is easy to reproduce and transmit from one country to another.'

Rolland: In every country music passes through several stages. The differences observed at any particular time may possibly be due to a difference of the particular stage of development. Music has its childhood, growth, and decay. The first song of emotion finds expression through a form which is scarcely adequate, then comes a perfect harmony between emotion and external form, and finally a certain formalization, a stereotyping and decay. If life continues, a new overflow and a new cycle begins again.

Tagore: It is the same in every form of art; in literature also we find that a new urge creates its own form. After some time a form which was once new becomes old and worn through constant usage and is no longer adequate.

Rolland: Yes, and so with life also. We have the eternal flow from form to form.

Tagore: Master-minds create new forms. Then come men without gift who imprison art in rusty fetters, and a time comes for breaking through bonds again.

Rolland: In Europe we are in the last phase: we feel we are imprisoned in a cage.

Tagore: Yes, perhaps you have become too intellectualised; everything which is vital and humane is getting killed.

Rolland: There is a tendency for our whole life to degenerate into a huge mechanical organization.

Tagore: Its signs are appearing everywhere over the face of your beautiful old Europe. We find everywhere the same mask, monotonous and devoid of beauty. The Italian cities which I visited are all becoming too modern in their appearance. But Florence was beautiful; the people there retained a certain detachment of mind which appealed to me very strongly. Without this detachment the life of art cannot exist.

Rolland: Yes, they still have a more rustic side to their life. Lately, Florentines have been looking back to their ancestors. This is probably the secret of Florence being a great artistic centre.

The talk took a lighter turn as tea was brought in. We all came out on the balcony. There was a brilliant glow in the west, but a little cloud came up. A few birds were singing in the neighbouring trees. The poet came back to the subject that they had been discussing a little earlier.

Tagore: I first heard European songs when I was 17-year old, during my first visit to London. The artist was Milson, who used to have a great reputation in those days. He sang nature-songs, giving imitation of birds' cries, a kind of mimicry, which appeared extremely ludicrous to me. Music should capture the delight of birds' songs, giving human form to the joy with which a bird sings. But it should not try to be a representation of such songs. Take the Indian rain-songs. They do not try to imitate the sound of falling raindrops. They rekindle the joy of rain-festivals, and convey something of the feeling associated with the rainy season. Somehow the songs of springtime do not have the same depth; I do not know why.

Rolland: When are your spring festivals held?

Tagore: In Bengal towards the end of February and in early March when the southern spring-breeze begins to blow; the days are hot while nights are cool and pleasant. This is also the season for the peasant to start work in the field. Is it purely association which gives beauty to the rain-songs? Or is it something which is really inherent in them? It is true that we get accustomed to hear rain-melodies more frequently in the rainy season; it is possible, these tunes bring back to our mind the joy and delight of the rainy season itself. But then the spring and summer melodies possess equally strong associations and yet they do not stir us so profoundly.

Rolland: Perhaps the melodies themselves have peculiar differences.

Tagore: In poetry a particular word possesses a subtle atmosphere of its own literary associations. The peculiar value of such words will never be intelligible to foreigners; they cannot be appreciated as being supremely beautiful by merely listening to them, or even by merely understanding their literal meaning, for the association will be lacking. In English take the following lines from Keats:

> .... magic casement opening on the foam
>
> Of perilous seas, in faery lands forlorn.

If I translate it into Bengali, it would become meaningless; it would have no significance for Bengali readers: '...magic casement, opening on the foam of perilous seas, in faery lands forlorn.' The phrases lack in living association to our people. Similarly it is possible that a certain clause, a certain grouping of notes, gradually acquires a value through growth of association. We may have musical phrases acquiring new values like words in literature through long continued usage.

Rolland: This kind of image formation occurs in European music, for example, in Bach whose careful phrasings have been carefully studied. Much of the beauty of his music is due to the use of certain musical forms which he borrowed from the earlier music of the 17th and 18th centuries and which he used effectively with the instinct of a genius. In pastoral music, certain groupings are used continually which are even now in vogue. If these particular groupings are used in non-pastoral music, even then they would create an atmosphere of pastoral life. It is probable that your associations of rain-songs are also brought about in the same way.

Rolland was much interested in Indian music and asked many questions. 'What are your chief instruments?'

Tagore: The *Vina* which gives extremely pure notes: it has not the flexibility of the violin, but preserves the purity of our melodies in a characteristic way.

He was still thinking about the suggestiveness of literature and came back to Keats.

Tagore: Although Keats cannot be translated into Bengali, I can understand the beauty of his poems. We lack the proper associations to start with, but after some familiarity with the ideals and with some knowledge of the surroundings in which these poems were written, we also can acquire the facility of appreciating them. So in spite of individual or geographical peculiarities of form, there is something which is universal in poetry. It requires education and also the growth of familiarity, but, given these things, poetry can be appreciated by every one. Similarly, what is pleasant to the European ear must have something in it which is universal. Indian music also must have an appeal to foreigners who have the necessary training.

Rolland: Yes, after getting away from the part which is merely superficial or fashionable. Certain peculiarities belong only to the surface which reflect the passing fancy of a particular time.

Tagore: In pictures, or in plastic art, the material consists of the representation of things which are in a way familiar to most people and can easily be apprehended by every one. But phrases in music are not familiar; so when we build up an architecture of music the whole thing appears fantastic to a foreigner. This is why it is much more difficult for a foreigner to understand foreign music than to appreciate foreign art.

After a little while, the poet went on to speak about the sources of inspiration in art and literature.

Tagore: The starting point for all arts, poetry, painting or music, is the breath, the rhythm which is inherent in the human body and which is the same everywhere, and is therefore universal. I believe musicians must often be inspired by the rhythm of the circulation of blood or breath. A very interesting study would be a comparison of four tunes of different countries. With more developed music things become more complex, and the underlying similarities cannot be systematically traced.

24 June 1926

II. VILLEUVE

Tagore: I want to tell you about my Italian visit. In India I was full of hesitation whether I should come to Italy at all. In an Italian steamer in which I came I had a long talk with the captain. He was full of admiration for Mussolini and fascism. He told me how things in Italy had changed for the better during the last few years. My Italian friends in India had also said the same thing. On my arrival in Rome I met the French ambassador. He and others all said that Mussolini had saved Italy from utter ruin. I said that that was not the most important thing. I was however trying to understand their point of view. They all agreed in thinking that during the great war something had happened which made Italian people extremely undisciplined. They all confessed to something in the Italian people which was against order and self-government. They said that those who cannot govern themselves must be governed by some external agency. If a large majority of people themselves confess that they have lost the capacity for self-government or self-control, it seems reasonable to admit that a different course would become applicable in their case. Then I saw Mussolini. In certain ways he has a striking appearance and I thought that his personality may have had a direct appeal to the Italian people. I tried to reconcile the whole situation in the following way.

With the tremendous growth of science you have become in almost everything, Government or State, like everything else in Europe, impersonal. The great advance of science gave you the power to create machineries of all kinds and

Europe thought that the human factor can be eliminated in machinery. In fact, as machinery was supposed to be absolutely free from mistakes, it was thought that society could be saved better by mechanical organization than by human personalities; but the great danger is that if something goes wrong with the machine there is an immediate deadlock. Owing to the great war the social and administrative body in Europe broke down and there was great misery; the people who suffered cried for help and found that they could not get any help from machines but had to depend on individuals. If at this stage somebody comes forward with a forceful personality and announces that he has saved them, then the people naturally accept him as their saviour; specially when they saw that Mussolini succeeded in clearing away the wreckage of the parliamentary machine and substituted his word as law. The common people, in spite of all their weakness, are human beings. The personality of Mussolini could not but have a great effect on them, specially at a time when they had lost faith in their old mechanical contrivances.

Rolland: The question is whether it would be worth-while to lose one's reason in order to live.

Tagore: It all depends on the actual facts. A situation may come about in which a temporary surrender of one's initiative may be welcome. I was told that Italy had become a land of lunatics. It was the best that could happen for the people themselves to put the whole country under the control of a masterful personality who alone could bring back order. Once this was achieved, they could hope for higher things to come back in time. I have been told that this is what actually happened. Mussolini has succeeded in bringing back law and order to the people. Now they are prosperous and happy, in fact far better than they were just after the war. I am told that formerly peaceful citizens could not go out without weapons and ran the risk of being assassinated and looted at any moment. One thing is now changed, that foreigners can now travel with security in every part in Italy and I was assured that all this was due to the forceful personality of Mussolini.

Duke Scottie in Milan told me that his mouth is shut. My guide Formichi told me that Duke Scottie was an incorrigible anti-Fascist. While I had been talking with the Duke, from time to time he got extremely nervous so that I did not get an opportunity of having a quiet talk with the Duke.

Rolland: The most undesirable thing to my mind is that nobody could speak out. I realize the difficulties of the situation in Italy. England, France and Italy were the three countries which had given the parliamentary system a trial on a big scale. England is in a very fortunate position because her parliamentary education began centuries ago and a sound, reliable civic consciousness has steadily grown up and matured. When parliamentarism is in danger, voluntary organizations simultaneously spring up to defend it and lend their support. This has made political conditions in England extremely suitable. In France love of liberty is strong among the individuals but there is very little organization. They cannot resist effectively the encroachment on the liberties of the people. They submit easily. In Italy it is still worse. There is very little initiative among the populace; they submit to the least sort of organized force. In the case of France I have myself known many critical periods. I remember in 1877 General Boulanger was almost on the point of becoming the Dictator of France. If he had shown a little more initiative he would certainly have become the Dictator. Most of the people were Republicans, but they would have failed to resist him. My own brother was at a Teachers Training School where everybody was Republican. Many of them wanted to issue a manifesto protesting against Boulanger, but out of about 130 only 8 actually signed and the rest were afraid, although the Dictator was not actually in power. They were afraid of their future.

I believe the same thing, or still worse, is actually happening in Italy. In reality only a small group of Fascists, very ardent, very sincere, have got power. I have lived in

Italy for a long time and my own impression is that the people are extremely undisciplined. The very huge crowd which immensely admires Mussolini today would crush him tomorrow if he shows the least weakness. I remember them shouting *Viva Crespi* one day and break his statue the next day. I have seen them breaking the doors of the French embassy one day and threaten the German legation the next day. Mussolini will remain in power so long as he is absolutely *in form* and strong. If he shakes a little the whole country will rapidly turn against him.

I feel sorry that a large number of ardent idealists who are followers of Mazzini were prevented from speaking to you in Italy. A young Italian came to see me. He had started several philanthropic and educational institutions before the war and had gathered a group of teachers, but all this was broken up as he had not subscribed to Fascism and would not agree to the instruction of the Fascist organization in his own institution. He saw the Minister of Education himself and asked the Minister, 'Do you want me to lose my soul?' To that the Minister replied, 'It is written in the Gospel that you must lose your soul to win it.' And he said he could not advise any teacher to help him with the work of the institution, for it would be over with him immediately. I have heard the same song from Dr Salvamini, the great historian of Mazzini and Italian liberty. He had to leave Italy and settle in England, which also was only possible because he had some private fortune. Mussolini has issued a decree under which exiles from Italy lose their rights of citizenship and their properties in Europe are confiscated. I have also seen Fascist papers writing editorials about the 'sacred' murder of Salvamini.

A young man of about twenty-five came to see me from Milan. He was a delegate who spoke as a representative of the people. He told me: 'We have suffered physical oppression but the greater oppression was that our mouths were forcibly shut. I have come to talk to you so that you may tell Tagore.' The young man went to Germany. I shall try to put you in touch with him.

I realize fully how the present dominance of the Fascist has come about. The political crisis after the war was aggravated by the failure of the socialists who proved doubly unfit for governing the country. I recognize that the seizure of power by Mussolini was inevitable. It was a logical necessity. Conditions in Italy at that time were somewhat similar to those in France at the end of the 18th century when Bonaparte came to prominence. A great deal depends upon the man but even Napoleon has done greater harm to France than good. I believe Italy is in a much worse condition, because Mussolini has not got the personality of Napoleon. The people of Italy are more impulsive and Mussolini is playing with fire. He is constantly speaking against foreign governments and is insisting on the patriotic ambition of his countrymen. When he speaks to big gatherings and asks, 'To whom does Nice belong, to whom does Savoy belong?' they all shout together 'To us.' He is rousing them and he is appealing to their hatred of other nations. I have no doubt that he is the greatest menace to the whole of Europe.

25 June 1926

III

Tagore: Do you think that Geneva is likely to play an important role in the world of international relationship?

Rolland: It may, but a good deal depends on factors over which Geneva has no control.

Tagore: The League of Nations seems to me to be but one of the various forces which are at work here. At the present moment it is by no means the most instrumental for the readjustment of international relationships. It may or may not develop into a power for bringing greater harmony in the political world. I have much faith in the various international groups and societies and the individuals working in this place, and my hope is that they will eventually create in Geneva a genuine center of international activities which will shape the politics of the future.

Rolland: We find a large number of people eagerly looking for a message from the East. India, they think—and I may add, rightly—is the country that can in this epoch give that message to the world.

Tagore: It is curious to note how India has furnished probably the first internationally minded man of the nineteenth century. I mean Raja Rammohun Roy; he had a passion for truth. He came from an orthodox Brahmin family, but he broke all bonds of superstition and formalism. He wanted to understand Buddhism, went to Tibet, studied Hebrew, Greek, Arabic, Persian, English, French; he traveled widely in Europe, and died in Bristol. Spiritual truth for him did not mean a sort of ecclesiasticism confined within sectarian sanctuaries; nor did he think that it could be inflicted upon people outside the sect by men who have professional rights to preach it as a doctrine. He realized that a bond of spiritual unity links the whole of mankind and that it is the purpose of religion to reach down to that fundamental unity of human relationship, of human efforts and achievements.

Rolland: I have often wondered at the spirit of religious toleration in India; it is unlike anything we have known in the West. The cosmic nature of your religion and the composite character of your civilization make this possible. India has allowed all kinds of religious faith and practice to flourish side by side.

Tagore: Perhaps that has also been our weakness, and it is due to an indiscriminate spirit of toleration that all forms of religious creeds and crudities have run riot in India, making it difficult for us to realize the true foundation of our spiritual faith. The practice of animal sacrifice, for instance, has nothing to do with our religion, yet many people sanction it on the ground of tradition. Similar aberrations of religion can be found in every country. Our concern in India today is to remove them and intensify the larger beliefs which are our true spiritual heritage.

Rolland: In Christian scriptures, too, this theme of animal sacrifice dominates. Take the opening chapters: God gave preference to Abel because he had offered a lamb for sacrifice.

Tagore: I have never been able to love the God of the Old Testament.

Rolland: ... The emphasis is wrongly placed, and the attitude is not spiritual in the larger sense.

Tagore: We should stress always the 'larger sense'. Truth cannot afford to be tolerant where it faces positive evil; it is like sunlight, which makes the existence of evil germs impossible. As a matter of fact, Indian religious life suffers today from the lack of a wholesome spirit of intolerance, which is characteristic of creative religion. Even a vogue of atheism may do good to India today, even though my country will never accept atheism as her permanent faith. It will sweep away all noxious under-growths in the forest, and the tall trees will remain intact. At the present moment even a gift of negation from the West will be of value to a large section of the Indian people.

Rolland: I believe that scientific rationalism will help to solve India's question.

Tagore: I know that India can never believe in mere intellectual determination for any long period of time; balance and harmony will certainly be restored. That is why a temporary swing in one direction may help us to arrive at the central adjustment of spiritual life. Science should come to our aid to be humanized by us at the end.

Rolland: Science is probably the most international element in the modern world; that is, the spirit of co-operation in scientific research. But we have today poison gas at the disposal of politicians. It is tragic that scientists are at the disposal of military powers who are not in the least interested in the progress of human thought and culture.... The problem today is not so much the antagonism of nations as the clash between different classes in the body of a nation itself. This does not, of course, justify or minimize to any degree the real curse of aggressive nationalism and the spirit of war.

Tagore: Words are too conscious; lines are not. Ideas have their form and colour, which wait for their incarnation in pictorial art. Just now painting has become a mania with me. My morning began with songs and poems; now, in the evening of my life, my mind is filled with forms and colours.

1930

SALVADORI AND TAGORE

[*The reports in Italian papers of interviews with Rabindranath Tagore aroused a great deal of concern among Italians in exile in Switzerland, and when the poet was at Zürich he was interviewed by the wife of one of their leaders, Professor Salvadori who was himself too ill to visit Tagore.*]

'You, who are so good,' asked Signora Salvadori, 'why did you come to Italy, now the land of violence and persecution?'

The poet replied:

Tagore: Let me tell you why I came to Italy this time. As you know I had been invited by your people in Milan last year. I was strongly moved when I found that the people loved me and wanted me to be with them for some time. I feel ill, however, and had to return to India before fulfilling my engagements in other towns. I promised to come back in the following summer.

In India the reports of Fascist atrocities reached me from time to time, and I had serious misgivings about coming back to Italy. About this time Professor Formichi came to Santiniketan, bringing with him from Mussolini a wonderful gift of books and a valuable collection of art reproductions for my institution. He also brought an appreciative letter from Mussolini himself. His gift struck me as particularly appropriate for helping us in our work of building up an international institution of fellowship which should be a true centre for the meeting of East and West. The services of Professor Formichi and Dr Tucci which have been lent to us also helped in our work. In my message to Mussolini I expressed my thanks to him for all this, but this was purely in connection with my own work, and had no reference to his political activities.

Professor Formichi and Dr Tucci encouraged me to come to Italy, but my misgivings were not dispelled, and at one time I had practically decided to give up my projected tour in Italy. However, I had my promise to fulfil. I also had a strong desire to meet and spend a few days with Romain Rolland, and this seemed the last chance of doing so. So at last I came to Italy and was taken to Rome.

I had no opportunities to study the genesis or the activities of the Fascist movement and I did not express any opinion about it. In fact in most of my interviews I was careful to explain that I was not competent to say anything either for or against Fascism, not having studied it.

About Mussolini himself I must, however, say that he did interest me as an artist. His personality was striking. As a poet the human element—even in politics—touches me more deeply than abstract theories. Modern civilization is too impersonal for me. The expression of the personal man in his work may or may not be good, may even be terrible, but when it makes itself powerfully evident it is fascinating. Moral judgment and the interest invoked by a dramatic personality are two entirely different things. Mussolini struck me as a masterful personality. He seems not only to have strength of determination, but a quick instinct for realizing his opportunities which has enabled him to obtain such perfect mastery over a whole people. His great dramatic personality brought to my vision a man riding upon a wild horse who by his marvellous strength checked almost an insane people and controlled them.

Signora Salvadori: I understand: you were interested in his character. He is certainly interesting, but he did not actually achieve all this by his own strength. The Socialists had already realized their own failure even before Mussolini came into power. He is maintaining his power by violence and by crushing the freedom of speech.

Tagore: The people with whom I came into contact in Italy were almost unanimous in assuring me that Mussolini had saved Italy from anarchy and utter ruin. The reports of the Fascist methods that reached me in India were of a revolting nature and came chiefly from English sources. Lately we have lost our faith in all such reports from the West in which the representatives of a people are accused of public crimes. For we know that along with their army and navy and aircraft the Western nations have also perfected their organizations for a world-wide propaganda of misrepresentation. Yet I could not altogether ignore these reports. I was therefore particularly impressed when I found Mussolini being praised by foreigners—notably by Englishmen residing in Italy—who regarded him as a saviour of Italy.

Signora Salvadori: It is not true. This is the opinion of people who are in favour of Fascism. Foreigners who are not friendly to Fascism cannot give free expression to their opinion in Italy. People who hold contrary views were not allowed to see you.

Tagore: I have realized that. I had no occasion to come into touch with any individual holding a contrary opinion. This seemed to me neither natural nor wholesome. We are justified in feeling suspicious of the true character of an idea for whose sake it becomes necessary to terrify a whole people into unanimity of expression.

Signora Salvadori: It is not true that Mussolini had saved Italy from financial ruin. The financial position of Italy was better before Mussolini came into power. Look at the *lira,* it was 70 to the pound, and it is now 130. There was great unrest in Italy certainly after the war, but this unrest was not Bolshevism. Foreigners do not know, and merely repeat conventional tales. Italy was actually on the way to recovering from the unrest when Mussolini started his campaign. But what makes us unhappy is that you have unintentionally helped to support Fascism. We know it is unintentional, for you are too good to do so.

Tagore: I did not support Fascism, though I did express my admiration for Mussolini as possessing the personality which alone can effect the miracles of creation in human history. I was careful to make this distinction. About Fascism the only thing of which I was assured by almost everyone I met was that it had saved Italy from economic ruin.

Signora Salvadori: That is not true.

Tagore: Even had it been true it would not affect my position. Even if Italy is prosperous—although you deny this very fact—it is of no avail. As an outsider I must claim something more. If Italy does not contribute something which is great, which is for all men and for all time, we cannot be satisfied. If, on the contrary, Italy, in the pursuit of her political power and material gain, has sacrificed some ideal of humanity she deserves condemnation, not only for her own sake but for the sake of us all. In this she becomes a universal menace, imperilling the foundation of human relationship. Your Garibaldi fought for the cause of independence which was not restricted to his own country. He fought for an ideal, so all humanity is grateful to him.

In an interview which I gave just before my departure from Rome I said: 'I am not really competent to judge what the Italian people think and wish. I hope they will realize that the mere pursuit of material wealth will never make them great. They will be a great world power only when they give the world permanent gifts of the spirit. Otherwise national prosperity and political power die with them. These are consumed in the process of enjoyment: but products of the spirit are for all time and for all countries.'

Before leaving Mussolini I had the opportunity to tell him what I felt,—that mere discipline of law and order is not a final gain, it is only of value if it gives expansion to that background of freedom which is necessary for all great creations of the spirit.

I have explained my own position. I should now like to hear what you have got to tell me—your own experience.

I can quite understand how even foreigners—for example, Englishmen residing in Italy—could condone acts of violence committed in the name of political necessity. This has become possible because of the callousness which possesses the world today. The world has, since the war, become accustomed to violence. This is why the English people could take part in and tolerate the atrocities committed in Ireland during the 'Black-and-Tan' madness. In Europe people now-a-days do not seem to feel keenly about outrages committed by the men in power. I cannot but think that such deeds of ferocity as you speak of would have shocked the moral sense of Europe before the war.

Signora Salvadori: But nothing appears in the papers in Italy. They dare not publish anything. In Florence 18 people were shot in one night. A father in bed was attacked, and while the children were shouting: 'Don't kill our father,' they shot him in his bed. You don't know what we have suffered. I myself heard the screams of a woman whose husband was killed before her eyes. But nothing in the papers—never!

Tagore: I wish I had known for certain the dark deeds that were being done in Italy, then I would not have come to that country—I certainly would not. I had not met any of the people who suffered. But now that I have seen you I realize my own responsibility.

Signora Salvadori: We have no means, we are helpless, we have no money, and we cannot do anything. We do not know how to inform other people. I hope you will help us. Italy is now buried in lies everywhere. It is so bad for the young generation—this teaching them love for Fascism and for morbid patriotism.

Of course there are a few honest Fascists who do not know the violent side, and who, not knowing, sincerely believe in Fascism. But most people are terrorised into acquiescing in it. We who have suffered know what it is in reality.

Tagore: Let me tell you before we part that I have a genuine love for the Italian people, and I fervently hope that this great period of pain through which they are passing will not coerce them into accepting an ambition for fatness of prosperity in place of spiritual greatness. Once Italy was the luminous centre of the West. In the art galleries of Rome and Florence the evidence of her marvellous creative power, both in its variety of perfection, has been overwhelming in its effect on a visitor like myself who comes for the first time to witness it. This exuberant impulse of creation which once overflowed the western continent must still be lying in suspense in her being, and I hope it will not be smothered into a stillness of death by any reign of terror and lure of greed, that once more it will find its true work and rescue Europe from the dominion of the machine.

1926

ANGELICA BALBAN AND TAGORE

I was in Vienna when Tagore, the Indian poet and philosopher was lecturing there, about two years after the assassination of Matteotti. This murder had evoked such a reaction to the Fascist *regime* that *emigre* opinion was shocked at the announcement that Tagore has been a guest of the Fascist Government in Italy. Modigliani, who had participated as an attorney in the 'trial' of Matteotti's murderers, was in Vienna at this time and he asked me to accompany him to an appointment with Tagore and to act as his translator.

Tagore was staying at the fashionable hotel, where he was obviously an object of idolatry among the wealthy patrons.

'There is no need to tell me the details of what is going on in Italy,' he said. 'I have been there and I do not know any thing I could say or do about it.'

I would have left immediately had not Modigliani begun to speak in Italian. I started to translate his remarks, Tagore interrupted me.

'Are you the person who gave the interview about Mussolini that was published a few months ago?'

His secretary answered before I could speak, 'Yes, this is the lady whose interviews and articles have interested you so much.'

The whole atmosphere changed and Tagore became an understanding and even apologetic human being.

'Your interpretation of Mussolini's character,' he said, 'coincides with the impression he made upon me—a coward and an actor. When I asked the English ambassador if he thought my impression was correct, he said, it was not—that Mussolini was a great courageous man. However, he did not convince me and I was glad to have a confirmation, in your interview of my impression. I should like you to tell me more.'

'I shall have to begin by saying,' I answered, 'that the Italian people who have attempted more than any other people, to apply your own attitude towards war, do not deserve that you should accept the hospitality of a man who came to power through violence and assassination.'

'Please do not misunderstand me,' he interrupted, 'when I came to Italy I knew nothing about the situation nor could I get in touch with reality. You are the second person who has given me any idea of what Fascism is: The first one I met also after had left Italy. You may be sure that I will make a statement of what I think about the fascist *regime*.'

The secretary told me that Tagore had numerous clippings of Fascism which he was eager to have translated.

One of the next issues of the Viennese Daily *Neue Freie Presse* contained a long article by Tagore dealing with this subject. It ended with the statement: 'To be ruled by a tyrant is a great misfortune for any country. But to know that one has worshipped an individual who owes his success only to his negative quality is a tragedy....' This comment, which I quote only from memory, contained the kernel of the tragedy of Italy. When all the factors which contributed to Mussolini's rise to power are unveiled—which can happen only after his fall most of those who today pretend that 'he must have some good qualities' will declare that they have always known that he was an imposter and an adventurer.

Their recognition of this fact may come too late. They themselves may be the victims of some similar demagogue in their own country whose rise they have encouraged through similar tolerance and ignorance of the conditions which make for Fascism. Hitalarism in Germany and Austria, undeclared war in Abyssania, China and Spain would not be possible if not for the complicity of public opinion in the social and economic condition from which war and fascism arise.

1926

INTERVIEW WITH F.L. MINIGERODE

ON CIVILIZATION

'What does Asia think of Christian civilization? Rabindranath Tagore—Nobel prize-winner for literature in 1913 and founder of the International Institution at Santiniketan, in Bengal—repeated the question slowly,' writes F.L. Minigerode in the *New York Times*.

'It would be difficult to imagine a more dignified, a more aristocratic man than Tagore. His long, snowy hair and snowy beard; his slender and delicate hands; his fine face (the face of a man who must have thought fine thoughts all his life), seemed supremely belonging to the bearer of a message of goodwill.

'Rabindranath Tagore is often called a "mystic." But he strikes one as being too full of the milk of human kindness to be mystical in quite the usual sense.

'Abruptly he straightened and leaned forward. Then, slowly in a voice that spoke the English tongue in accents making every word clear and musical, he repeated again the question: "What does Asia think of Christian civilization?" And now the answer was forthcoming.

'"Europe," he began, "has lost prestige tremendously throughout all Asia and Asiatics are more than ever convinced that; spiritually, Europe has nothing to give them. Asia in the years gone by, used to look-upon Europe with something akin to reverence. Today, Asia thinks that Europe does not speak the truth."'

MAGNIFICENT DREAMS

'As a boy I looked eagerly forward to the time when I should pay my first visit to Europe. I dreamed of magnificent things there—not material things, but fine thoughts, fine characteristics. I looked forward to a meeting, there people with conscience that guided not only the individual but the nation. I had, however, counted too much upon the spirituality that seemed to abound in the early days of the nineteenth century, when Keats and Shelley and Byron and a host of others seemed to be sounding a trumpet call to higher things. They had fired my imagination with ideals.

'Later Abraham Lincoln rose to superb heights. Garibaldi impressed me as a man in search of a fight for right. The writings and histories of such men had influenced me strongly; made me believe that in Europe I should find a true consciousness in men, in peoples, in nations; that I should discover a continent where all the people were striving for high ideals—I was poignantly disappointed.

'In my travels through the so-called highly civilized countries—in Europe, in America, in Japan—I have found all the existing influences carrying the nations headlong toward material things, to the exclusion of spiritual things. These material things are of little worth. Today the great nations and their great men measure success in terms of bulk. This means that they are not great.

'It is no great achievement to understand and put to use the forces of electricity. A man has not accomplished much merely because his factory can turn out a thousand motor cars in a day. It is all done by rule and line, and man can easily master the details of such things. But who can fathom the intricacies of the human being? Great surgeons know the flesh, but who attempts to learn the spirit of men?

'The multiplication table has become greater than the Ten Commandments. Let us have everything on a big scale, seems to be the watchword of the day. Western civilization has put everything on a scale of mass production, except the thoughts and influences at work in the human mind. Those are sadly neglected.

'But what the peoples of Asia observe with most burning apprehension is the aggressive spirit of nationalism and imperialism which the nations of Europe cultivate. It is a menace to the whole world. Europe's political demoralization is so acute that it must necessarily react on Asia, whose peoples are the victims of Western exploitation.'

Tagore had mentioned Japan, and Mr Minigerode asked him how, in his opinion, Japan had been changed spiritually by her steadily increasing contact with the ideas of Europe.

'It has changed her completely,' he said, 'The spirit of bigness, of material prosperity of aggrandisement holds her tightly. The ancient Samurai spirit is dead. Japan has joined the march of territorial expansion.'

'The moral self-respect of a people is greater than all material glories. Imperialism stifles self-respect and makes men slaves. It does not allow them to think and speak for themselves. Western civilization came into being because the power to rule was distributed among a whole people. There was an individual dignity, an individual consciousness of importance. Dictatorships put an end to such individuality.'

'Speaking of dictators, Dr Tagore, you have recently been received with great cordiality by Mussolini—yet with your love of freedom for the individual you surely do not approve Fascist methods?'

'My popularity waned quite suddenly in Italy,' he replied, 'When I had told them my true opinion of a Government that permitted little or no individual freedom, I found myself deserted by all who had before been ready to honour me.'

'In Italy the worship of unscrupulous force is the vehicle of nationalism, and this force keeps alive the fire of international jealousy. It may ultimately be the means of bringing about universal devastation. The world is knit closely together in these days of fast steamships, railways and aeroplanes. Boundaries are but imaginary lines that do not actually separate one nation from another. Any process of destruction once underway will sweep beyond these frontiers. Mountains and seas are no longer barriers.'

The Italian adventure has had many echoes. According to cable reports, the Italian Press afterward published flattering comments attributed to Dr Tagore, which made it appear that he was thoroughly in accord with the principles of Fascism but the poet after he had left Italy, felt compelled to deny. He issued a statement, part of which follows:

'The methods and basic principles of Fascism concern all humanity and it is absurd to imagine that would ever support a movement that ruthlessly suppress free speech, that compels obedience to its commands that are against the convictions of individuals and that follows the blood bespattered path of violence and secret crime.

'I have declared over and over again that the aggressive spirit of nationalism and imperialism observed by most Western nations like a religion, constitutes a menace to the whole world. The moral retrogression that it has produced in European politics has very devastating consequences, especially for the people of the East who are at the mercy of Western methods of exploitation.

'So even if it were not almost criminal, it would at least be very foolish of me to admire a political ideal that comes out openly for brutal violence as the moving force of civilization. And if one considers this barbarism, which is not at all impossible of combination with material prosperity, as desirable, its cost is fearfully high.'

For many years Rabindranath Tagore has been preaching his gospel of peace and universal brotherhood. His ideal is the perfect whole, not the whole broken up into parts continually warring against each other. 'The universe,' one of his disciples once wrote, summing up the philosophy of Tagore, 'is to be viewed as a single family where the different neighbours are the members, each contributing its quota to the welfare of the whole. All peoples will then have a place in the sun.' And in Rabindranath's own image we read:

'As the mission of the rose lies in the unfoldment of the petals which implies distinctness; so the rose of humanity is perfect only when the diverse races and the nations have evolved their perfect distinct characteristics, but all attached in the stem of humanity by the bond of love.' He has further said: 'There is a moral law in this world which has its application both in individual and to organized bodies of men. You cannot go on violating these laws in the name of your nation yet enjoy their advantage as individuals. We may forget truth for our convenience, but truth does not forget us. Prosperity cannot save itself without moral foundation. Unless man can see the gaping chasm between his full storehouse and his humanity, until he can feel the unity of mankind, the kind of barbarism which you call civilization will exist.'

'I remembered,' says Mr Minigerode, 'Dr Tagore's having said that if Christ came to New York he would be forcibly turned back for lack of dollars, if for no other reason, and also that if Christ had been born in America the Ku Klux Klan would have destroyed Him.'

'Do you think we are really as bad as all that!'

He countered the query with one of his own.

'Is it not true today that such an utterance as "Blessed are the meek" is political blasphemy? Suppose Christ said in America: "Blessed are the poor." It would be judged economic heresy. And if He told your country that it is as easy for the prosperous to reach the Kingdom of Heaven as for a camel to pass through the eye of a needle, would He not be thrown into prison? Perhaps America would not go so far as to inflict physical punishment upon Christ because of his utterances. But the fact remains, I think, that to be either meek or poor in America to....[1]

'Do you class America with the Great European Powers that utterly lack spirituality, or do you think there is a spiritual torch still burning?'

1. A few words in the sentence are illegible.

'I am convinced that America is searching—certainly some Americans are searching—for ideals,' he answered. 'Whether these seekers for better things will be evolved because of the overwhelming members in the opposite camp, or whether they will eventually make their voices heard throughout the world and be a great power for the good of all peoples, I am not qualified to prophesy. All men must hope that they will succeed.'

1926

H.G. WELLS AND TAGORE

Tagore: The tendency in modern civilization is to make the world uniform. Calcutta, Bombay, Hong Kong and other cities are more or less alike, wearing big masks which represent no country in particular.

Wells: Yet don't you think this very fact is an indication that we are reaching out for a new world-wide human order which refuses to be localized?

Tagore: Our individual physiognomy need not be the same. Let the mind be universal. The individual should not be sacrificed.

Wells: We are gradually thinking now of one human civilization on the foundation of which individualities will have great chance of fulfilment. The individual, as we take him, has suffered from the fact that civilization has been split up into separate units, instead of being merged into a universal whole, which seems to be the natural destiny of humankind.

Tagore: I believe the unity of human civilization can be better maintained by the linking up in fellowship and co-operation of the different civilizations of the world. Do you think there is a tendency to have one common language for humanity?

Wells: One common language will probably be forced on mankind whether we like it or not. Previously a community of fine minds created a new dialect. Now it is necessity that will compel us to accept a universal language.

Tagore: I quite agree. The time for five-mile dialects is fast vanishing. Rapid communication makes for a common language. Yet this common language probably would not exclude national languages. There is again the curious fact that just now, along with the growing unities of the human mind, the development of national self-consciousness is leading to the formation or rather revival of national languages everywhere. Don't you think that in America, in spite of constant touch between America and England, the English language is tending toward a definite modification and change?

Wells: I wonder if that is the case now. Forty or fifty years ago this would have been the case, but now in literature and in common speech it becomes increasingly difficult to distinguish between English and American. There seems to be much more repercussion in the other direction. Today we are elaborating and perfecting physical methods of transmitting words. Translation is a bother. Take your poems—do they not lose much by that process? If you had a method of making them intelligible to all people at the same time, it would be really wonderful.

Tagore: Music of different nations has a common psychological foundation, and yet that does not mean that national music should not exist. The same thing is, in my opinion, probably true for literature.

Wells: Modern music is going from one country to another without loss—from Purcell to Bach, then Brahms, then Russian music, then oriental. Music is of all things in the world the most international.

Tagore: May I add something? I have composed more than three hundred pieces of music. They are all sealed from the West because they cannot properly be given to you in your own notation. Perhaps they would not be intelligible to your people even if I could get them written down in European notation.

Wells: The West may get used to your music.

Tagore: Certain forms of tunes and melodies which move us profoundly seem to baffle western listeners; yet, as you say, perhaps closer acquaintance with them may gradually lead to their appreciation in the West.

Wells: Artistic expression in the future will probably be quite different from what it is today; the medium will be the same and comprehensible to all. Take radio, which links together the world. And we cannot prevent further invention. Perhaps in the future, when the present clamor for dialects and national languages in broadcasting subsides and new discoveries in science are made, we shall be conversing with one another through a common medium of speech yet undreamt of.

Tagore: We have to create the new psychology needed for this age. We have to adjust ourselves to the new necessities and conditions of civilization.

Wells: Adjustments, terrible adjustments!

Tagore: Do you think there are any fundamental racial difficulties?

Wells: No. New races are appearing and reappearing, perpetual fluctuations. There have been race mixtures from the earliest historical times; India is the supreme example of this. In Bengal, for instance, there has been an amazing mixture of races in spite of castes and other barriers.

Tagore: There is the question of race pride. Can the West fully acknowledge the East? If mutual acceptance is not possible, then I shall be very sorry for that country which rejects another's culture. Study can bring no harm, though men like Dr Haas and Henri Matisse seem to think that the eastern mind should not go outside eastern countries, and then everything will be all right.

Wells: I hope you disagree. So do I!

Tagore: It is regrettable that any race or nation should claim divine favoritism and assume inherent superiority to all others in the scheme of creation.

Wells: The supremacy of the West is only a question of probably the past hundred years. Before the battle of Lepanto the Turks were dominating the West; the voyage of Columbus was undertaken to avoid the Turks. Elizabethan writers and even their successors were struck by the wealth and the high material standards of the East. The history of western ascendancy is very brief indeed.

Tagore: Physical science of the nineteenth century probably has created this spirit of race superiority in the West. When the East assimilates this physical science, the tide may turn and take a normal course.

Wells: Modern science is not exactly European. A series of accidents and peculiar circumstances prevented some of the eastern countries from applying the discoveries made by humanists in other parts of the world. They themselves had once originated and developed a great many of the sciences that were later on taken up by the West and given greater perfection. Today, Japanese, Chinese and Indian names in the world of science are gaining due recognition.

Tagore: India has been in a bad situation.

Wells: When Macaulay imposed a third-rate literature and a poor system of education on India, Indians naturally resented it. No human being can live on Scott's poetry. I believe that things are now changing. But, remain assured, we English were not better off. We were no less badly educated than the average Indian, probably even worse.

Tagore: Our difficulty is that our contact with the great civilization of the West has not been a natural one. Japan has absorbed more of the western culture because she has been free to accept or reject according to her needs.

Wells: It is a very bad story indeed, because there have been such great opportunities for knowing each other.

Tagore: And then, the channels of education have become dry river beds, the current of our resources having systematically been diverted along other directions.

Wells: I also am a member of a subject race. I am taxed enormously. I have to send my check—so much for military aviation, so much for the diplomatic machinery of government! You see, we suffer from the same evils. In India the tradition of officialdom is, of course, more unnatural and has been going on for a long time. The Moguls, before the English came, seem to have been as indiscriminate as our own people.

Tagore: And yet there is a difference. The Mogul government was not scientifically efficient and mechanical to a degree. The Moguls wanted money, and so long as they could live in luxury they did not wish to interfere with the progressive village communities in India. The Muslim emperors did not dictate terms and force the hands of Indian educators and villagers. Now, for instance, the ancient educational systems of India are completely disorganized, and all indigenous educational effort has to depend on official recognition.

Wells: 'Recognition' by the state, and good bye to education!

Tagore: I have often been asked what my plans are. My reply is that I have no scheme. My country, like every other, will evolve its own constitution; it will pass through its experimental phase and settle down into something probably quite different from what you or I expect.

1936

EINSTEIN AND TAGORE

I

Einstein: Do you believe in the Divine as isolated from the world?

Tagore: Not isolated. The infinite personality of Man comprehends the Universe. There cannot be anything that cannot be subsumed by the human personality, and this proves that the truth of the Universe is human truth. I have taken a scientific fact to illustrate this—Matter is composed of protons and electrons, with gaps between them; but matter may seem to be solid. Similarly humanity is composed of individuals, yet they have their inter-connection of human

Tagore and Gandhi
(*Courtesy*: Rabindra Bhavan, Visva-Bharati)

Einstein and Tagore
(*Courtesy*: Rabindra Bhavan, Visva-Bharati)

Rolland and Tagore
(*Courtesy*: Rabindra Bhavan, Visva-Bharati)

relationship, which gives living solidarity to man's world. The entire universe is linked up with us in a similar manner, it is a human universe. I have pursued this thought through art, literature and the religious consciousness of man.

Einstein: There are two different conceptions about the nature of the universe: (1) The world as a unity dependent on humanity. (2) The world as a reality independent of the human factor.

Tagore: When our universe is in harmony with Man, the eternal, we know it as truth, we feel it as beauty.

Einstein: This is a purely human conception of the universe.

Tagore: There can be no other conception. This world is a human world—the scientific view of it is also that of the scientific man. There is some standard of reason and enjoyment which gives it truth, the standard of the Eternal Man whose experiences are through our experiences.

Einstein: This is a realization of the human entity.

Tagore: Yes, one eternal entity. We have to realize it through our emotions and activities. We realize the Supreme Man who has no individual limitations through our limitations. Science is concerned with that which is not confined to individuals; it is the impersonal human world of truths. Religion realizes these truths and links them up with our deeper needs; our individual consciousness of truth gains universal significance. Religion applies values to truth, and we know truth as good through our own harmony with it.

Einstein: Truth, then, or Beauty, is not independent of man?

Tagore: No.

Einstein: If there would be no human beings any more, the Apollo of Belvedere would no longer be beautiful.

Tagore: No.

Einstein: I agree with regard to this conception of Beauty, but not with regard to Truth.

Tagore: Why not? Truth is realized through man.

Einstein: I cannot prove that my conception is right, but that is my religion.

Tagore: Beauty is in the ideal of perfect harmony which is in the Universal Being; Truth the perfect comprehension of the Universal Mind. We individuals approach it through our own mistakes and blunders, through our accumulated experience, through our illumined consciousness—how, otherwise, can we know Truth?

Einstein: I cannot prove scientifically that truth must be conceived as a truth that is valid independent of humanity; but I believe it firmly. I believe, for instance, that the Pythagorean theorem in geometry states something that is approximately true, independent of the existence of man. Anyway, if there is a *reality* independent of man there is also a truth relative to this reality; and in the same way the negation of the first engenders a negation of the existence of the latter.

Tagore: Truth, which is one with the Universal Being, must essentially be human, otherwise whatever we individuals realize as true can never be called truth—at least the truth which is described as scientific and can only be reached through the process of logic, in other words, by an organ of thoughts which is human. According to Indian Philosophy there is Brahman the absolute Truth, which cannot be conceived by the isolation of the individual mind or described by words, but can only be realized by completely merging the individual in its infinity. But such a truth cannot belong to Science. The nature of truth which we are discussing is an appearance—that is to say what appears to be true to the human mind and therefore is human, and may be called *māyā,* or illusion.

Einstein: So according to your conception, which may be the Indian conception, it is not the illusion of the individual, but of humanity as a whole.

Tagore: In science we go through the discipline of eliminating the personal limitations of our individual minds and thus reach that comprehension of truth which is in the mind of the Universal Man.

Einstein: The problem begins whether Truth is independent of our consciousness.

Tagore: What we call truth lies in the rational harmony between the subjective and objective aspects of reality, both of which belong to the super-personal man.

Einstein: Even in our everyday life we feel compelled to ascribe a reality independent of man to the objects we use. We do this to connect the experiences of our senses in a reasonable way. For instance, if nobody is in this house, yet that table remains where it is.

Tagore: Yes, it remains outside the individual mind, but not outside the universal mind. The table which I perceive is perceptible by the same kind of consciousness which I possess.

Einstein: Our natural point of view in regard to the existence of truth apart from humanity cannot be explained or proved, but it is a belief which nobody can lack—no primitive beings even. We attribute to Truth a superhuman objectivity; it is indispensable for us, this reality which is independent of our existence and our experience and our mind—though we cannot say what it means.

Tagore: Science has proved that the table as a solid object is an appearance, and therefore that which the human mind perceives as a table would not exist if that mind were naught. At the same time it must be admitted that the fact, that the ultimate physical reality of the table is nothing but a multitude of separate revolving centres of electric forces, also belongs to the human mind.

In the apprehension of truth there is an eternal conflict between the universal human mind and the same mind confined in the individual. The perpetual process of reconciliation is being carried on in our science and philosophy, and in our ethics. In any case, if there be any truth absolutely unrelated to humanity then for us it is absolutely non-existing.

It is not difficult to imagine a mind to which the sequence of things happens not in space, but only in time like the sequence of notes in music. For such a mind its conception of reality is akin to the musical reality in which

Pythagorean geometry can have no meaning. There is the reality of paper, infinitely different from the reality of literature. For the kind of mind possessed by the moth, which eats that paper, literature is absolutely non-existent, yet for Man's mind literature has a greater value of truth than the paper itself. In a similar manner, if there be some truth which has no sensuous or rational relation to the human mind it will ever remain as nothing so long as we remain human beings.

Einstein: Then I am more religious than you are!

Tagore: My religion is in the reconciliation of the Super-personal Man, the Universal human spirit, in my own individual being. This has been the subject of my Hibbert Lectures, which I have called 'The Religion of Man'.

14 July 1930

II

Tagore: I was discussing with Dr Mendel today the new mathematical discoveries which tell us that in the realm of infinitesimal atoms chance has its play: the drama of existence is not absolutely in character.

Einstein: The facts that make science tend toward this view do not say good-bye to causality.

Tagore: Maybe, not; but it appears that the idea of causality is not in the elements, that some other force builds up with them an organized universe.

Einstein: One tries to understand in the higher plane how the order is. The order is there, where the big elements combine and guide existence; but in the minute elements this order is not perceptible.

Tagore: Thus duality is in the depths of existence—the contradiction of free impulse and the directive will which works upon it and evolves an orderly scheme of things.

Einstein: Modern physics would not say they are contradictory. Clouds look one from a distance, but, if you see them near, they show themselves in disorderly drops of water.

Tagore: I find a parallel in human psychology. Our passions and desires are unruly, but our character subdues these elements into a harmonious whole. Does something similar to this happen in the physical world? Are the elements rebellious, dynamic with individual impulse? And is there a principle in the physical world which dominates them and puts them into an orderly organization?

Einstein: Even the elements are not without statistical order; elements of radium will always maintain their specific order, now and ever onward, just as they have done all along. There is, then, a statistical order in the elements.

Tagore: Otherwise the drama of existence would be too desultory. It is the constant harmony of chance and determination which makes it eternally new and living.

Einstein: I believe that whatever we do or live for has its causality; it is good, however, that we cannot look through it.

Tagore: There is in human affairs an element of elasticity also—some freedom within a small range, which is for the expression of our personality. It is like the musical system in India which is not so rigidly fixed as is the western music. Our composers give a certain definite outline, a system of melody and rhythmic arrangement, and within a certain limit the player can improvise upon it. He must be one with the law of that particular melody, and then he can give spontaneous expression to his musical feeling within the prescribed regulation. We praise the composer for his genius in creating a foundation along with a superstructure of melodies, but we expect from the player his own skill in the creation of variations of melodic flourish and ornamentation. In creation we follow the central law of existence, but, if we do not cut ourselves adrift from it, we can have sufficient freedom within the limits of our personality for the fullest self-expression.

Einstein: That is only possible where there is a strong artistic tradition in music to guide the people's mind. In Europe music has come too far away from popular art and popular feeling and has become something like a secret art with conventions and traditions of its own.

Tagore: So you have to be absolutely obedient to this too complicated music. In India the measure of a singer's freedom is in his own creative personality. He can sing the composer's song as his own, if he has the power creatively to assert himself in his interpretation of the general law of the melody which he is given to interpret.

Einstein: It requires a very high standard of art fully to realize the great idea in the original music, so that one can make variations upon it. In our country the variations are often prescribed.

Tagore: If in our conduct we can follow the law of goodness, we can have real liberty of self-expression. The principle of conduct is there, but the character which makes it true and individual is our own creation. In our music there is a duality of freedom and prescribed order.

Einstein: Are the words of a song also free? I mean to say, is the singer at liberty to add his own words to the song which he is singing?

Tagore: Yes. In Bengal we have a kind of song—*Kirtan* we call it—which gives freedom to the singer to introduce parenthetical comments, phrases not in the original song. This occasions great enthusiasm, since the audience is constantly thrilled by some beautiful, spontaneous sentiment added by the singer.

Einstein: Is the metrical form quite severe?

Tagore: Yes, quite. You cannot exceed the limits of versification; the singer in all his variations must keep the rhythm and the time, which is fixed. In European music you have a comparative liberty about time, but not about melody. But in India we have freedom of melody with no freedom of time.

Einstein: Can the Indian music be sung without words? Can one understand a song without words?

Tagore: Yes, we have songs with unmeaning words, sounds which just help to act as carriers of the notes. In North India music is an independent art, not the interpretation of words and thoughts, as in Bengal. The music is very intricate and subtle and is a complete world of melody by itself.

Einstein: It is not polyphonic?

Tagore: Instruments are used, not for harmony, but for keeping time and for adding to the volume and depth. Has melody suffered in your music by the imposition of harmony?

Einstein: Sometimes it does suffer very much. Sometimes the harmony swallows up the melody altogether.

Tagore: Melody and harmony are like lines and colours in pictures. A simple linear picture may be completely beautiful; the introduction of colour may make it vague and insignificant. Yet colour may, by combination with lines, create great pictures so long as it does not smother and destroy their value.

Einstein: It is a beautiful comparison; line is also much older than colour. It seems that your melody is much richer in structure than ours. Japanese music seems to be so.

Tagore: It is difficult to analyse the effect of eastern and western music on our minds. I am deeply moved by the western music—I feel that it is great, that it is vast in its structure and grand in its composition. Our own music touches me more deeply by its fundamental lyrical appeal. European music is epic in character; it has a broad background and is Gothic in its structure.

Einstein: Yes, yes, that is very true. When did you first hear European music?

Tagore: At seventeen, when I first came to Europe I came to know it intimately, but even before that time I had heard European music in our own household. I had heard the music of Chopin and others at an early age.

Einstein: There is a question we Europeans cannot properly answer, we are so used to our own music. We want to know whether our own music is a conventional or a fundamental human feeling; whether to feel consonance and dissonance is natural or a convention which we accept.

Tagore: Somehow the piano confounds me. The violin pleases me much more.

Einstein: It would be interesting to study the effects of European music on an Indian who had never heard it when he was young.

Tagore: Once I asked an English musician to analyse for me some classical music and explain to me what elements make it the beauty of a piece.

Einstein: The difficulty is that the really good music, whether of the East or of the West, cannot be analysed.

Tagore: Yes, and what deeply affects the hearer is beyond himself.

Einstein: The same uncertainty will always be there about everything fundamental in our experience, in our reaction to art, whether in Europe or in Asia. Even the red flower I see before me on your table may not be the same to you and me.

Tagore: And yet there is always going on the process of reconciliation between them, the individual taste conforming to the universal standard.

CONVERSATIONS IN RUSSIA

For a long time Rabindranath Tagore had been anxious to visit Russia. In 1926 received an invitation from the Soviet Government, but was taken seriously ill with influenza at Vienna towards the end of October. It was already late autumn, and news of an early winter was coming in from all sides. Vienna itself was under snow. It was with the greatest difficulty that he was finally persuaded to give up the idea. In 1929, on his way back from Canada he intended to go across Russia by the Trans-Siberian Railway, but unfortunately ill health again prevented him from doing so.

In 1930 his long felt desire was fulfilled. While he was in Berlin that year, the great Soviet educationist Mr Lunacharsky came there to invite the poet to Russia. The poet accepted the invitation. On the 11th of September, 1930 he arrived in Moscow, accompanied by Dr Harry Timbres, Miss Margot Einstein of Berlin, the poet's grandnephew Saumyendranath Tagore and his secretaries, Aryanayakam and Amiya Chakravarty. The poet was received at the white Russian Baltic Station by the representatives of the USSR Society for Cultural Relations with Foreign Countries: D. Novomirsky, head of the Anglo-American Section; A. Eshukoff, head of the Exhibition Department, and M. Dobin, head of the, Foreign Reception Bureau, and by prominent members of the Moscow Writers' Association, including the author Alexiev, the eminent constructivist poetess Vera Iber and others. A reception was arranged at midday on Friday, the 12th September in the VOKS building. Prof. F.N. Petroff, President of the Society, explained the aims and objects of the new experiments in Russia. The following notes of the conversation will give some idea of the topics discussed by the Poet.

CONVERSATION AT THE VOKS RECEPTION

Petroff: Please excuse me for my inability to speak your language. I am glad to welcome you to our country. It is a great inspiration to us that you take such interest in our new order of civilization in the Soviet Union.

Tagore: I thank you for your cordial welcome. I know you are making a tremendous experiment in this country. I am not in a position to give any considered opinion about it, but I cannot help expressing my admiration for your courage, for your keen enthusiasm to build up your social structure on the equitable basis of human freedom. It is wonderful to feel that you are interested not merely in your national problems but in the good of humanity as a whole.

Petroff: This rebuilding of society on a basis of equality is an inevitable consequence of the abundance of tribes and castes in Russia. We have had to deal with this baffling problem of heterogeneity all through our history. The attempt to realize that our differences are negligible in the light of a common need and a common urge of civilization has imparted great enthusiasm to all our workers, and we fervently believe that we shall be able to offer definite solutions to many of the outstanding problems which have troubled humanity in the past.

Tagore: By offering education to vast multitudes of your people who were kept imprisoned in the darkness of ignorance, millions of human beings who never got any chance to realize their humanity, and were obliged to yield to exploitation and oppression in order to preserve their precarious existence, you have made an invaluable contribution to human progress. You are creating a new world of humanity, and for the first time in history, acknowledging the dignity of man in your scheme of practical work.

Petroff: We believe, however, that the spread of mass education can only be possible under suitable economic conditions. It is because we could gain full control of the economic resources of Russia that we have been able to spend so much for education and for various forms of cultural work that have now been introduced for the first time in a vast agricultural country.

Tagore: That is true. No aspect of life can in reality be deducted from another. Education is necessarily connected with economic problems.

Petroff: After gaining economic control, our first care has been to educate the children before they go to school. We bring them up from their very first days in a properly organized social environment, which itself is at once the basis and the superstructure of all educational systems. Nor do we neglect the parents of the children; we carry on a vigorous educational movement among adults. In this way we hope to develop a new race of men with a free and independent outlook, co-operating for the mutual good of society as a whole.

Tagore: Don't you believe that much of what you do today has behind it the accumulated forces of active reaction against the oppressive regime of the past government? It is wonderful that this reaction should have been translated into higher forms of activity and not dissipated in mere retaliatory politics. You have of course, as I am sure you will freely admit, made grievous mistakes at the time of your first accession to power, but the sense of responsibility that this power brought along with it has quickly given you a full sense of reality, and you seem to lose no opportunity now of merging your racial individualities into a harmonious social existence. I, as an educationist, am concerned vitally with all the great movements you have initiated for the good of the peasant masses. As you know, our country, like yours, is an agricultural one, and we have amongst our peasantry all the obstacles of ignorance, of bigotry, and superstition that you have already overcome to a great extent with the help of education. If we can learn from your experiences in this line, we shall be able to grapple with rural problems in India in an efficient manner.

Petroff: Our first educational weapon is to launch an intensive campaign in the villages directed to make the peasants conscious of their own dignity, of their inherent rights of which they had been deprived for so long, and of all the possibilities that lie open to them. We are not ashamed to be propagandists, and our propaganda itself is educative. It is scientific, it is human, it is moral, and carries all the fervour of social service that we are capable of igniting in our minds and hearts.

Whatever line of work we undertake today has always the welfare of the people as its direct inspiration. We do not want to enjoy any exclusive privileges at all, because that kind of enjoyment is anti-social and therefore non-human, perhaps even inhuman. All the storehouses of wisdom, of joy, of well-ordered social benefits are open to everyone of us, because everyone of us has equal human rights to them.

Tagore: I have come to study your educational methods, to draw strength from the atmosphere of creative efforts which surrounds you. I have my educational colony in India which is linked up with the surrounding villages. With meagre means I and my colleagues there try our best to serve our neighbours, to invite them to our festivals, to supply them with medicine, to demonstrate to them the efficiency of up-to-date methods of agriculture. Whatever you can show me, therefore, of your educational work will be of very great use to me indeed. I wish I had more time and energy to study your work properly, but I shall do all that I can to utilize my visit to your country.

Petroff: Sir, your name is known and loved in the whole of Russia. We have over 25 current volumes of your works, and a vast public reads them. We shall be only too happy and proud to show you whatever you want to see of our work, and we feel sure you will appreciate our educational activities.

AT THE FEDERATION OF SOVIET WRITERS, MOSCOW

On the evening of the same day a concert was arranged jointly by VOKS and the Moscow Association of Writers in honour of Rabindranath Tagore at the club house of the Association. Among those present were Prof. P.S. Kogan (President of the Academy of Arts); Prof. Pinkevitch (Director of the Second Moscow State University); Albert Rhys Williams, the writer, Madame Litvinova and a number of eminent Soviet writers, such as Ognyed (author of Diary of Kostya Ryaptseva, Life of a Soviet School Boy), Vera Inber, Fedor Gladkov (who wrote the much-talked-of *Cement);* Eseev (poet, a former futurist and close adherent of Vladimir Mayakovsky) and others. Prof. Petroff opened the proceedings with the following speech of welcome:

Representatives of Soviet public life, art and science see among them today Rabindranath Tagore, one of the greatest of living poets and thinkers.

Rabindranath Tagore is one of those men who have followed with the closest attention and interest the great events developing during the last ten years in the history of humanity. It is obvious that one so gifted with spiritual and poetic insight could not have gone away without seeing this most important page of human history, that page which bears the name of the great October Revolution.

We, who have taken part in the October Revolution and have assisted at the construction of new forms of human culture, extend a warm welcome to one who has come amongst us, as a profound thinker, to study our culture, to study our strivings for the renewal of human society, and thus of human personality itself.

Rabindranath Tagore is an active worker on the forefront of popular education, as well as a poet and thinker. He is endeavouring, in the educational institution founded by himself in Santiniketan (near Calcutta), to solve problems regarding the formation of the human personality. This branch of work occupies an important place in his activities and makes great demands upon his energy and strength. He has come here to learn about the endeavours of our country, to understand how, in the new and revolutionary conditions, the human personality, destined to advance human progress in economic, social and cultural conditions which are all new, expands and formulates. Rabindranath Tagore wishes to understand how the human personality can in the conditions of Socialist reconstruction, perfect itself and become a varitable creative force in the spheres of art, science, and in human progress of every description.

We welcome visits by friends who come with an open mind and a pure soul to our country to study our efforts, to try and understand the aspirations of the masses towards a new human life, a new and free system for the perfection of human nature.

Many are the lies which have been spoken and written about us, and monstrous are the rumours industriously spread abroad. There are many who say that culture is languishing in our country, and others that culture has perished altogether in Soviet Russia. It is also said that the Bolsheviks, after accomplishing the greatest revolution in the world, have been unable to cope with the problems thence arising, and have been unable to substitute that which they have destroyed with something else of equal value.

We have only one answer to all this: come and see for yourself, and meditate upon what we are doing, try to understand our aspirations, study our achievements—not only in the spheres of economics, of construction, of industry and agriculture—but our achievements in the solution of the most subtle problems of human creation in the spheres of pedagogics, of art, of poetry and of the science of social life. Realize the special feature introduced into this creative work when the collective, the massed, the emancipated people came forward to replace the isolated aspirations of the individual, with the whole collective force of goodwill of their national creative powers.

Our Soviet culture is of interest at the present stage of revolutionary creation inasmuch as, emancipating both materially and spiritually the many races inhabiting the USSR, it has enabled the million-strong mass of the backward peoples, as well as the toilers of Russian extraction, to apply their powers and their energy to the progress of all humanity, and these backward peoples are now taking the most active part in that historical movement which we in our country call Socialistic construction. Anyone who has seen the Uzbek theatre and heard Turkoman music, anyone acquainted with the creative manifestations of our Caucasian people, and with the achievements in art and science in the Ukraine, must realize that the problems of mass culture are solved in our country, not by one, but by many nationalities, by the numerous races in the USSR who are progressing, in their own national forms, towards the creation of an international, free, proletarian culture. This in itself is bound to make an impression upon all peoples aspiring towards liberation. All the peoples and races beyond the territory of the USSR are following with profound attention and interest the way in which the USSR peoples, liberated from the Tsarist regime and the yoke of a religious-police system, and proceeding towards free creative work in new, in Socialist economic conditions, are living and carrying out their affairs.

We believe that our friend, Rabindranath Tagore, who has come to visit us, will approach our intellectual processes and endeavour to understand what is going on in our country with that serious thoughtfulness which he has shown in all his creative work. We rejoice when a great personality of the contemporary historical moment, such as Tagore, comes to us in true fellowship and speaks with perfect frankness of what he has seen and felt in our Union.

Permit me, in the name of VOKS, whose only aim is to demonstrate to the whole world, as impartially, vividly and fairly as possible, all that is going on in our Union, to welcome you; permit me, as a member of the representatives of science and in the name of the representatives of the artistic circles grouped around our Society, to welcome you as a close friend, and to hope that you will understand us and express in fairness and justice your opinion of our Socialistic reconstruction to the whole world.

He was followed by Profs. Kogan and Pinkevitch and by the Soviet author Shaklar, the latter speaking on behalf of the Moscow Writers' Association.

REPLY BY RABINDRANATH TAGORE

I thank you for the honour you have done me in inviting me to your country and also to this feast this evening where I have had the opportunity of meeting with some of the greatest representatives of intellectual life in your country. Unfortunately, I do not understand your language, and the language in which I am speaking is neither yours nor mine. I will therefore be brief.

I have come to this country to learn. I want to know how you are solving in your country the great problem: the world problem of civilization. Civilization today has taken man far away from his normal humanity. It has torn individual personality away from society. Modern civilization has given birth to an extraordinarily artificial life; it has created diseases, evoked specific sufferings and given rise to many anomalies. I do not know what ought to be done to cure modern civilization of its ills. I do not know if the path you have chosen in this country for the solution of this problem is the right one. History will judge the extent to which you have been successful. I do not wish to criticize you. I am filled with enthusiasm for the way in which you have, for the first time, afforded to all the opportunity of acquiring education. For this I would applaud you. I am myself profoundly interested in problems of education. My idea, my dream, has been to create free human beings who should be surrounded by an environment of creative work. Under modern civilization the human personality is imprisoned in a cage, shut off from the rest of society. In your country you have put an end to this evil. I have heard from many and am beginning myself to be convinced, that your ideas are very much like my own dream for a full life for the individual, for complete education. In your country you are not only giving the individual scientific education, you are making of him a creative personality. In this way you are realizing the greatest, the highest ideal of humanity. For the first time in history you are giving the hidden wealth of the human mind a chance to express itself. I thank you for this with all my heart.

I myself have been working in my own way in my own institutions, and my idea of education is that it should be imparted in contact with life itself; it should be a part of life. By living a true life one can have proper education, and not through the complete withdrawal from the realities of life which you so often see in the colleges and schools in the civilized world, those brick-built prisons in which children are denied the true goods of life.

Since I have come to this place I have been able to realize that your ideal of education is very similar to mine, that the people are living a complete life through which their mind is prepared to receive education in its full richness and not merely to hoard isolated facts of scientific instruction or information. You have been stimulating the people's mind for creative work which is the highest privilege of man. It has not been possible for me to give effect to this idea in an adequate manner in my own institutions. In this country you have been able to give it a proper form, and you have succeeded in giving the movement a great impetus. I realize that it will be an immortal gift to humanity from your country, this idea of education for everybody.

I can only thank you in these few brief words. I am still waiting to see in detail something of the work of education which you are carrying out in your various institutions.

Unfortunately, I have very little time to spare, and also I cannot forget the fact, I am reminded of it every day—that I am no longer young. Yet I hope I shall be able to see something which I can carry back to my own land in my memory and which will help us in our own work. I offer you my heartiest thanks for giving me this great opportunity to learn from you about your pioneer work in the field of people's education.

THE FIRST PIONEER COMMUNE

On the evening of the 14th September the Poet visited the first Pioneer Commune, Isigansky Ploschand, Iovarischsky Pereulok, No. 25, Moscow.

On reaching the staircase of the Commune Building the Poet was greeted by pioneer songs, the boys and girls standing in line on both sides of the steps and joining in the chorus. After the Poet had taken his seat in the central hall, a young pioneer girl of fourteen read a message of welcome in English.

REPLY TO ADDRESS OF WELCOME

My friends, I am deeply touched by the warm welcome you have accorded to me. As I look at your bright young faces full of hope and a glorious future, I feel stirred to my depths and know that the purpose of my visit to Russia is realized. For, believe me, I have come here, not so much to see what you have done and are doing now, which is great, but to visualize the future which you are creating with such fervour for the welfare of the whole of humanity. In every country I visit I want to come in close touch with the young who have the great privilege of looking ahead and of building up with their lives the basis of a new order of civilization. You know I am a poet, and my work is to give expression to living impulses and youthful hopes, and so I can be one with you today in your dreams of the future.

Besides, I can come close to you because I have spent a great part of my life with children. I have my school in Bengal where I live with them, and where I try to bring them up in an atmosphere of complete life. My idea is to provide them with all possible opportunities for the development of a creative life, and I trust them in their free initiative to make the best use of them.

I believe in freedom, in that freedom which naturally takes upon itself responsibilities in order to express adequately the deeper human impulses of love and service. I have given this freedom to the children of my school, and I am interested to know how you young pioneers are using the freedom you possess for the good of your community and what methods you follow to give expression to the ideal of the new age which you have realized in your country. I hope this evening to know in detail about your work and your way of life.

I thank you warmly for your reception, and I assure you that I feel very happy indeed to be here with you this evening.

TALK WITH THE CHILDREN

A boy: We are unlike the bourgeois scouts. They want rewards, they want military honours, they want everything for themselves individually, not for the good of every one. We pioneers want nothing for ourselves. Whatever good we do for everybody is also of benefit to us.

Tagore: You will be interested to know that we have in our school *Brati-balakas* and *Brati-balikas,* two organizations for boys and girls which are like yours. I do not believe in Boy Scouts' and Girl Guides' organizations because they have to take all kinds of oaths, and then, as you say, there are amongst those organizations some wrong notions of a military kind. Our boys and girls go out to serve the villagers, to put out fires when fires break out in the neighbourhood, they distribute medicine, they show the villagers how to live properly and well. I am very happy indeed to know that you enjoy doing service of this kind because, as you say, by helping the village people you are helping yourselves, you are serving the whole country.

THE CENTRAL PEASANTS' HOUSE

On the morning of the 16th September the Poet visited the Central Peasants' House.

On his arrival at the Central Peasants' House Rabindranath Tagore was received in the main clubroom by the Superintendent of the House, the House Council, and some 150 peasants who were boarding there at the time, representatives from the nearest and the far-distant points of the Soviet Union.

The small meeting of welcome that followed was opened by the Superintendent who explained to the peasants that the Poet had come to visit them in order personally to meet them and to learn about them. The Superintendent welcomed the Poet on behalf of the assembled peasants, and hoped that this first meeting between the great Indian Poet and the Soviet peasants would lay the foundation for a still deeper contact between the peasant masses of both countries.

In his brief reply the Poet emphasized the importance and significance of the strenuous work being carried on by the peasants and workers of the Soviet Republic in the building up of a new life, a new humanity. He expressed his admiration for the great spirit of goodwill which inspired this new effort, this great undertaking which demanded the utmost self-sacrifice and self-denial on the part of the Soviet population.

TALK WITH THE PEASANTS

A number of questions were then put to the Poet, and he answered them to the full satisfaction of his audience.

Question: What is the position of the National Policy in India today and what is the reason for the strife between Hindus and Mussalmans?

Tagore: I find from personal observations that this strife has been going on for the past twenty-five years only. Before this period there was, as far as I can recall—and I have lived for many years in the village—no such animosity and enmity between them. I am certain that this strife has been accentuated by the overwhelming ignorance and illiteracy of the Indian peasants. These feelings of religious hostility can, in my opinion, be liquidated only by the introduction of mass education. The possibility of educating the masses, unfortunately, does not exist today in India.

Question: Have you written anything about the peasants in your works, and what are your views regarding the future of the Indian peasants?

Tagore: Not only have I written about peasants but I am working among them, endeavouring, as far as I can, to educate them. I am not only educating children in my schools, but also carrying on this work in the surrounding villages. This work is, of course, of a modest nature in comparison with the gigantic educational work that is being carried on in the Soviet Union.

Question: What is your opinion of the collectivization that is being developed in this country?

Tagore: I realize the great importance of this work (collectivization) that is being carried out by the peasants, but I cannot answer this question as, unfortunately, I know very little about it. Lack of knowledge of how this problem is being solved in the Soviet Union is one of the chief reasons of my visit to your country.

Question: What is known in India concerning our collectivization and about the work of our country generally?

Tagore: Unfortunately, very little, as the existing press in India as well as in other countries is reticent and untrustworthy about all facts concerning your country.

Question: Have you heard before of the existence of the Peasants' Houses and of their work?

Tagore: No, only since my coming to Moscow have I learnt of the existence of these welfare centres for the peasants. Now I would like to hear from the peasants at this meeting of their own opinion about collectivization and its full significance for the agricultural population.

A young Ukrainian peasant of the name of Semenchiko, about 32 years of age, replied: 'I am working on a Collective Farm which was organized two years ago. Our Collective farm consists of big gardens from which we supply canning factories with vegetables and wheat. We have an 8-hour working day and each fifth day is a holiday' (The 5-day week is now introduced throughout the country and works under the name of the uninterrupted working week').

'The average crop is twice as large as that of any of the neighbouring individual peasants. In the beginning about 150 individual farms were merged into the common unit. In the spring of 1929, half of them left us owing to faulty understanding and misguided application of the instructions given by Comrade Stalin (the General Secretary of the All-Union Communist Party). He had emphasized that the fundamental principle of collectivization was *Voluntary Social Participation* in the organization of these collective farms. This basic principle was not correctly understood in a number of rural areas, and due to its inadequate application and the resulting bureaucratic mistakes, many peasants withdrew from the collective farms. But now, owing to supplementary explanations and the courageous efforts of the remaining collectivists, about a fourth of those that had left have returned. And today we are stronger than ever. We are building new living houses for our members, a new dining-hall and a school.'

On this same question further information was advanced by a peasant woman from Siberia. She had been a member of a Commune Farm for ten years. She asked the Poet to bear in mind the intimate connexion between the women's movement and the Collective Farms. She explained how the woman of today was more self-reliant than her sisters of even a decade ago. She said: 'We have specially organized brigades of women collectivists which travel from one part of the country to the other, working among the women, rousing them up, and pointing out to them in detail the economic and cultural advantages of collectivization. In order to lighten the strenuous life of the women collectivists in their farm work, and with a view to making their status truly equal to that of their men comrades, there are in every Collective Farm a nursery, a kindergarten, and a communal kitchen.'

A farm-labourer from the famous State Farm (Sovkhoz) 'Gigant' also described how the collectivist idea was being realized in Russia. 'This farm embraces 100,000 hectare of farm land. Last year, we had 3,000 workers. This year that figure will slightly decrease although the output per man will increase. This is due to the introduction of advanced methods of agriculture such as scientific manuring, the use of tractors and other machinery. We have now more than 300 tractors. We also have an 8-hour working day. Those of us who work longer receive overtime allowances. During the winter months when there is insufficient work for all the workers, some two-thirds of them are permitted to leave the farm to seek work in the cities (building, road-mending etc.). During their period of work in the towns they will receive one-third of their summer wage from the farm and their families continue to reside in the rooms given them at the farm.'

Tagore: I should like to know the opinion of some of the individual peasants who are here regarding the Collective Farm, and the views of anyone here present concerning the principle of private property and whether they regret their surrender of their individual farm-holdings.

A brief pause ensued before the peasants got up to reply to this question. A number of them confessed that they entertained orthodox views on this subject as the idea of collectivization was not clear to their minds; still more of them were shy and embarrassed.

Eventually, a peasant from Bashkir Republic (Central Asia) spoke up. He was still an individual farmer, but in a short time he would enter the neighbouring Collective Farm. Pointing out his reasons for this desire he said: 'The collective method of land exploitation yields a far better and a higher ratio of crop than the individual system. We need machinery for the better cultivation of the land. We individuals cannot afford to purchase machines. Further, even if we owned machines, we could not cultivate the small strips of land that each individual peasant owns. Only through the collectivization of these small plots into large collective farms can we really begin to build a new order of social existence.'

A woman peasant from the Tamboy region (some 150 miles south of Moscow) then took the floor and said: 'There can be no doubt of the superiority of life in Collective Farms to that outside them, and I do not think anyone regrets this change of conditions.' Several other peasants confirmed this opinion. Someone from the audience cried out, 'How can we regret changing from our former small, dirty huts to our present large, sanitary, hygienic collectivist houses?'

Tagore: I had the pleasure of meeting yesterday M. Karakhan who said that he was particularly proud of the work done by the Soviet Government and the Soviet social organizations in the sphere of the emancipation of women and the education and upbringing of children. In my conversation with him, I expressed my doubts regarding the future of family life, and even of its existence.

He explained that the Soviet authorities had no explicit desire to destroy family life. The state was trying to assume greater responsibilities for the bringing up of children. If this led indirectly to the extinction of family life that would only prove that family life had no survival value for the future civilization of mankind. I should like to hear what your opinions are upon this matter, and whether you believe that family life will continue to exist under the collectivist social system.

The young Ukrainian Semenchiko, who had spoken before, replied: 'What I will tell you will show whether family life is being destroyed or not under the new social regime. When my father was alive, he used to work six months of the year in the cities and for the remaining six months (in summer) I was sent with my brothers and sisters to work as shepherds for the wealthy peasants, and therefore we seldom saw our father. Now, I see my son everyday after he returns from the kindergarten, and we are the best of friends.'

Another peasant, a woman, also spoke, stating it as her opinion that the introduction of crèches and kindergartens has really helped husband and wife to reach a better understanding and happier relations. They fostered the growth of a deeper sense of responsibility and appreciation of their duty as parents.

A young Caucasian woman who had been living, excepting for the last four years, in a small village in the Caucasian mountains, spoke with great pathos and understanding. Addressing the interpreter she said: 'Tell the Great Poet, Rabindranath Tagore, that we women living in the Soviet Union, and particularly in the Trans-Caucasian Republics, consider that we are really free and happy only since the October Revolution. The dark days of the past before 1917 have now become distant. We are building up a new life in which we are participating fully, conscious of our duties and responsibilities. We are prepared to go to the extreme length of self-denial for the realization of the ideal we cherish in our hearts. Let the Great Poet know that the various peoples and nationalities of the Soviet Union wish him to convey to the people of India their warmest greetings and sympathy in their dark hours.'

Tagore: Our people are still ignorant, our women are helpless, they need the light of the new age in order to find their place in the world of humanity.

The same woman from the Caucasus said: 'I would leave my home, my children, all that I have, in order to be able to work amongst your people and to help them!'

Tagore: Who is that Mongolian-looking young man on the left?

The Interpreter: He is the son of a collective farmer in the Kirghisian Republic. He has come to Moscow to study in the Higher Textile Industrial Technicum. In three years' time he will become an engineer and return to his Republic to work on a big plant built since the Revolution.

The Superintendent of the Central Peasants' House in closing this meeting said: 'The visit of the Poet to the Soviet Union is of the greatest importance. The coming of such an eminent personage to this country, such an outstanding figure of the cultural world, means a new and bigger step in the mutual contacts between the toiling peoples of India and the Soviet Union. We hope the Poet will assist in the spreading of genuine and objective information in India concerning the efforts and activities of the workers and peasants of the First Workers' and

Peasants' Republic in History.' The meeting terminated with the singing of 'The International'.

EXHIBITION OF DRAWINGS

The exhibition of the paintings of the Poet was opened at the State Moscow Museum of New Western Art on the afternoon of the 17th September. In his introductory speech Prof. Petroff said, 'Today we are experiencing the pleasure of meeting Rabindranath Tagore, not only as a great poet and philosopher, but also as an outstanding painter of the day. We greet the great Poet and Painter who has come to our country to observe our building of a new economic, political and social order. We particularly appreciate his visit as a man of great vision and deep intuitive understanding of life's essential realities.'

Prof. Sidorov spoke on the essence of the creative art of the Poet as a painter. Prof. Ettingov of the People's Commissariat of Education expressed his warmest welcome on behalf of the Commissariat.

Prof. Kristy, the Director of the Tretiakov-Gallery in his speech of welcome said:

'We greet you, revered philosopher and writer, in the name of the greatest museum and region-study department of Moscow, and in the name of the People's Commissariat of Education, directing the affairs of art in the Soviet Union.

'We all know Rabindranath Tagore, philosopher and writer, but it was a pleasant surprise for us to learn that he is also a painter. It is with special pleasure that we have arranged an exhibition of his work in order to acquaint our intellectuals and our working masses with them. We are glad that our guest has come to us at the moment when his own native land is on the eve of emancipation, and that he has come to us when we are ourselves making heroic efforts for the reconstruction of our material and spiritual world.

'We believe that by acquainting himself with our country he will take back much that is useful for his own. For ourselves, we believe that our close contact with this great representative of an old and cultured nation and the consequent fertilization of our own ideas will result in far-reaching benefits for us both.'

Reply by Rabindranath Tagore: 'I return warm thanks for the welcome extended to me. I appreciate intensely this opportunity to get in touch with some of the best minds and best hearts of your country. My most intimate gift to you are my pictures and I hope that in them we shall truly meet each other. Only this has made me venture to bring my pictures here and exhibit them. I myself value them chiefly because they enable me to get into direct touch with the Western people. Words have failed me, the help of the interpreter has created further distractions in the path of our mutual understanding—let me hope that my pictures will be the messengers of thought between us and bring us close to each other on the plane of harmonious understanding.'

In his concluding remarks Prof. Kristy said:

'We are sincerely grateful for what we have just seen. When we came here we knew Rabindranath Tagore merely as a great philosopher and a poet and supposed that for him art would be merely the hobby of a great man. But the more we acquaint ourselves with his paintings, the more we are struck with the creative skill shown in his pictures. We consider these works to be a great manifestation of artistic life, and that his methods will be, like all high technical achievements assimilated by us from abroad, of the greatest use to our country.'

The Exhibition was very successful, and a large number of people including representatives from various art and educational institutions visited it.

TALKS WITH ART CRITICS

Tagore: I thank you for your welcome and the words of appreciation. I know that the best communication between nations is the communication of mind and heart. The best products of each country belong to all humanity. This is the proper field of exchange—the field of culture. And I shall be only too glad to show you what I have done in this latest manifestation of my own creative mind.

It came to me all of a sudden without any training or preparation, and so it has its psychological value, I believe. In other parts of Europe I must confess, however, those who are very critical of art or products of art, have given me assurance that my pictures not only have a psychological interest, but also a higher interest of art, and they have acknowledged me as an artist, for which I feel very proud. I want now to know what you think of my attempts, because I value your opinion of art very highly indeed.

I have felt a need to bring my pictures to you also because through pictures I can come into direct touch with your mind. I cannot do this with my words owing to the barrier of language. But my pictures, they will speak to you without the medium of an interpreter.

Critic: What is the idea of this picture?

Tagore: No idea. It is a picture. Ideas are in words and not in life.

Critic: What is remarkable in your work is the spirit of youth, and that is why these paintings are so interesting. The spirit of youth meets no difficulty in finding its proper mode of expression and your pictures have created their own technique. Have you ever painted before?

Tagore: Never.

Critic: You are a first-class artist. Every new picture makes a stronger impression and the entire audience is thrilled by this. We are very interested to know when these were made?

Tagore: These are early ones. They are mainly linear, colours come in later on.

Critic: Something resembling very much the works of Vrubel, whom you have never seen perhaps?

Tagore: I do not believe I have seen any of his pictures.

Critic: We shall be glad to show them to you. We shall be glad to take your paintings and exhibit them as our own—as those of a Russian artist!

Critic: We ask whether your paintings have any names?

Tagore: None at all. I cannot think of any names. I do not know how to describe my pictures.

Critic: Is this a portrait of Dante?

Tagore: No, it is not a portrait of Dante. I did it on the steamer on my way from Japan; last year my pen followed its own impulse which led to this figure you see before you.

Critic: (*with regard to a picture made the day before*) An impression of Moscow?

Tagore: Well, I did it yesterday. I do not know if Moscow has anything to do with it—perhaps it may be so, who knows!

Critic: We wish to express our deep pleasure. Professor Kristy says he has known you for a long time as a great poet, and here he expected to see some productions of a dilettante-artist, but what he has seen has amazed him. He was struck by the virility of the paintings he had the pleasure to see. He is sure that your paintings represent a very great event in the history of art. He believes your pictures will have a deep effect on our artists and give them a fuller sense of life.

Tagore: It gives me great delight to be able to gain your approbation and to know that this came from the expert critics and artists of your land. I almost feel vain about my productions. My pictures being too new, I am not yet accustomed to this, and I always feel the greatest delight when they are praised because I have some diffidence in not having any standard within myself, and have to rely upon those who have a great background of artistic experience.

TALKS WITH STUDENTS

In Moscow many distinguished scholars like Prof. Veltman, Prof. Shor and others came to see him, and as usual he had a large number of interviews with scientific workers and students. Notes of conversations with students kept by Dr. Timbres are given below.

Tagore: I thank you very much for giving me this opportunity of coming into close touch with you.

But I do not know how to have proper communication with you. Through translations we cannot say very much. I do not feel encouraged to talk in English about any subject which is important and serious. I would like to know about your aspirations and also if you still have any misgivings about the society under which you are working and growing up. But these are serious questions which cannot be answered through translations. If you have any curiosity to know about anything which I am doing or any other subject concerning India, I shall be glad to answer your questions.

Maria Steinhaus: Before I ask you a question I would like to greet you in the name of the scientific workers of Moscow and tell you how glad we are to meet you. Your famous name is known all over our country, and we know that you are interested in our schools and educational work. And our comrades would be glad and happy to show you our work.

I have heard that yesterday you spoke about your educational work in India, and I would like to know how you have combined education with the realities of life.

'You ought to know one thing—that I am by nature a poet. From my very young days, my only vocation was to express my ideas in verse, give shape to my dreams in my poems.

'What was it that impelled me to take up this work for which I am not naturally fit?

'When I was young, as usual, I was sent to a school. Some of you may have read from the translation of my Reminiscences about the misadventures I had when I began my career as a student in a school. It was a miserable life, which became absolutely intolerable to me. At that time I did not have the capacity to analyse the reason why I suffered; but then when I grew up, it became quite clear to me what it was that hurt me so deeply to be compelled to attend my class in that school where my parents sent me.

'I have my natural love for life, for nature, and for my surroundings where I have my dear ones; and to be snatched away from these natural surroundings with which I had all my deeper life of relationship, and to be sent as an exile to the school, to the class with its bare white walls, and its stare of dead eyes, frightened me every day. When I was once inside these walls, I did not feel natural. It was a fragment torn away from life, and this caused me intense misery because I was uprooted from my own world and sent to surroundings which were dead and unsympathetic, disharmonious and monotonously dull.

'It was not possible for the mind of a child to be able to receive anything in those cheerless surroundings, in the environment of dead routine. And the teachers were like living gramophones, repeating the same lessons day by day in a dull manner. My mind refused to accept anything from my teachers. With all my heart and soul I repudiated what was put before me. And then there were some teachers who were utterly unsympathetic, and did not understand at all the sensitive soul of a young boy, and tried to punish him for the mistakes he made. Such teachers in their stupidity did not know how to teach, how to impart education to a living mind. And because they failed, they punished their victim. And this was how I suffered when I was thirteen years old.

'And then I left school, and in spite of all the efforts of my guardians, I refused to go to school.

'Since then I have been educating myself, and that process is still being carried on. And whatever I have learned, I have learned outside the classes. And I believe that that was a fortunate event in my life—that avoiding the schoolmaster when I was still young. And whatever I have done in later life, if I have shown any special gift or originality, I feel certain it was owing to the fact that I did not have a respectable education drilled into me.

'I took to my own work. I retired to a solitary place near the Ganges, and a great part of my life I lived in a houseboat, writing my poems, stories and plays, dreaming my dreams.

'I went on till I gradually became known to my own countrymen and claims were made on me from all parts of the country for writings and for various kinds of help. But I kept to my solitude for a long time. It is very difficult for me to say what it was—how the call came to me to come out of the isolation of my literary life, and live among my fellow-beings to share their life and help them in their living.

'And it is also a surprise to me how I had the courage to start an educational institution for our children, for I had no experience in this line at all. But I had confidence in myself. I knew that I had very profound sympathy for children. And about my knowledge of their psychology, I was very certain. I felt that I could help them more than the ordinary teachers.

'I selected a beautiful place, far away from the contamination of town life. I myself, in my young days, was brought up in that town, in the heart of India, Calcutta, and all the time I had a sort of homesickness for the open country where my heart, my soul, could have its true freedom. Though I had no experience of the outer world, I had in my heart a great longing to go away from my enclosure of those walls and from that huge, stony-hearted stepmother, Calcutta. I knew that the mind has its hunger for the ministrations of mother-nature, and so I selected this spot where the sky is unobstructed to the verge of the horizon. There the mind could have its fearless freedom to create its own dreams, and the seasons could come with all their colours and movements and beauty into the very heart of the human dwelling. And there I got a few children around me and I taught them. I was their companion. I sang to them. I composed musical pieces, operas and plays, and they took part in the performances. I recited to them our epics, and this was the beginning of this school. I had only about five or six students at that time. People did not have any confidence in a poet for bringing up their children and educating them. And so I had very few students to begin with.

'My idea was that education should be part of life itself, and must not be detached from it and be made into something abstract. And so when I brought these children around me, I allowed them to live a complete life. They had perfect freedom to do what they wished, as much liberty as was possible for me to give them. And in all their activities I tried to put before them something which would be interesting to them.

'I tried to arouse their interest in all things, in nature's beauty and the surrounding villages, and also in literature. I tried to educate them through play-acting, through listening to music in a natural manner, and not merely by class teaching.

'They knew when I was employed in writing a drama, and they took an intense interest as it went on and developed, and in the process of their rehearsals they acquired a real taste for literature, more than they could through formal lessons in grammar and class-teaching. And this was my method. I knew the children's mind. Their subconscious mind is more active than the conscious one, and therefore the important thing is to surround them with all kinds of activities which could stimulate their minds and gradually arouse their interest.

'I had musical evenings—not merely music classes, and those boys who at first did not have any special love of music would, out of curiosity, listen to our songs from outside, and gradually they too were drawn into the room and their taste for music developed. I had some of the very great artists of our land, and while they went on with their work, the boys could watch them and saw day by day how those works of art developed.

'An atmosphere was created, and what was important, this atmosphere provided the students with a natural impulse to live in harmony with it. In the beginning it was easier to feel this, when I had only a few students; I was then almost their only companion and teacher and it was truly the golden age of our school. I know that the boys who had then the privilege of attending my school look back on those days with much love and longing. But as their number grew, it became more and more expensive for me to carry on the school in my own way.

'According to the old tradition of our country it was the responsibility of the teacher to give education to those who came to him to be taught, and in our country students used to have free tuition and also free lodging in their teacher's house. The teachers acknowledged their responsibility: they themselves had the privilege of being educated, and they owed it to society that they should help their students in return, and should not claim anything in the shape of fees or remuneration.

'And I also began like that. Free tuition, lodging and boarding and all necessities of life, I supplied to my students out of my own poor resources. But you can easily imagine that under modern conditions of life it was not possible to continue like this, because now you have to get the help of teachers whose salaries are high, and there are other expenses which daily seem to increase. I could not maintain the old tradition that it was the duty and the privilege of the teacher to impart education to his students, and that an educational institution was not a shop where you could buy commodities with money. I was compelled to give up this idea, and now gradually it has taken the shape of an ordinary school.

'Only I tried my best to have certain things in the school which they did not have in the orthodox schools. The teachers shared the common life with the boys, it was a community life. In the sports and festivals the teachers and the students fully co-operated with each other. It was not like a cage in which the birds are fed from the outside, but it was like a nest which students themselves co-operated in building with their own life, with their love, with their daily work, and their play.

'I believe that we still have this true to a great extent. It is difficult to maintain this atmosphere owing to the fact that my colleagues with whom I have to work were brought up in a different tradition, not having the same chance as I had to play truant when they were young. They have their own ideas about education, and it is difficult to wholly get rid of them. And so something alien to the central ideal does creep into this institution through those who are there to help me. I had in the beginning to struggle very hard with my teachers, not with the students, as very often happens in other schools. I had to take sides with the boys when they were punished for no fault of their own, but of their teachers. I had to be firm and defend the boys, which often offended the teachers. I remember, one day, a new teacher came and when he found that some of the boys were doing their lessons up on the tree, he was furious because of this want of discipline on their part. I had to protect the boys from the schoolmaster. I told him that when these boys grew up to his age they would not have the great privilege of climbing up the trees to do their lessons; they would become more respectable and keep from mother-nature.

'But I believe that an atmosphere has been created and it is there. The school has grown. The number of students is increasing year by year, which is not always an advantage. But it cannot be helped.'

'Another feature which is of later growth is that the number of girls has been increasing. The co-education system is quite a new thing in India. But it is working perfectly in my school. We have had no cause for complaint. Very often the boys and girls go out together on excursions; the boys help the girls by bringing fuel and fetching water, and the girls cook the dinners for the boys and everything is managed by mutual help. That is a great education in itself.

'There is another factor which I consider to be important. I always try to get from outside of India, from Europe and from the Far East, lecturers, who came to the school to teach and also to share the simple life of the school with our students. This contributes to the creation of a favourable atmosphere. Our boys are very natural in their relationship with the foreign guests and visitors. My idea is that the mind should find its freedom in every respect, and I am sure that our children have, through their early training, freedom from the barriers of country and race, and creeds and sects. It is always difficult to get rid of these prejudices after we grow up. It is often sedulously cultivated in our school-books, and also by the patriots who wish the boys to be proud of the exploits of their own country by running down other countries. In this way nationalistic prejudices are cultivated. With the help of my visitors from abroad I have tried my best to make our boys' minds hospitable to the guests who come to us, and I think I have been successful.

'Then there are other activities. We have in the neighbouring villages some primitive people who need our help. We have started night-schools for them and our boys go there and teach. Then we have the village work in connexion with our institution; and there our boys have the opportunity to study the conditions of our village life and to know how to help them efficiently through scientific and up-to-date methods of cultivation and of fighting diseases. To impart not merely academic information, but how to live a complete life is, according to me, the purpose of education.

'The only thing I have not been able to provide our boys with is science, owing to the enormous expense it would entail, which in a poor country like ours is difficult to meet. I have not yet been able to arrange it. Our students and I hope that some day it will be possible for me to make up their this deficiency.

'This is the idea which I have in my mind and in spite of my lack of means, my poor resources, I have done something. Those who have been able to visit our institution can tell you how we have been helping the villages. It is not only for providing needed relief to the villages but also for the educational value of the work itself that children should be trained in the heart of such activities. The villages are the cradles of life, and if we cannot give them what is due to them, then we commit suicide. Modern civilization is depriving the villages of life-stuff, and draining away everything from the villages to the pampered towns. To counteract this I have brought my students around this village work which we have started in order to give them the proper training for helping the villagers.

'I think this is, in short, the idea which I have in mind in my school.'

VILLAGE SCHOOLS IN INDIA

Question: What is the condition of women in India as compared with the position of women in this country?

Tagore: This is a very comprehensive question.

Question: What is the social origin of the generality of your pupils? Are they peasants, workers and so on?

Tagore: In the neighbourhood of the village where we are working, we have opened a special school for the villages. You may ask why I should make such a distinction. Why should I not allow the children of the villages to come and attend the other school which is for the children of the upper class people. The reason is that these students who come from comparatively rich families, all want to pass their examinations and get their degrees in order to earn their livelihood. Therefore, it is not possible to give to them the ideal kind of education. For instance, they cannot waste their time in manual training, or even in such cultural training as music and art, and they want to cram themselves for their examinations and somehow get through. I had to submit to this because otherwise there would be no chance of having a single student in my school. One of the reasons is that our country is exceedingly poor, and it is natural for these boys to want to earn their livelihood and maintain their family when they grow older, and they must have some opportunity to pass their examinations in their schools. So I had to start a parallel school where the villagers who do not have ambitions for finding government employment or employment in merchant offices, come and join. There I am trying to introduce all my methods which I consider to be absolutely necessary for a perfect education. Before long, this village school, I believe, will be the real school, the ideal school, and the other one will be neglected.

Question: A representative of the literary organization of the people would like to know which are the most interesting currents in Indian literature. Are there in India any institutions for training workers for literary activity?

Tagore: We do not have any organized effort to help the working men to stimulate their creative activities. There have been started various night schools, but that is for the purpose of teaching them how to read and write and to get elementary information of various kinds. We cannot say that we have many schools which are of a higher class than that. One of the reasons is that we should not have any students even if we did start such a school. With some encouragement we can induce villagers to attend the night schools in order to be able just to read and write, for they consider this quite enough. Only occasionally there are a few intelligent individuals who have the ambition to join the higher classes, and pass through their examinations to get degrees. But their number is very small, and even they after passing their examinations lose touch with their village. They do not want to live in the village. They try to come to the town and take up some kind of work which they consider to be of a higher nature.

So we hardly have any institution for training the peasants or the working-men in order to do their own vocation properly in an educated manner. I think the only exception in Bengal which I may mention is this school which I have started in the neighbouring village near our institution. There the real people of the village get a proper training, a real education, not merely a smattering of some elementary subjects.

FAREWELL MEETING AT DOM SOYOUZOV

On the evening of the 24th September, the day before the Poet's departure from Moscow a big public meeting was arranged in Dom Soyouzov, the Central House of Trade Unions. This House was formerly the General Meeting Hall of the Moscow aristocracy and was known as 'Dvoryanskoye Sobraniye' in pre-revolution days. More than 2,000 persons were present. On the dais, with Rabindranath Tagore in the centre, sat the distinguished personages of Moscow including Prof. Petroff, Prof. Kogan, D. Novomirsky, A. Eshukoff and a number of eminent writers and artists.

Prof. Petroff opened the proceedings with a few words. The Soviet poet Shingalee then recited the Ode to Rabindranath Tagore which he had specially composed for the occasion.

FAREWELL SPEECH BY RABINDRANATH TAGORE

I am highly honoured at the invitation to appear in this hall and I am grateful to Dr. Petroff for the kind words he has said about me. I am thankful to the people for giving me the opportunity of knowing this country and seeing the great work which the people are doing in this land. My mission in life is education. I believe that all human problems find their fundamental solution in education. And outside of my own vocation as a poet I have accepted this responsibility to educate my people as much as lies in my individual power to do so. I know that all the evils, almost without exception, from which my land suffers are solely owing to the utter lack of education of the people.

Poverty, pestilence, communal fights and industrial backwardness make our path of life narrow and perilous owing to the meagerness of education. And this is the reason why, in spite of my advanced age and my weak health, I gladly accepted the invitation offered to me to see how you are working out the most important problem of education in this country. I have seen, I have admired and I have envied you in your great opportunities. You will know that our condition in India is very similar to yours. She has an agricultural population which is in need of all the help and encouragement that you have given the people in this country. You know how precarious is the living which depends exclusively upon agriculture, and so how utterly necessary it is for the cultivators to have the knowledge of up-to-date methods of producing crops in order to meet the increasing demands of life.

Our people are living on the verge of perpetual famine, and do not know how to help this because they have lost their faith and confidence in their own humanity. This is the greatest misfortune of our people, three hundred millions of men and women burdened with profound ignorance, without any hope in life.

So I came to this land to see how you deal with this problem, you who have struggled against the incubus of ignorance, superstition, and apathy which were once prevalent in this land among the working-men and the peasantry. The little that I have seen has convinced me of the marvellous progress that has been made, the miracle that has been achieved. How the mental attitude of the people has been changed in such a short time, it is difficult for us to realize, we who live in the darkest shadow of ignorance and futility. It gladdens my heart to know that the people, the real people who maintain the life of society and bear the burden of civilization, are not deprived of their own rights and that they enjoy an equal share of all the advantages of a progressive community.

And I dream of the time when it will be possible for that ancient land of Aryan civilization also to enjoy the great boon of education and equal opportunities for all the people. I am thankful, truly thankful to you all who have helped me in visualising in a concrete form the dream which I have been carrying for a long time in my mind, the dream of emancipating the people's minds which have been shackled for ages. For this I thank you."

IMPRESSIONS OF MOSCOW

On the 25th September, just before the Poet's departure from Moscow a reporter from *Izvestia* came to see him. We give below the reported interview in full.

The Poet was asked to say what things in Moscow had impressed him the most.

He replied: 'The Orphans at the Home of the Young Pioneers showed great confidence in their ability to realize their ideal for a new world. Their behaviour to me was so natural. Their conduct impressed me very deeply. Then at the Peasants' House I met the peasants. We questioned each other quite frankly. Their problems are similar to the problems of the peasants in my own country. I was deeply impressed by the attitude of mind of your peasants.

'Places which I have not been able to visit have been visited by my secretaries. My doctor tells me of the fine work you are doing in sanitation, hygiene, scientific research. You are accomplishing a great deal in these lines under conditions not nearly as favourable, economically at least, as in other countries. My secretaries tell me of your splendid work in training students of agriculture, in caring for and training the homeless children left by war and famine, and of the outstanding experiment in practical education being carried on by Mr Shatsky in his colony. Mr Shatsky did me the honour of coming to visit me. I find that the ideal of his institution I also share. I am certain that your methods of education would be of great benefit in other countries where there is so much in education that is merely academic and abstract. Yours is much more practical and therefore moral, and it is in closer touch with the varied aspects and purposes of life.'

On being asked if he would express a few words in regard to his general impressions of Moscow, the Poet replied:

'I wish to let you know how deeply I have been impressed by the amazing intensity of your energy in spreading education among masses, the most intelligent direction which you have given to this noble work and also the variety of channels that have been opened out to train their minds and senses and limbs. I appreciate it all the more keenly because I belong to that country where millions of my fellow-countrymen are denied the light that education can bring to them. For human beings all other boons that are external and superficial, that are imposed from outside, are like paints and patches that never represent the bloom of health but only disguise the anaemic skin without enriching the blood. You have recognized the truth that in extirpating all social evils one has to go to the root, which can only be done through education, and not through police batons and military brow-beating.

'But I find here certain contradictions to the great mission which you have undertaken. Certain attitudes of mind are being cultivated which are contrary to your ideal.

'I must ask you: Are you doing your ideal a service by arousing in the minds of those under your training, anger, class hatred and revengefulness against those not sharing your ideal, against those whom you consider to be your enemies? True, you have to fight against obstacles, you have to overcome ignorance and lack of sympathy, even persistently virulent antagonism. But your mission is not restricted to your own nation or own party, it is for the betterment of humanity according to your light. But does not humanity include those who do not agree with your aim? Just as you try to help peasants who have other ideas than yours about religion, economics, and social life, not by getting fatally angry with them, but by patiently teaching them and showing them where the evil lurks in secret, should you not have the same mission to those other people who have other ideals than your own? These you may consider to be mistaken ideals, but they have an historical origin and have become inevitable through a combination of circumstances. You may consider the men who hold them as misguided. But it should all the more be your mission to try to convert them by pity and love, realizing that they are as much a part of humanity as the peasants whom you serve.

'If you dwell too much upon the evil elements in your opponents and assume that they are inherent in human nature meriting eternal damnation, you inspire an attitude of mind which with its content of hatred and revengefulness may some day react against your own ideal and destroy it. You are working in a great cause. Therefore, you must be great in your mind, great in your mercy, your understanding and your patience. I feel profound admiration for the greatness of the things you are trying to do, therefore I cannot help expecting for it a motive force of love and an environment of a charitable understanding.

'There must be disagreement where minds are allowed to be free. It would not only be an uninteresting but a sterile world of mechanical regularity if all of our opinions were forcibly made alike. If you have a mission which includes all humanity, you must, for the sake of that living humanity, acknowledge the existence of differences of opinion. Opinions are constantly changed and rechanged only through the free circulation of intellectual forces and moral persuasion. Violence begets violence and blind stupidity. Freedom of mind is needed for the reception of truth; terror hopelessly kills it. The brute cannot subdue the brute. It is only the man who can do it.

'Before leaving your country let me once again assure you that I am struck with admiration by all that you are doing to free those who once were in slavery, to raise up those who were lowly and oppressed, endeavouring to bring help to those who are utterly helpless all through the world, reminding them that the source of their salvation lies in a proper education and their power to combine their human resources. Therefore, for the sake of humanity I hope that you may never create a vicious force of violence which will go on weaving an interminable chain of violence and cruelty. Already you have inherited much of this legacy from the Tsarist regime. It is the worst legacy you possibly could have. You have tried to destroy many of the other evils of that regime. Why not try to destroy this one also? I have learnt much from you, how skilfully you evolve usefulness out of the helpfulness of the weak and ignorant. Your ideal is great and so I ask you for perfection in serving it, and a broad field of freedom for laying its permanent foundation.'

INTERVIEW WITH THE 'JEWISH STANDARD': ON THE PALESTINIAN PROBLEM

'I respect the Zionist ideal and admire the selflessness of those who work for it.' Tagore replied when I asked whether he is a pro-Zionist. 'I have followed as closely as I can the steady and continuous progress of the transformation of your ideal into reality. You have made extraordinary headway. But now your political orientation is leading you into a blind alley, a path without issue. Even if England wanted to bring about an Arab-Jewish partnership she could not do so. Arab-Jewish harmony must be achieved in Palestine.'

'How can this harmony be achieved?' the interviewer asked.

'I am not a statesman, nor do I pretend to know the answer to your query', wearily countered the poet. 'I do know the Arabs, and I believe that I know the Jews. And that is why I feel that political and economic co-operation between them can be achieved. The Jews are an old people. They have withstood persecution, torture, and have refused to lose their identity. Their strength lies in their culture and religion. Yours is a spiritual heritage that grows stronger with age, that cannot be assimilated or absorbed. The Arabs also are an endurable people. Their religion and culture come from the same mould as those of the Jews. Spiritually the Arabs have borrowed much from the Jews. Viewed fundamentally, you and they are one family—yes, one great family. Family quarrels are always virulent'—the philosopher smiled—'but they are adjustable.

You have learned to live among people much further from you than the Arabs, people foreign to you in every respect. Even in America, the land of machine culture, you have managed to be both Jews and Americans. Can you not manage to be Jews and Palestinians at the same time?'

An almost supernatural calm came over Tagore's face as he leaned back and listened to the echo which his own words had awakened. Hesitantly I disturbed his peaceful repose: 'But Zionism, Dr Tagore, is trying to find an escape from this dual life of the Jew. It is intended for those who cannot or do not want to assimilate with other nations. If Jews have to differentiate between Jewish nationalism and Palestinism, as you suggest, then Palestine will be merely another America, France or Germany as far as the Jews are concerned.'

In the rhythmic voice that gives a poetic flavor even to his conversation Tagore answered: 'I understand Zionism in the same sense as my great friend Einstein. I regard Jewish nationalism as an effort to preserve and enrich Jewish culture and tradition. In today's world this programme requires a national home. It also implies appropriate physical surroundings as well as favourable political and economic conditions. I realize this. Palestine, however, can provide these only if the Jews will include the Arabs in their political and economic programme. Your spiritual and cultural programmes do not need to sacrifice anything to obtain this political co-operation. I visualize a Palestine Commonwealth in which the Arabs will live their own religious life and the Jews will revive their resplendent culture, but both will be united as one political and economic entity.

'I see that there is skepticism in your eyes and you think these the ramblings of a naive poet. You wonder how it can be done. I do not doubt the abilities and special gifts of the Jewish people. If you will set your hearts upon convincing the Arabs that their political and economic interests are identical with yours, if you will show them that by your work in Palestine you are building for Arabs and Jews alike, without regard for your cultural differences, the Arabs will in time become your most loyal allies.'

The interviewer humbly submitted that this was what the Zionists had been doing in the past. And yet, in August of last year....

[Arab attacks on Jews in Palestine, following disputes over Jewish use of the Wailing Wall, Jerusalem.]

Rabindranath Tagore did not let me conclude the sentence. A shadow flitted over his beautiful countenance: 'Don't speak about those ugly incidents now. It is because of what happened that I speak as I do. Until recently Arab nationalism was primarily spiritual, though different in aspect from the Jewish. For centuries the Arabs have neglected their land, because spiritually they were above political nationalism. Western civilization calls this state primitive and uncivilized. In any case, the Arabs are newcomers to the Western game of political nationalism and their minds can easily be confused—as they have been confused. They got the idea that their spiritual or religious life was endangered by the Jewish homeland. The intensive integration of the Jewish people into Palestine was misinterpreted by them. Demagogic leadership helped this along. Zionism, which well-trained Western diplomatic minds sometimes find hard to understand, was altogether new and strange to the Arab primitiveness. I am trying to explain that the Arabs' psychological adjustment to a Jewish homeland must necessarily be a gradual process.

'Jews must have patience and resourcefulness in dealing with the Arab. You who are a blending of Western and Eastern civilization must be indulgent teachers. Despite political obstacles you must keep your spiritual heritage intact. Notwithstanding sacrifices you must plod along on the road to an understanding with your co-nationalists of Palestine.

'Einstein's religion—with which I agree fundamentally though we differ in some minor aspects—is opposed to petty chauvinism, to rigid political nationalism. His cosmic faith cannot be disturbed by White Papers or other instruments of European diplomacy. It is such faith which will lead you to that broad nationalism which you can establish in Palestine as an example to the whole of humanity. Don't become enmeshed in paragraphs and clauses. The Jews of all nations know that political protection means nothing. Treaties have never saved you from persecution. They never will.

'Come to your co-Palestinians in a free spirit and tell them: 'You and we are both old races. We are both stubborn races. You cannot subdue us, and we will not try to change you. But we can both be ourselves, retain our identity and still be united in the political aims of Palestine, the Commonwealth of Jews and Arabs.' I know that you will not be understood at your first approach. Forget the Western conception of prestige and pride and keep on working with this end in view: 'A Palestine Commonwealth in which Arabs and Jews will live their own distinct cultural and spiritual lives. Then you will, you must succeed.'

Tagore leaned back exhausted. Speaking almost to himself, he added, in a low whisper: 'The Palestine problem cannot be solved in London by any negotiations between the British Government and the Zionist leaders. The success of Zionism depends entirely upon Arab-Jewish co-operation. This can be obtained in Palestine only by means of a direct understanding between the Arabs and the Jews. If the Zionist leadership will insist on separating Jewish political and economic interests in Palestine from those of the Arabs ugly eruptions will occur in the Holy Land.'

Closing his eyes, Rabindranath Tagore murmured softly: 'What we poets have dreamt the Jews can create in Palestine if they free themselves of the Western concept of nationalism.'

1930

INTERVIEWS IN PERSIA

I. DISCUSSION WITH THE EDITOR OF 'ISPHAHAN'

Question: After welcoming you, Sir, to this land which holds you in high honour, may we be permitted to ask whether you have so far enjoyed your tour in this country?

Poet: Your country is beautiful and your hospitality is overwhelming. I have had a most enjoyable time in all the places I have visited.

Question: Has the beauty and as you kindly put it, the hospitable nature of our people, had any effect yet on your thoughts and writings?

Poet: I am gathering inspiration; I am sure when I leave Persia I shall carry home within my heart experiences which will be of permanent value to me. As yet I have seen only a few places in your country—Bushire is a port town situated practically in a desert, yet with great care you have preserved some gardens within it. Shiraz is lovely with birds, blossoms, trees and its springtime climate which I enjoyed very much. In Khalil-Abad garden I used to watch the purple outline of the hills in the background; the shady trees gave me rest.

Question: We know you visited the tombs of Saadi and Hafez.

Poet: Those experiences have gone deep into my heart. You know I had my first introduction to Hafez through my father who used to recite his verses to me. They seemed to me like a greeting from a far away poet who was yet near to me.

25 April 1932

II. DISCUSSIONS WITH EDUCATIONISTS AT TEHERAN

Poet: I am glad to meet you here today and have this opportunity of discussing with you about some fundamental principles of education which we owe it to the modern generation to establish in our educational institutions. To me the most important issue seems to be the task of widening the mental horizon of the students, of imparting to their studies the background of internationalism which will enable them to realize the true character of our interlinked humanity and the deeper unities of our civilizations in the West and the East.

Educator 1: I express on behalf of my colleagues and myself our profound thankfulness to you for reviving in your educational colony the spirit of internationalism which is the spirit of Asia.

This spirit as you know, Sir, is not foreign to our Persian civilization. In the olden days Shapur's University was a refuge for students of Rome who met with no racial bias from our people when they flocked round our teachers for knowledge. After the invasion of the Arabs, in the Nizamic schools we had Jewish, Arab and Assyrian students. Our educational traditions have consistently maintained this supernational attitude in all matters relating to quest of truth. It is because of this tradition which we yet carry in our blood that we can accept your great message with an open heart.

Poet: I rejoice to hear that you share with me a deep faith in cultural federation between different peoples and races. In India we have offered hospitality to various indigenous and foreign cultures and attempted to evolve our own civilization by assimilating influences from far and wide. It is only now that in our artificial universities we have gone in wholly for parrot-like repetition, in imitation that is uncritical, in memorising lessons without using our own initiative of mind and courage of judgment. It produces eternal schoolboys who gather informations that never ripen into true knowledge and wisdom.

My dream is to offer to our students a continental background of mind, a background in which have been co-ordinated the experiences of ages, the intellectual and spiritual experiments made in Asia for long generations.

Europe has evolved a continental culture which is like a common coffer to which the different peoples of Europe contribute their best gifts. Owing to this collaboration Europe has become great. She has successfully exploited the rich potentialities of her peoples and come to the forefront in the march of life. Asia too must reorganize her continental life and vitalize her scattered cultures by recognizing their affinities and expressing them in literature, arts, science and civic life. Barriers of national segregation must be broken through, superstitions of religions and social incompatibility must be relentlessly fought against. In a daring quest of all that lies deepest in our common humanity Asia must unite and hold out her hands to the West in friendly co-operation.

Educator 2: Sir, we are sure that your hopes will be justified because a whole civilization expresses its deepest needs, its greatest fulfilment through its men of genius. A prophet is the product of circumstance, appearing at a critical period of a country's history. Now all the great nations of Asia are thinking of their past glories, they are waking up to their responsibility, to their national inheritance. They are seeking a great message which will ignite their dormant consciousness and bring about an illumination of their fullest personality. You appear, sir, as a prophet and spokesman of Asia's great dreams, through you we are beginning to realize the nature of the work which we educators have before us. Though we get your message through the unsatisfying medium of translation, your noble physiognomy and the music of your speech bring it very near to our soul.

Poet: We must no longer be satisfied with isolated domestic lamps, we must have a festival of lights which will express the effulgence of our humanity in Asia and justify us before the modern age. Otherwise we can never hope to be recognized by the world at large, we shall remain obscure, and the bondage of obscurity is the worst form of slavery that can shackle a nation. We must gain freedom, freedom which is a gift of self-expression, not an opportunity for self-indulgence in material comforts. During our great past our free peoples sent their torch-bearers to different countries to carry the radiant message of love, of great thoughts and deeds, to acquaint their neighbouring peoples with the highest realizations of their seers and sages. Asia in those days had the freedom of soul to bestow and to accept all that she considered great and enduring; it is that highest form of freedom which we must today win for our coming generations by opening up through an education of complete life the richest potentialities of their character. This education of a complete life involves training to recognize the kinship of our common humanity through a correct reading of history, of science, of the arts, in the light of man's spiritual truth.

Utilitarian education has its value but it is deprived of all significance if in its fragmentary pursuit of narrow immediate ends it fails to arouse in the mind of students the impulse of larger purposes, of aspirations which comprehend the fullness of our personality. In the East we must never forget to link up our educational institutions with the fundamental values of our undivided spiritual life, because that has been the greatest mission of our ancient universities, which, as you have said, in spite of political vicissitudes, never allowed their vision of humanity to be darkened by racial considerations. Asia owes it to humanity to restore her spirit of generous co-operation in culture and heal the suffering peoples of the modern age now divided by cruel politics and materialistic greed which vitiate even the citadels of education.

In order to have this intermingling of minds in Asia we must rid our minds that are dark and against reason, of all the aberrations of local history that repel others and with a spirit of intellectual detachment seek out the treasures that have universal value.

Educator 1: Material progress is essential but it must know its limits. You have made wonderfully clear to us today our task as educators to inspire our students with a correct sense of values which may be described as the one great purpose of education. Every student of history knows how nations have perished either from dire paucity of material needs or from a surfeit of them. The East and the West, roughly speaking, present before us today a spectacle of these two extreme conditions. Europe by concentrating on material achievement has exploited nature and man at the expense of her soul. She has evolved a unity of civilization because of the urge of a common purpose which has permeated her continental life. But that is not enough—the results are too evident to need explanation. Asia still retains the vision of a synthetic cultural life where the good is the good of our whole nature, of all the peoples;—but as you have made evident to us now, failing to establish her ideals on the basis of a united, a continental civilization, she has become ineffective.

Sir, you have raised the banner of Asia's self-expression, your ideas of education are a new revelation to the modern age. We are proud that through you our continent offers to all humanity the promise of a new path which will lead us out of the debris of the present, out of all the delusions and oppressions which insult our human nature and bring us into mutual conflict. You can be assured that we shall never forget your message, that our renascent nation will strive its utmost to put your ideas into effective operation.

Poet: I thank you for your sympathy and your faith which strengthen my hopes for the future. Our institution in Bengal depends on your co-operation for its success. We must keep in touch with each other and be guided by the experiences we both gain in our efforts to train the minds of the young towards a fellowship of culture which will bring humanity together in love and understanding.

3 May 1932

III. DISCUSSIONS WITH DASHTY, A MEMBER OF THE IRANIAN ASSEMBLY

Poet: My time in Persia is coming to an end. I have not been here for long, yet I do not feel like a stranger. It is surprising that though I do not know your language somehow I have come very close to you and can easily communicate with you and feel the warmth of your friendship. There is not much difference between your people and ours, the general outlook on life and temperament seems to be very much akin.

Dashty: Languages are after all secondary; of primary importance is our psychological make-up which manifests itself directly through the medium of gestures and expressions.

You told me in Bushire that you have come to us in Persia to discover the old India. Quite true, our real spirit is old Indian; it comes from a past when we shared a common culture. Even now an inner affinity persists, and it is this that makes you feel at home with us.

Poet: Yes, the path was open for me before I was born. As a matter of fact, in our home in Bengal the spirit of Iran was a living influence when I was a child. My revered father and my elder brothers were deeply attached to Persian mystical literature and art.

Going further back one discovers that at one time the Bengali language freely borrowed words from your vocabulary which we use now without knowing their origin. When you find this, you must know that something of your culture flows through our daily life; for words are merely symbols of thoughts and attitudes which they represent. Even before the Mohamedan rule in India there was active cultural interchange between India and Iran; in our classical art and literature direct traces of this are to be discovered.

I do not indeed find your life and habits at all unfamiliar, it is very easy for me to adjust myself to your ways and to realize your spirit.

Dashty: I hope we have not tired you too much. We all wanted to see you and get the inspiration of your personality. It has not been possible for us to spare you as much as we should have done.

Poet: You know, that is what I wanted. I had been longing to meet different groups of your people, to know individuals irrespective of their vocation, their station in life. I confess that sometimes the strain of engagements has told on my health but I have never minded this. It has been a great inspiration for me to meet your people to converse with them on present-day affairs in Persia which are of vital interest to us.

A Gentleman: Have you already started a centre of Persian culture in your university in Bengal?

Poet: Yes, because I have always felt that it is necessary for us both to know each other, not only because of our common ancestry but because there is something in your literature and art which deeply appeals to us. The Persian temperament is poetic, you love music and merry conversation, you share our love for nature's beauty.

If you were rigidly pious 'Mullahs' corresponding to our Hindu priests, we could not have dared to invite you. Unfortunately two of our biggest communities in India have yet too many representatives of this type of bigotry and that is why we cannot come together. I claim the collaboration of your scholars and artists whose influence will unite us culturally and modify our differences which are not really fundamental.

Dashty: How do you like Persian music?

Poet: Very much indeed. Some of your recent innovations I do not fully understand. It seems to me that they have not yet been fully assimilated by the native genius of your music. They are too reminiscent of Europe; in any case, they do not move me so much as your classical music.

Dashty: We are of the same opinion. We feel that the introduction of harmony is too recent to have successfully enriched our music; but may be gradually we shall evolve a music which will be all the more beautiful because of these innovations.

Poet: It must be so. You have all along had a wonderful gift of assimilating influences from outside and coming out more fully with the expression of your own unique culture. In music too you are sure to gain by European influence. I have always felt sad that European music has not had any direct influence on our own, that great European composers such as Beethoven have, unlike great European poets or philosophers, wielded little or no influence on Eastern cultural movements. For European music is unquestionably great and without doubt our own music will be all the richer if it can absorb, into its living texture, creative influences form European music.

Dashty: I am one of those who believe that Persia should assimilate 100 per cent of American culture. I am not afraid of foreign influence; indeed, I believe, that nothing can radically change our temperament, so that we may safely go in for Americanization. We shall then be American in our methods but thoroughly Persian in our culture. I believe you try to follow the same principle in Santiniketan.

Poet: The time has come when we must think deeply about human civilization. You must have read Spengler's book on European civilization. It raises searching questions about the destiny of the modern Western civilization and gives us dangerous parallelism from history.

When you speak of hundred per cent Americanization you must remember that America herself is faced today with an imminent crisis and has yet to achieve a stability which will prove the soundness of her social and political machinery.

I was talking today to a German scientist—Dr Stratil-Sauer of Leipzig—who has come here all the way from Berlin by motor car for geological exploration, and he was telling me the same thing about Europe. The whole Western civilization is undergoing a severe trial. The reckless mechanization of life which has gone on in the West is already having a drastic reaction.

We in the East must ponder seriously before we go in for hasty imitation of Western life in its totality. There is a profound maladjustment somewhere at the very basis of European life. Everywhere there is a material well-being but happiness has vanished. And how could it be otherwise? Pierce through the veneer of modernity and you find almost primitive barbarism staring at you. What is high-pressure modern life for the multitude but a ceaseless preoccupation with physical needs—a hot pursuit of dress, expensive cars, elaborate food and housing, that is to say, of materials which satisfy the elementary needs of our animal existence? Such a life has no time for self-realization, for human fellowship, for all that make man's existence significant and precious. Certainly, this is the modern form of barbarism which exhausts all its resources merely to climb up the steep summit of living surrounded by emptiness.

Dashty: Our soul accepts what it may; we cannot determine consciously how much to receive or reject exactly. The whole process of assimilation is a subconscious one so that there is perhaps no fear of only outside influence totally submerging or exterminating the basic character of our civilization. If we try to profit by American modes of life and hold them before our people we shall probably adopt only a few of them and that will be all to our benefit. Greek ideals, for example, have left their legacy in the great architecture and sculpture of India; but at the beginning of Greek influence we would probably have feared that India was doing harm to its traditions by accepting Greek motifs and technique to experiment upon. In Persia similarly we have had periods of extraneous influence but this has only vitalised our Persian genius. We have quickly shaken off the imitative phase and retained something from it which have helped us.

Poet: Why then do you emphasize upon American modes of life and how can you isolate and specify a particular country when you want the healthy contact of science, which is neither American nor Western but universal in its truth? I am not condemning America in particular but only pointing out that when you say you want to imitate a particular country or people you can only copy things and external facts, you cannot assimilate truths which lie at the foundation of our human character. If any nation or a people have been successful in giving shape to ideals which are of perennial value, what we have to learn from them is their capacity to absorb and establish these ideals; we must not merely copy the results that others have produced. That is my point—I am not against absorbing truths which are of universal value; as a matter of fact, it is our human birthright to claim such truths as our own. But I am against borrowing ready-made models or emphasizing upon the need of imitating isolated external facts which are particular to a particular race or a nation. Let our emphasis be on Truth, not on particular facts which have had their special evolution under inevitable local circumstances.

Dashty: I quite agree. I mentioned America as an example.

Poet: The German scientist told me that Europe is sick of her mechanised high-speed life which adds materials but fails to satisfy the soul. As a result of this, there are many of them who seek out remote spots where they can forget the rush and fever of a purposeless existence; they go to the South Sea Islands, Madagascar, Middle Africa and so on where they can wash themselves clean of Western ways of living. He told me of a great Leipzig professor who gave up his scientific work and all that he held dear in his life to search for inner peace which he found in a Tibetan monastery. It may be a reaction but it indicates very grave problems which the modern age can no longer ignore. In Darmstadt, after the War, German students with pale emaciated faces used to flock round me and ask: 'Sir, we have lost faith in our teachers, they have misled us. What shall we do with our lives?' They expected an Eastern poet to give them something which would satisfy their spiritual hunger, some philosophy of life which the Western world needed for its salvation.

Dashty: Yes, we must work to bring the Western Spirit of Science and the Eastern Philosophy of Life together. Materially we must be secure, spiritually we must develop our human wealth of character.

Poet: That is what I say. We must get out of the tangle of doctrines and the infatuation of material results in order to achieve a balanced harmony of life which, as you indicate, takes cognizance of our complete human personality comprehending the physical as well as the spiritual aspects of our nature. This harmony, however, can never be established unless we have sufficient detachment of mind to judge for ourselves, to minister to the essential and reject all that is ephemeral and delusive in building the foundation of our national life. It would be fatal if we surrender our critical faculty to a mood of indiscriminate emulation. We in the East, however poor we may now be materially, must reserve the right of judging what we consider to be beneficial or not for humanity, of selecting for ourselves a path which suits the evolution of our civilization. By exercising this right of judgment we shall not only be serving our own country but do our inescapable duty to the whole world of humanity of which we form a part.

Dashty: We thank you, Sir, for your words of wisdom which, we assure you, we shall treasure in the depths of our life.

1932

TAGORE ON FILMS

'[Tagore] deplored the prevalence of films representing sex-relationships, gushing sentimentality, night clubs, crime or ludicrous adventures, which he said, were having a most mischievous effect upon the Indian population. It was seldom realized that the average Indian possessed a deep artistic consciousness, and they would always respond to any film of an elevating character or spiritual background.

'The films at present shown could only be regarded in most cases as a libel upon Western civilization. Many of the films which were presumed to represent Indian Orientals constantly misrepresented the life and manners of the East.

'He warmly commended "The Light of Asia" film which in its beauty and dignity counteracted such misrepresentations, and he hoped the work initiated by the Indian players in such a film would be followed up by other films representing Oriental ideals in their proper aspects. The value from the moral educative standpoint of such a film was incalculable. He had great faith in the people, and he believed that a levelling up of the tone of the films generally shown was not only very desirable, but would be welcomed by the majority of film audiences.

'Rabindranath Tagore welcomed the formation of the British Empire Film Institute and was so impressed with the value of its work that he consented to join its Grand Council. Every movement, he said, that aimed at encouraging the emergence of higher standards of art in this industry deserved every support.'

1926

INDEX

A

B

C

D

U

V